2 ILLINOIS CENTRAL COLLEGE

P9-DFE-182

WITHDRAWN

8/09

I.C.C. LIBRARY

DEMCO

DANGEROUS BUSINESS

ALSO BY PAT CHOATE

Hot Property: The Stealing of Ideas in an Age of Globalization

Save Your Job, Save Our Country (with Ross Perot)

Agents of Influence: How Japan's Lobbyists in the United States Manipulate America's Political and Economic System

The High-Flex Society: Shaping America's Economic Future (with J. K. Linger)

America in Ruins: The Decaying Infrastructure (with Susan Walter)

Being Number One: Rebuilding the U.S. Economy
(with Gail Garfield Schwartz)

DANGEROUS BUSINESS

THE RISKS OF GLOBALIZATION FOR AMERICA

PAT CHOATE

I.C.C. LIBRARY

Alfred A. Knopf ＊ *New York* ＊ 2008

HC
103
.C49
2008

THIS IS A BORZOI BOOK
PUBLISHED BY ALFRED A. KNOPF

Copyright © 2008 by Manufacturing Policy Project
All rights reserved. Published in the United States by Alfred
A. Knopf, a division of Random House, Inc., New York, and
in Canada by Random House of Canada Limited, Toronto.
www.aaknopf.com

Knopf, Borzoi Book, and the colophon are registered
trademarks of Random House, Inc.

Library of Congress Cataloging-in-Publication Data
Choate, Pat.
Dangerous business : the risks of globalization for America /
by Pat Choate.—1st ed.
p. cm.
"A Borzoi book."
Includes bibliographical references and index.
ISBN 978-0-307-26684-2
1. United States—Economic conditions. 2. United States—Economic policy.
3. Corporations—Political aspects—United States.
4. Globalization—Economic aspects—United States. 5. Globalization—
Social aspects—United States.
6. United States—Foreign economic relations.
I. Title. II. Title: Risks of globalization for America.
III. Title: Globalization for America.
HC103.C49 2008
337.73—dc22   2007052249

Manufactured in the United States of America
First Edition

6/09 B&T 25.95

In Memory

George Becker

*Who bravely fought
for the United States
in war and peace*

Contents

DANGEROUS BUSINESS

Prologue

The extraordinary enigma we must seek to understand is that
despite an expanding economy, violence increases, the number of
those living in poverty grows and urban slums spread in cities
throughout the world. How is it that our greatest period of technological and scientific achievement has come to endanger the conditions that allow life on earth? There is a growing realization that
something fundamental has gone wrong and a pervasive feeling
that those in power do not know what should be done.
                          —Sir James Goldsmith, *The Trap*

After the fall of the Berlin Wall in 1989 and before the creation of the
World Trade Organization (WTO) in 1995, the toughest geopolitical question the world faced was how to integrate into the global economy the 4 billion people who had long been separated from the West by their political
systems, which were primarily Communist or socialist. The solution chosen by the United States, Europe, and Japan is what became known as
"globalization."

In 1994, months before the U.S. Congress was to vote on ratifying the
United States' membership in the World Trade Organization, the main
institution for globalization, Sir James Goldsmith, one of Europe's most
flamboyant financiers and a staunch WTO opponent, came to Washington
to meet with like-minded people, of whom I was one, in preparation for a
similar political battle in Europe.

A citizen of both England and France, a member of the British establishment, an aristocrat who owned a three-star restaurant in Paris, a person
who traveled on his own two-bedroom Boeing 757, and a man with three
families, Sir James was greeted in Washington with some uncertainty. Our
doubts immediately disappeared, however, when we exchanged views
with him.

Goldsmith's concern was that an unfettered global trade regime, as envisioned under the World Trade Organization, would "shatter the way in
which value-added is shared between capital and labor. That agreement
has been reached through generations of political debate, elections,
strikes, lockouts, and other conflicts. Overnight that agreement will be
destroyed. The social divisions that this will cause will be deeper than anything ever envisaged by Marx."

Transnational corporations, he argued in his book, *The Trap,* would seek the lowest-cost labor in nations with the weakest environmental and worker safety regulations. Those companies would shift as much of their manufacturing as they could, as well as their service work. The interests of these corporations, which owe allegiance to no country, are divorced from those of society.

Surely, he said, it would be a mistake for a nation to adopt an economic policy that would make its corporations rich if they transfer production abroad and eliminate their national workforce but would bankrupt them if they remain and continue to employ their country's workers. This was the trap.

Sir James and his allies failed to persuade European governments to reject the WTO and create a less ideological, more practical system of global trade, just as WTO opponents in the United States failed.

By joining the WTO, the United States altered its trade policies with other nations radically. The domestic social compact forged among corporations, workers, and society over the prior century was fractured and soon began to shatter. Millions of American workers and the communities in which they lived were left to their own devices. Moreover, those were only the most visible and most immediate consequences of this great policy shift. Which brings us to the subject of this book: the dangers of globalization.

We are now deeply trapped in the world that Goldsmith feared. Millions of American workers are moving from higher-paying jobs with health insurance and pensions to lower-paying positions with no benefits. Lifetime jobs are being replaced with short-term, dead-end work, undermining our middle class. The U.S. industrial base is being hollowed out to the point that the nation is unable to produce domestically the weapons and technologies required for an assured national security. The federal government has gone deep into debt, with foreign owners holding almost half of its obligations. The U.S. trade deficit has soared to more than $700 billion per year. Washington has surrendered, through dozens of trade treaties, its sovereign right to act unilaterally against other nations that violate their trade obligations to the United States. The economies of most developing states, such as Mexico, are so ravaged by these policies that millions of their citizens cannot find work at home and millions have illegally entered the United States in search of jobs. Foreign laborers are being abused in dozens of countries by U.S.-owned corporations to a degree and on a scale that future historians will view as economic war crimes. And as Goldsmith predicted, the global environment is being rapidly destroyed.

These historic changes are neither political accidents nor the consequences of immutable cosmic forces. They flow directly from the policy decisions of our last three presidents and Congress, who year after year have purposefully ignored the outsourcing of American jobs and the resulting decline in U.S. living standards, even as they pursue more open-ended trade treaties while not providing even the most elementary safeguards for American workers and consumers.

The globalization policies of Presidents George H. W. Bush, Bill Clinton, and George W. Bush collectively constitute the worst economic policy mistake in American history. Their policies have enabled leaders of transnational companies and global finance to enrich themselves and advance their interests at the expense of the larger society. These companies and financiers and the campaign fund–driven politicians they support are transforming the United States into a corporately governed nation, the mass of whose citizens face an increasingly bleak future.

The challenge we face is to institute a new approach to globalization that will create a broad-based prosperity with stability and economic justice, sovereignty with vision, and security with peace, while not endangering the conditions that allow life on Earth.

The central question surrounding further integration of the world economy (globalization) is not whether the U.S. economy will become ever more entwined with those of other nations, for it will. The issue is how will this be done, by whom, and in whose best interest. This book explores three fundamental questions:

1. Why did the government of the United States, the world's trading and economic powerhouse, choose to integrate its economy with those of the rest of the world without providing the most basic safeguards for the nation and its people?
2. Can the United States maintain its standard of living, pay its debts, retain its sovereignty, and ensure its national security under its present policies?
3. Can the United States gain the benefits of globalization without plunging into economic ruin?

AND HOLD THE
MELAMINE, PLEASE

I was stirring martinis for two dinner guests one night in 2007 when the telephone rang. My wife answered it, and about twenty seconds later she asked me to join her conversation with Kim, a friend of ours who is a logistics director for a national chain of pet stores. Kim wanted to know if we fed Dolly, our aging English bulldog, canned food. It seemed an odd question for a Saturday-evening call. But it wasn't.

Relieved that we did not, she told us that earlier that day the Food and Drug Administration (FDA) had issued a massive recall of "wet" (canned) dog and cat food manufactured by Menu Foods, a company located in Canada whose products were sold by dozens of other food companies under their various brand names. The food was poisoned, and it was killing thousands of healthy dogs and cats in ghastly ways: vomiting, bleeding, diarrhea, thirst, starvation, and seizures, followed by death.

Kim, the owner of two rescued miniature Doberman pinschers, had spent that Saturday energetically ensuring that all the recalled products were off her stores' shelves. Simultaneously, she and her colleagues were being bombarded with questions from veterinarians and irate pet owners, for whom she had no answers.

No one knew if this penetration of the U.S. food system was because of terrorism, ineptitude, or simple greed. Neither the Canadian company nor the FDA, moreover, knew why the food was killing pets, only that it was. Worse, the FDA was unsure whether its recall included all the poisoned products.

In the weeks that followed the initial recall, Americans had a "canary in the mine" epiphany. They learned that the United States now imports more food than it exports and much of it comes from developing countries that regularly use unsafe ingredients and unsanitary processing practices, many of which were outlawed a century ago in the United States.

New York Times columnist Paul Krugman captured the concerns of many Americans in a piece titled "Fear of Eating," wherein he said, "Yesterday, I did something risky: I ate a salad. . . . For all you know, there may be *E. coli* on your spinach, salmonella in your peanut butter and melamine in your pet's food and, because it was in the feed, in your chicken sandwich."

Though humorously stated, Krugman's angst was no joke. *The Nation* reported that "In the six years since 9/11, food-borne pathogens and toxins have quietly killed ten times the number of Americans who died in the terrorist attacks."

Eating might be dangerous, even deadly, and not simply because of obesity. For most of the previous century Americans had conducted their lives and raised their families with the confidence that their food and medicine supplies were safe. No longer. In the spring of 2007, with one revelation after another, they learned that impure drugs, tainted seafood, rancid meats, poisoned toothpaste, and adulterated mouthwash, among dozens of other goods, mostly imported, have penetrated the U.S. market on a massive scale.

In a headlong rush into globalization, we discovered, the U.S. government had simultaneously thrown open its markets to these foreign imports yet withheld from the FDA and the Department of Agriculture the resources needed to inspect the surge of foods and medicines entering the country. The Bush administration's FY 2009 budget called for closing five of the FDA regional offices, four of twenty district offices, and seven of thirteen regional testing laboratories as a "cost-saving" measure—meaning more imports and fewer inspections.

In a tangible, nontheoretical, and immediate way, we learned that unfettered globalization does not meet our most elementary demand—assurance of the personal safety of our children and ourselves. American-style globalism is a very Dangerous Business.

The pet food debacle is instructive, for it is similar to dozens of similar scandals, and it reveals the problems of unregulated globalism in an intimate way that touches everyone.

This particular scandal became public on March 16, 2007, when Menu Foods, the Canadian-based manufacturer of pet foods, voluntarily recalled 60 million units of its "cuts and gravy" products made between December 3, 2006, and March 6, 2007. This little-known Canadian corporation was the real manufacturer of wet pet foods for most of America's largest suppliers, including Procter & Gamble, Colgate-Palmolive, Purina, Wal-Mart, Safeway, and PetSmart. Owners who were paying high prices for certain brands under the assumption that they were buying a superior product for their pets were getting the same contaminated food as in the low-priced cans. Altogether, Menu Foods produces almost 75 percent of Canada's private-label wet foods and 50 percent of those sold in the United States. The first recall included eighty-six different dog and cat food brands. Later, more brands were added to the list.

Initially, FDA scientists thought the residue of a rat poison used in Chinese wheat fields might have tainted one of the ingredients. Within days, however, researchers at the University of Guelph in Ontario and at Cornell University in New York State pinpointed the real source of contamination, making it clear that this was no innocent accident.

The scientists isolated a manufactured chemical substance, melamine, that had been mixed into the wheat gluten that Menu Foods used in its wet pet foods. Wheat gluten is dough made by mixing wheat flour and water and then kneading and rinsing it until the starch is removed. Gluten gives dough its elasticity and baked goods, such as bread and cakes, their toothsomeness. The nutritional value of gluten is high, providing about 80 percent of the proteins in wheat.

The melamine was an alien ingredient and should never have been mixed with the gluten or put into any food. Melamine is used primarily to make other chemical products, such as fertilizers, paints, and plastics. But when put into foodstuffs, it produces a false test result that tricks people into thinking they are getting a higher protein value than they are. The American Veterinary Medical Association reports that even tiny amounts of melamine form "extremely insoluble" crystals that block animals' kidney function. Without treatment, the blockage can lead to a torturous death.

The United States imports more than a half-million pounds of food-quality glutens annually, and most of us, in fact, eat glutens in some form virtually every day. Because glutens are so common, their use is so widespread, and the food processing industry is now so concentrated, the contamination of even a small portion of the food supply is a frightening prospect. Just as a single food producer poisoned almost half the U.S. production of wet pet foods, the same thing could just as easily happen to food for humans because of the concentration in that industry.

Once the FDA knew that melamine was the contaminating element, its investigators immediately began searching for the source. China was the first suspect. Because of the economics of the pet food industry, which is fiercely competitive, big retailers are constantly driving producers to lower their costs. A tiny fraction of a penny per unit can make the difference between winning and losing massive contracts with retailers such as Wal-Mart. To stay in business, therefore, manufacturers must use the least costly components. Those are most often found in China's unregulated commodities market.

Menu Foods' records documented that the wheat gluten in the recalled pet foods had been purchased from ChemNutra, a Las Vegas–based importer of Chinese food products. ChemNutra had won the contract by charging 20 cents per pound less than its U.S. competitors. In turn, it had purchased its supplies from the Xuzhou Anying Biological Technology Development Company in Xuzhou, China, the lowest-price producer.

By mid-April, the FDA had pulled from the U.S. market 889 separate items of 100 different brands of pet foods made by three producers. By then, its investigators had discovered melamine in corn glutens used as animal feed in the United States. FDA officials announced that melamine had been found in the urine of hogs in North Carolina, California, and South Carolina, and that similar melamine-laced animal food had been distributed to farms in New York, Ohio, and Utah. The FDA and Department of Agriculture also found evidence that as many as 3 million chickens that had eaten contaminated feed might have been sold for human food and presumably consumed. But agency officials assured the U.S. public that they faced "no risk" from eating melamine-tainted beef, pork, and chicken.

After the FDA scientists identified the Chinese supplier, the State Department requested permission from the Beijing government to have FDA staff inspect its factories and examine its order books to determine if more poisoned goods were already in the United States or on the way. Despite the potential health risks to American consumers, the Chinese government stonewalled U.S. officials, initially denying that there were any melamine connections to the pet food poisonings. Then it announced that its own investigators would inspect the gluten factories themselves and share their information with the FDA.

But, after more and more foods sold in the United States were identified as being tainted by imports of Chinese melamine-laced feeds, as more pets died, as more outraged American pet owners vented their anger, and as Congress prepared for public hearings, Beijing suddenly relented and allowed FDA inspectors into the Chinese factories. Simultaneously, that government reiterated its official stance that melamine had had nothing to do with the pet deaths, even as other officials announced a ban on the use of melamine in all Chinese-made food products.

By late April, the tainted glutens had been narrowed to two Chinese companies. But before the FDA investigators could arrive, the owner of one factory razed his brick structure and destroyed all evidence. The Chinese government arrested him and put the other owner under investigation.

FDA officials soon discovered that the two companies had evaded quality checks on their products by labeling them as exports, which are not subject to inspection in China. With the FDA investigation and the arrest of one supplier, the scandal seemed contained.

But, of course, it wasn't. On May 7, 2007, *The New York Times* ran, as its lead story, "From China to Panama, a Trail of Poisoned Medicine" by Walt Bogdanich and Jake Hooker. Their report revealed that thousands of people around the world have died because unscrupulous Chinese manufacturers were selling diethylene glycol (DG), a syrupy, sweet, and deadly industrial solvent, as glycerin, a safe, sweet syrup used in products such as cough medicines, toothpastes, and many foods. The citizens of Panama were the latest victims.

In 2006, workers at Panama's National Health Service mixed 260,000 bottles of cold medicine with what they thought was 99.9 percent pure glycerin but was actually the solvent DG. Subsequently, the authorities traced 100 deaths directly to the poisoned cold medicine and have evidence that another 265 people may also have been killed by it.

The *Times* traced the forty-six barrels of the poison syrup used by the Panamanian health officials through trading companies operating out of three countries: China, Spain, and Panama. During their journey, the contents of the barrels were never tested. The three governments and the three trading companies relied on a false certificate of purity that should have been instantly suspect because it did not list the producer or prior owners. The *Times* learned that the Chinese government owns one of the companies that sold the DG to Panama's health service.

Lest anyone think the Chinese people are themselves safe from such deadly commerce, consider this: in May 2004, the Xinhua news agency reported that as many as 200 babies had died because they had been fed fake infant formula sold in Anhui and Shandong provinces. Investigators were examining 141 production facilities that were selling forty-five types of substandard infant formula to village grocery stores. One popular formula contained only one sixth of the nutrients required to meet a baby's dietary requirements for development. Hundreds of other babies suffered severe malnutrition and brain damage.

Chinese pharmaceutical and food industries are so little regulated and Chinese food and drug laws are so weak that such regulations might as well be nonexistent. In 2005, the government investigated 310,000 reports of counterfeit medicines and subsequently destroyed 530 illegal pharmaceutical factories. The same year, as in virtually every other recent year, between 200,000 and 300,000 Chinese died because of counterfeit medicines. As regulatory enforcement, it was too little, too late—more a political placebo to calm the people of China than real law enforcement. Of the 530 destroyed factories, only 214 cases continued to prosecution. And of these, the laws are so weak that they virtually preclude criminal prosecution of the responsible individuals.

The obvious question is this: If the government of China will not protect its own people from poisoned food and drugs, why should the United States government expect it to protect the American people from such dangers? In fact, neither the citizens of China nor those of the United States can rely on the Chinese government to monitor the production of the bulk active pharmaceutical ingredients used in the manufacture of drugs produced there and shipped here. Strikingly, the selling of such ingredients to drug counterfeiters, manufacturers of illicit drug products that look like legitimate drugs but may or may not contain the proper ingredients, is still legal under Chinese law.

As for the scandal in Panama, Beijing has officially determined that it has no jurisdiction to deal with any acts in China that led to the deaths of so many Panamanians. That government does not even require the inspection of bulk products used in foods and medicines if they are shipped abroad. In plain terms, China takes no responsibility for the export of poisoned, contaminated, or deadly products, whether they are used in genuine or counterfeit goods. China, moreover, is no different from Russia, India, and dozens of developing nations. It just happens to be the largest exporter of contaminated and counterfeit goods.

Which brings us back to our "canary in the mine." The list of tainted Chinese goods imported into the United States includes far more than just pet foods. In the one-month period of April 2007, FDA inspectors seized 107 shipments of tainted food imports from China, plus more than 1,000 shipments of dietary supplements, toxic cosmetics, and counterfeit medicines. Among the seized goods were dried apples coated with a cancer-causing chemical, frozen catfish filled with banned antibiotics, scallops coated with rotting bacteria, and mushrooms tainted with harsh pesticides.

While Chinese exporters were caught selling tainted goods more often than those of other nations, India and Mexico were not far behind. In the twelve months from mid-2006 to mid-2007, the FDA rejected 1,901 shipments from China, 1,782 from India, 1,560 from Mexico, 862 from the Dominican Republic, and 82 from Denmark. Candy from Mexico contained pesticides, and cantaloupes were raised there with water from sewage-polluted rivers. Spices from India were contaminated, and medicines were impure.

Most worrisome, the FDA reported that this catch of poisoned foods, cosmetics, and medicines was far from inclusive since the agency had the staff to inspect only 1 percent of such imports. The other 99 percent moved into the U.S. market.

This is a glaring security failure that can be traced directly to a lack of federal funding. The agency's 2,000 inspectors are responsible for the oversight of almost 300,000 food plants, of which 190,000 are abroad. Global trade has changed the nature of inspections as more of the U.S. food supply is imported. Between 1999 and 2007, imports of food rose by 50 percent. Yet in that same period, the food samples analyzed in FDA labs dropped from almost 4 percent of import shipments to less than 1 percent. The FDA inspection of foreign seafood-processing facilities has decreased even more. In fiscal year 2003, Congress provided the FDA $211,000 to physically inspect foreign facilities where seafood is prepared for export to American consumers. In 2006, Congress cut that to $22,000 and in 2007 to zero. Of the 190,000 foreign food firms that export into the United States, the FDA inspected fewer than 100 in 2007.

Inexplicably, the U.S. government sends contaminated foods back to the shippers rather than destroying them. Thus, these foreign exporters often resend the same putrid shipments back to the United States, knowing that the odds are 99 to 1 that they will succeed the next time. As one FDA official explained, "If you send a problem shipment to the United States, it is going to get in and you won't get caught, and you won't have your food returned to you, let alone get arrested or imprisoned."

The U.S. government largely ignores China's dumping of rotten food on the American market mainly because well-connected U.S.-headquartered food processors want to sell their agricultural products to China. If the United States rejects Chinese imports, the Chinese will restrict U.S. food imports. When the FDA blocked the importation of some Chinese seafood in June 2007, Beijing immediately responded by prohibiting pork and chicken imports from the United States, claiming they contained banned chemicals. The two U.S.-based companies the Chinese targeted were Tyson Foods, which had processed the chicken, and Cargill, which had sold the pork.

Not surprisingly, China's best allies in the trade "politics" of tainted foodstuffs are U.S.-based transnational agricorporations. In 2006, the U.S. poultry industry and the Chinese government successfully pressured the Department of Agriculture to allow the processing in China of chickens raised and slaughtered in North America—that is, Mexico, Canada, and the United States. American law allows this chicken to be sold without a country of origin label. Thus, most U.S. shoppers don't know when they are buying chicken raised and killed in Mexico, frozen and put into containers, shipped across the Pacific Ocean, processed in China, put back into containers, and then sent back across the ocean for distribution and sale in the United States. Think of this much-traveled delicacy as "transpacific chicken."

Now the Chinese government and some U.S. poultry dealers are pressing the USDA to allow the importation of chickens raised, slaughtered, and processed in China, the world center of avian flu. This is a shockingly bad idea since improperly processed chickens from China could easily bring some variant of that flu to the United States. Trade trumps consumer safety in American-style globalism.

To evaluate whether the United States can import food from China safely, Congress sent its investigators there to find out in the summer of 2007. They discovered many problems, several of which had originated in the United States. While China's General Administration of Quality, Supervision, Inspection and Quarantine (AQSIQ) certifies exporters, who must provide lab results and documentation before exports are approved, for instance, the FDA does not recognize that certification and allows Chinese imports without AQSIQ documentation, which means that exporters can evade even minimal Chinese regulation.

The congressional investigators were intrigued with Japan's approach, which is to allow thirty-six specific Chinese chicken-processing plants to ship into its domestic market. Japanese officials inspect those plants regularly, often with surprise visits. Japan also tests about 15 percent of the food imported from China, while the United States tests less than 1 percent.

Although the investigators reported that China's food supply does not meet either international or U.S. standards, they also advised Congress not to impose equivalent safety measures on food imported from China, as the Department of Agriculture does with meat, because China would not meet those standards, which would close off Chinese food exports to America. Commerce trumped safety.

Globalization, therefore, is about more than just trade. It is also about our personal safety and who assures it and geopolitics and who benefits. In an unregulated global marketplace, the only guarantees Americans have about the safety and quality of the foods and medicines they consume are U.S. laws, regulations, and inspections. They are wise to view any goods from China and other developing nations, particularly those made for human or animal consumption, as being suspect. We are years, if not decades, away from a time when the regulatory agencies of China and newly developing countries can be relied upon to protect our safety. The FDA and USDA are not just our first line of food and medicine security, they are our *only* line of safety.

Significantly, the FDA, in its 2002 *Performance Plan Summary*, warned, "The agency is unable to assure the U.S. public that it can prevent unsafe imports from entering the country." This is a scary bit of candor, but also an important message.

Yet agency officials have been testifying before Congress since at least 2002 that more than 80 percent of the bulk active ingredients that go into U.S. prescription drugs are imported and that the FDA has information on only 18 percent of the companies supplying these ingredients. Worse, the FDA has never inspected the facilities of more than 4,600 foreign companies that supply most of the ingredients used in prescription medicines sold in the United States.

The FDA also reports that its investigators have never inspected more than 600 Chinese firms and more than 400 Indian firms that manufacture drugs for export to the United States. Since China and India are also the world's two main counterfeiters of medicines and bulk pharmaceutical ingredients, this means that neither legitimate nor counterfeit medicines are inspected.

Alarmed by the possibility that American consumers might stop buying foods and medicines containing any ingredient from China, Beijing began a "safety" propaganda campaign in July 2007 to save the credibility of the "Made in China" label. Its show opened with the high-visibility execution of the head of China's food and drug regulation bureau for taking bribes and his failure to adequately supervise food and drug producers. Over the next four months, the Chinese government closed dozens of shady companies and arrested 774 people, whom it identified as "criminal suspects." The campaign was reminiscent of earlier, token PR campaigns, when Chinese officials announced that they had stopped the illegal reproduction of music and movie CDs, arrested a few people, piled thousands of seized CDs in a field, and then smashed them by running heavy construction machinery back and forth over the pile, even as the illegal copying continued.

President Bush announced in July 2007 the creation of a federal panel whose mission was to identify ways to minimize the dangers to American consumers from imported foods and medicines. A White House spokesman denied that these efforts were aimed at China. And they were not; they were aimed at worried Americans. The maneuver worked. By the end of 2007, China's exports of toys, foods, and other goods were soaring to record levels.

In November 2007, the FDA Science Board's Science and Technology Subcommittee presented a confidential report to the agency titled "FDA Science and Mission at Risk." It reminded the President and Congress that the FDA is responsible for protecting 80 percent of the U.S. food supply; regulating all drugs, human vaccines, and medical devices; and playing a central role in protecting America from the effects of terrorist attacks, employing means such as anthrax, smallpox, poisoning food, nerve agent attacks, and radioactive contamination, as well as natural threats such as SARS, West Nile virus, and avian influenza.

The authors concluded that the FDA's scientific base, workforce, and information infrastructure had been allowed to erode to the point that "American lives are at risk." They made recommendations for change that subsequently have been largely ignored. The FDA is so resource starved that it cannot meet its most basic missions.

In sum, the United States' approach to globalization has been to openly accept goods of all kinds from anywhere, including those for human consumption, even as the government's capacity to inspect those products for their safety is reduced.

In Pursuit of Raw Capitalism Half the imports from China are from corporations whose owners are headquartered in the United States, Japan, and Europe. The trade rules of globalization allow them to operate there and in dozens of other nations with virtually no environmental, labor, worker safety, or other regulations. Under those same trade rules, these corporations can export the goods into the United States and pay few if any tariffs. In numerous ways, our recent presidents and Congresses have inadvertently created a global trade legal environment in which the raw capitalism of the nineteenth century can thrive once again.

One consequence of such unfettered globalization is that it makes possible massive concentration of industries on a global scale. For most of the twentieth century, the government of the United States opposed mergers that would give the top four firms in an industry a combined market share of 40 percent or more. During the Reagan administration, federal antitrust officials transformed the 40 percent level into a screen for determining when to look at other factors such as market operations, price discrimination, and lack of entry into the market by competitors.

With the advent of competition from abroad in the 1970s, however, federal officials became decreasingly unable to determine whether monopolies existed by looking at U.S. market shares. In 1980, Lester Thurow wrote in *The Zero-Sum Society* that national antitrust laws no longer made sense as they only served to hinder U.S. competitors, which must live by a code that their foreign competitors can ignore.

Thurow was doubly perceptive. The application of antitrust law was, indeed, increasingly one-sided. And second, foreign competitors could ignore antitrust restrictions at home because their governments were often the architects and managers of national cartels. Germany, France, and Japan, like most other nations, supported the idea of national champions, backed them with monies and procartel regulations, and kept foreign competitors out of their markets or at a minimum set the terms by which they could operate there. China is the most recent entry into the "cartel club." As we will see, the government of China still owns its major industries and defines sharply how foreigners will operate there.

When Thurow wrote his book, the modern era of globalization was more than a decade in the future. Although the U.S. Justice Department and the Federal Trade Commission still file and win dozens of antitrust cases annually, mostly against U.S.-based violators, the larger concentration of industries is global in nature. Unfettered globalization allows a handful of firms to dominate entire industries worldwide. International aircraft, Internet equipment, Internet search engines, machine tools, robotics, and consumer electronics are only some of the most visible examples. Although such concentration can achieve great economies of scale in production, lower costs, and increase profits, these cartels also set worldwide prices, divide markets, keep out new entrants, and slow innovation. As these cartels have escaped national boundaries and laws, examining their activities has become correspondingly difficult, as has imposing any regulation.

Absent such examination and any meaningful regulation, globalization is bringing us the rapid cartelization of industries worldwide. The consequences are neither insignificant nor abstract, for they touch the lives of all Americans every day, beginning every morning with the food we eat at breakfast. Consider this story.

Tucson's Mountain Oyster Club (don't ask) serves the most unique hors d'oeuvres and some of the best steaks in America. That's no surprise, as the MO, as its members call it, was founded by the sons of Arizona ranchers when they returned from World War II. The young veterans wanted a private, informal club of their own, where they could get a good steak and a stiff drink and sometimes even make a fool of themselves without anyone noticing, especially their parents. Sixty years later, the MO retains the same informality, though in far better surroundings, and on any given evening many diners will be ranchers, their families, and guests wearing jeans, bolo ties, and cleaned-up cowboy boots.

My wife and I were dining there with our friends Howard and Sally Creswell, whose families were ranchers, and Wyndy Pyre, the widow of one of the founding members. As we were finishing our meal, their friend Tom Noonan and his wife joined us for coffee. Noonan, a tall, trim, white-haired cattleman, had driven to Tucson from one of his ranches in northern Mexico for a steak dinner. Ranchers do that.

The conversation eventually turned to ranching, and when I asked how globalization was affecting his industry, Noonan answered, "Big. Anyone who wishes to survive in the red meat industry," he said, "must get as big as they can, as fast as they can."

In the 1980s, the U.S. beef-packing industry had a couple of dozen companies, he explained, that had been served by a score of beef suppliers. But now four giant global corporations control more than 80 percent of the U.S. meatpacking industry and ten major beef producers supply them, of which he was one.

Such a sharp increase of industry concentration in such a short period seemed unlikely to me, so the next day I checked it on the Internet. Noonan knew his business. Between 1994 and 2005, more than 122,000 American cattle ranches and farms closed down or left the beef cattle industry. In 1980, the four largest U.S. meatpackers accounted for 36 percent of all steers and heifers slaughtered. By 1990, those four accounted for 72 percent. The number was 84 percent for steer and heifer slaughter in 2004 and 64 percent for hog slaughter.

Put into context, the meatpacking industry today is more concentrated than it was in 1919, when President Woodrow Wilson decided to bust the "Beef Trust." In 1919, Armour, Swift, Morris, Wilson, and Cudahy Packing held an estimated 50 to 75 percent of the market, a position that they divested in a consent agreement with the Federal Trade Commission in 1920.

With globalization, "big" is back. A 1999 Senate hearing on economic concentration in agriculture revealed that suppliers of seed, chemicals, feed, fuel, and other inputs have become highly concentrated. Simultaneously, the markets for beef, hogs, chickens, sheep, corn, and grains have also consolidated and are dominated by just a few agribusiness giants. Thus, a handful of giant transnational corporations control the production, transport, marketing, and pricing of much of the world's food.

Cargill-Monsanto, Novartis, Archer-Daniels, IBP, and ConAgra dominate agricultural production. Nestlé, Unilever, and Kraft control food processing. The world's principal food retailers are Tesco (United Kingdom), Royal Ahold (Netherlands), Carrefour (France), and Wal-Mart (United States). These corporations work together in endless ways. Through mergers, contracts, joint projects, partnerships, and other arrangements, these giant economic clusters link up producers, commodity traders, meat production, and processing in an ever-changing global network of deals. Cargill supplies Kroger's beef. Wal-Mart buys much of its meat from IBP, Farmland, and Smithfield. Ahold USA supplies dairy products to Dean Foods.

The arithmetic of this concentration is conspicuous. Four corporations, for instance, process 80 percent of all U.S. soybeans, three quarters of U.S. corn, and two thirds of U.S. wheat. Four companies control more than 84 percent of the U.S. cattle slaughter industry, 64 percent of all pork packing, and 50 percent of the chicken-processing industry. Four companies control 89 percent of the production of breakfast cereals.

Concentration is equally great in food retailing. In France, five companies sell 94 percent of all food bought in that country. Four retailers account for three quarters of all foods sold in U.S. cities. Their stores have many names and their products many brands. As we learned during the 2007 melamine-contaminated pet food controversy, one company can account for dozens, if not hundreds, of separate brand names. As we also learned, a mistake or sabotage in any one of these megaproducers can affect a major portion of the nation's food or drug supplies.

The reach of these corporate giants, moreover, goes far beyond Europe and the United States. France's Carrefour, the world's second largest food retailer, dominates sales in France and several South American countries, plus Taiwan. Royal Ahold (Netherlands) is the major food retailer for the rest of South America, plus Spain, Norway, and Sweden.

Farmers in developing countries throughout South America, Africa, and Asia are constantly vulnerable to price manipulations as the mega-industry buyers pit producers in one nation against those in another to lower the prices from all. Middlemen in developing nations finance farmers' production with extortion-level interest rates, fertilizers and seeds at artificially high prices, controlled milling and processing, high transport prices, and goods from company-operated stores sold on credit that are payable with the borrower's crop. If this seems familiar, it is how food trusts operated in the United States until the "trust-busting" of the early twentieth century.

The concentration in the U.S. agriculture and food industries is so tight and the political power of those corporations so great that they can politically deny consumers even basic information, such as the country of origin of many foods they buy. In 2002, Senator Tom Harkin (D-Iowa) and Senator Tom Daschle (D-N.D.), for instance, put a provision into the Farm Bill that requires country-of-origin labeling (COOL) for beef, lamb, pork, fish, perishable agricultural commodities, and peanuts. The provision went unnoticed by most food lobbyists and the large food producers and distributors until after President George W. Bush signed the legislation into law.

COOL had the strong political support of independent U.S. beef producers in those two senators' states and elsewhere because many Americans believe that many imported foods are produced in unsanitary conditions, while they think that those of U.S. producers are superior. Consequently, many American consumers will reject foreign-produced meats and vegetables, if they know the country of origin. Much is at stake for the big producers and retailers since they bring more than 1.7 million head of cattle into the United States every year, primarily from Mexico, Australia, Canada, and Uruguay. Without COOL, the corporations can hide the country of origin and more easily sell their less expensive, more profitable imported goods.

The transnational food corporations could not get the COOL law eliminated by Congress in 2003, so they set out to delay its implementation. Surprisingly—or perhaps not—their principal allies were the politically appointed officials in the Department of Agriculture (USDA), who in 2003 issued draft rules for the implementation of COOL that were so burdensome they made the law unworkable. Then, before the 2004 presidential election, the food corporations persuaded Congress to enact legislation that delayed COOL's implementation until September 30, 2006, even though President Bush had signed the bill into law on January 27, 2004. The excuse, of course, was that the USDA needed more time to devise workable rules.

To stop the "big" stall, advocates of COOL sponsored legislation in 2005 that mandated immediate implementation of the law. Twenty-one major agribusiness corporations and their trade associations collectively put 160 lobbyists to work on Capitol Hill; a quarter of them were former Department of Agriculture officials. On November 10, 2005, Bush signed another bill that further delayed the implementation of COOL until September 30, 2008. But in 2004, when the Bush administration wanted to protect politically powerful domestic catfish and shellfish producers from Asian imports, the USDA created a set of simplified rules for them that facilitated country-of-origin labeling and were not burdensome.

As matters stand in early 2008, consumers are allowed to know the source of the fish and shellfish they buy, but they are not allowed to know the country of origin of their beef, pork, lamb, perishable agricultural commodities, and peanut purchases. In August 2007, the Zogby polling firm released survey results that revealed that 95 percent of respondents feel that consumers have a right to know the country of origin of the foods they buy and 88 percent said they want all retail food labeled with country-of-origin information.

The fact that American consumers are not allowed to know the country of origin for many of the foods they eat reflects the money-driven political collusion between the transnational food corporations and the elected officials who control our government.

The idea is so basic that Adam Smith noted in *The Wealth of Nations*, "People of the same trade seldom meet together, even for merriment and diversion, but the conversation ends in a conspiracy against the public, or in some contrivance to raise prices." Stated in modern terms, collusion, not competition, is the default strategy in concentrated industries.

One of the most visible and significant concentrations is in the media industry. As of 2007, eight global conglomerates owned about 90 percent of the media markets of Europe and the United States. With the loosened U.S. media ownership requirements mandated in 1996 and 2003, one company can own two newspapers in any American city, three local television stations, two national networks, and eight local radio stations. Such media giants have interlocking directorates composed of a narrow group of investment bankers and heads of other transnational corporations, including private equity groups, oil producers, pharmaceutical makers, health care providers, and arms makers—virtually all of which are directly vested in transnational operations.

Ben H. Bagdikian, dean emeritus of the University of California at Berkeley Graduate School of Journalism, points out that the "dumbing down" of reportage and the resulting conflicts of interest can be numerous, even resulting in self-censorship in what is reported about topics such as globalization or the corporate activities of interrelated companies. Bagdikian observes that trying to be a first-rate reporter on the average American newspaper today is like trying to play Bach on a ukulele.

The most troubling aspect about today's economic concentration is that it is so large scale and so far flung that regulation is beyond the capacity of any individual government. Today, only the governments of the United States, Europe, and Japan, acting in concert, have the power to rein in the abuses of enterprises so large that many have annual revenues far greater than the gross domestic products of all but a few nations.

Weakening National Security Adam Smith also wrote in *The Wealth of Nations* that a nation should "depend as little as possible upon its neighbors for the manufactures necessary for its defense." Certainly, this was U.S. policy from 1790 until the end of the Cold War—that is, before this era of globalization. For Smith, security trumped commerce. In American-style globalization, commerce trumps security.

The presidential administrations of Bill Clinton and George W. Bush, with the end of the Cold War, adopted new assumptions about the nature of the wars America would face. The new premise of the Department of Defense (DOD) is that the United States will no longer have to fight wars that take a protracted time and require weapons and supplies that are constantly coming off the production line. "We don't plan on fighting that kind of war," a senior DOD official told *Manufacturing and Technology News* in 2005. "You fight from stockpiles."

The Iraq War, of course, is already longer than the U.S. engagement in World War II, and the list of undersupplied items for the fighting has been long and critical: body armor, vehicle armor, desert uniforms, helmets, desert boots, tanks, even bullets, among other items. By May 2004 the Army was running out of bullets and had to let emergency contracts to British and Israeli suppliers.

Although U.S. military expenditures have been maintained at high levels since the Cold War, defense industries in Europe and the United States have been consolidated and the DOD has entered into agreements with several nations to ensure a supply of defense goods and services. Thus, producers in the United Kingdom and many other nations can bid on contracts and supply the DOD from there and vice versa.

In 1996, the DOD announced that its procurement goal was to "maintain superior technology and industrial capabilities at an affordable price." One part of its twofold strategy is to rely on dual-use technologies—that is, items used in commercial products such as cell phones but also usable in military goods such as battlefield communications equipment. The other part is to take advantage of the cost and technology benefits offered by global suppliers. The DOD handbook on acquisition and technology instructs managers:

> *Reliable foreign suppliers are usually acceptable, and in fact are encouraged to allow the Department to obtain a wider competitive cost and technology base. Foreign dependence does not mean foreign vulnerability. The Department of Defense seeks to use foreign sources wherever advantageous and within the limitations of the law.*
>
> *If you have not used or even solicited foreign sources for your product or service in the past, you may have to research potential feasible firms. Work with your procurement officer to perform this research and to analyze this alternative.*

In short, the U.S. Department of Defense encourages its contractors to outsource components from low-cost foreign suppliers. Adam Smith, I think, would be aghast.

DOD also notes that market concentration—that is, a single source of supply—is not a reason to exclude foreign sourcing if the home country has political stability. Equally significant, the handbook says, "Sheer physical distance from the U.S. is *not by itself* a risk which merits foreign source exclusion." Subsequently, these new DOD policies have allowed China and the nations surrounding it to become major suppliers of weapons components the U.S. military buys.

Yet all of the DOD's *Annual Reports on the Military Power of the People's Republic of China* point out that China is a rising military threat to the United States. Apparently, policy makers believe if there is a U.S.-China military crisis, the flow of critical military supplies from that country, or nations close to it, to the United States will not be interrupted.

The Iraq War has revealed major problems with the current U.S. defense procurement strategy, not the least of which is the assumption that future wars will be short enough to supply from existing stockpiles. Equally significant, foreign producers of commercial technologies are often unwilling to divert production from their long-term customers in exchange for short-term DOD purchases. Though other governments may agree that the DOD can go to the head of the line, private companies may require prods that foreign politicians are reluctant to exert. In one such instance, a Swiss supplier refused to supply a critical component because the owner disapproved of the Iraq War. A second supplier was found, but only after a bit of scrambling.

Alan Tonelson, a defense analyst at the U.S. Business and Industry Council, observes that the DOD is making the dubious assumption "that most countries can be trusted to keep secrets, remain as responsible suppliers and comply with reciprocity agreements." Many critics also doubt the efficacy of DOD's "globalization" supply strategy. Representative Duncan Hunter (R-Calif.), former chairman of the House Armed Services Committee, has repeatedly asked DOD officials for a list of components they buy and the countries of origin. He wants to know which items are produced in foreign-based factories, how vital they are, and what alternate sources are available. The DOD maintains that it does not have such a list, a claim Hunter thinks is unlikely. Rather, he says, DOD outsourcing is now so extensive that the release of such information would cause a political backlash, for it would make it clear that the United States now relies on a defense industrial base that is increasingly located on the other sides of the Atlantic and Pacific Oceans.

Growing uncertainty about the safety of our food and drug supplies, the expanding global concentration of industries, the ever-increasing influence of corporate interests over our governance, and a deepening vulnerability in our national security are only some of the consequences, and risks, of a globalization process that is not monitored or regulated by any nation or organization.

In these opening years of the twenty-first century three megaforces are driving the United States' approach to the integration of our economy with the rest of the world: modern mercantilism, global corporatism, and elitist control of our government and the economy itself. They are each examined in the next section of this book.

I

Three Megaforces

One

MODERN MERCANTILISM

In 1989, Alan M. Webber, then the managing editor of the *Harvard Business Review*, returned from a trip to Japan and wrote to his readers:

> *The world is changing, and Japan is different. On both sides of the Pacific, the old, entrenched interests are hard at work denying these conclusions, pretending that business as usual will do, and silencing the observers and analysts who call attention to the new situation. Japan's motives are not hard to fathom; after all, every day the country gains in wealth, economic power, and global momentum. The longer Japan successfully confounds U.S. leaders into thinking that all the old rules still apply, the longer the transfer of wealth and power can continue unimpeded. It is not Japan's job to inform us of our blind stupidity.*

What Webber found in Japan was a nation actively pursuing a mercantile trade policy, the approach to global commerce where the government and industry work together to build national wealth through increased exports while maintaining an economic moat around their country to stop direct foreign investment, sharply limit imports, and build up huge financial reserves. Adam Smith would have immediately recognized this Japanese policy as mercantilism; however, even after more than a quarter century of engagement, U.S. leaders still do not.

If we fast-forward in time about twenty years, what Webber found in Japan in 1989 is happening all over Asia and in parts of South America today. And, as then, U.S. leaders and opinion elites do not recognize that they are witnessing a new rise of mercantilism, particularly in China. Rather, they view China's economic and trade activities as a steady march from socialism to market-oriented capitalism like that of the United States, though a bit more exotic.

China is actively creating a hybrid economy that the Chinese define as a "socialist market system" (SMS). While to many outsiders that system appears to be market-oriented and largely controlled by the private sector, it is neither. China is well along in creating an economy where the government owns and controls the strategic industries while secondary and service industries are left to private ownership, which the government also controls.

The giant enterprise called China, which accrued a historic global trade surplus of $262 billion in 2007, is pursuing export-driven, beggar-thy-neighbor trade policies that are so blatantly nationalistic they are undermining the World Trade Organization and putting the entire global trading system at risk. To understand China's approach to global economics, we must examine its basic elements.

Mercantilism In the sixteenth through eighteenth centuries, the dominant economic theory in Europe, mercantilism, held that national prosperity depended on a nation's supply of capital, which at the time was gold. The fastest way to acquire capital was to run a trade surplus with other nations by exporting more goods than were imported. To facilitate this economic dynamic, governments subsidized production and exports, at the same time imposing barriers on foreign imports. The idea was simple: to make exports so inexpensive that foreign consumers would prefer them over domestically made goods and conversely make imports so expensive that local consumers would prefer domestic goods over foreign-made ones.

England, under the intellectual influence of the economists Adam Smith and David Ricardo, gradually abandoned mercantilist policies in the nineteenth century and replaced them with an ideology of free trade and comparative advantage. The United States continued to pursue a mercantilist economic agenda until the early 1930s, when Roosevelt's secretary of state, Cordell Hull, began a move to a free-trade regime, which also promoted FDR's foreign policy objectives.

China is taking the mercantilist path abandoned by England and once used by the United States. The principal differences are that the United States did not own the major enterprises on which its economy depended, as the Chinese government does, and the U.S. government operated under a two-party, democratic system, while China is governed by one-party rule.

The ownership and democratic differences between the United States and China are fundamental. The Chinese government announced in December 2006 that seven industries were critical to the nation's economic security and would remain under strict government control. They are defense, power, oil, telecommunications, mineral resources, civil aviation, and shipping industries. This list, moreover, is not exclusive; Chinese officials noted that the government intended to expand the volume and structure of those industries so that they would become leading world businesses.

One-Party Rule by the Techno-Elite In a nation of 1.3 billion people, about 63 million Chinese are members of the Communist Party. Its principal national body is the Party Congress, which has about 3,000 delegates and meets every five years. The real control of the government resides in the Politburo Standing Committee (PSC), which since 2002 has consisted of nine persons drawn from the twenty-two-member Politburo. One of these nine serves as head of state (president) and another as head of government (premier). The number is kept uneven to prevent deadlocks.

All of the nine members of the Sixteenth Politburo Standing Committee (2002–2007) are trained engineers, experienced in various national development disciplines. One is a civil engineer, another is a geological engineer, three are electrical engineers, and four are mechanical engineers. All have extensive development experience in which they began at the bottom of organizations and worked their way up.

Unlike when Mao Tse-tung and political ideologues governed the nation, China's development planning now reflects leadership by a techno-elite. Major projects are phased. Industries are clustered to gain the efficiencies of colocation. Transport systems, from local industrial areas to seaports, are entwined. Basic infrastructure, such as electric generating power, is being given priority in planning and allocation of resources. Foreigners are involved when they can bring something China lacks, but their actions are controlled. The nation is developing along the lines set forth in Five-Year Plans, which set strategic directions and overall priorities. All of this is precisely the type of order that trained engineers would impose.

The point is that competent and experienced people lead China's government. For instance, Minister Wu Yi, a senior petroleum engineer who has represented China in trade discussions since 1991, is what U.S. Secretary of the Treasury Henry Paulson calls a "force of nature." Beyond having talented negotiators, China's leaders are systematically strengthening their nation's public infrastructure and consolidating and modernizing their industries so the enterprises can compete globally against those of Europe, Japan, and the United States.

Restructuring to Compete When the Communist Party seized control in 1949, it nationalized the economy. For the next thirty years, China's economic enterprises had little contact with the outside world and were considered by most Western observers to be quite backward. As recently as the late 1970s, most of China's industries were remnants of nineteenth-century investments or mirrors of those of the Soviet Union. Since 1979, however, China has been rapidly modernizing its economy, bringing to its production many of the world's most advanced technologies along with the leading management tools of major Western corporations.

To close the gap with other nations, China began reconstituting its state-owned industries in the 1980s. In the process, the government has encouraged foreign direct investment, joint ventures, the elimination of redundant production, the transformation of state industries into joint-stock ventures, the outright sale of some operations, and the liquidation of tens of thousands of failing ventures.

The magnitude of this challenge is daunting. In 2002, China's central government placed the responsibility for overseeing almost 200,000 state-owned enterprises in the state-owned Assets Supervision and Administration Commission (SASAC). Imagine SASAC as the world's largest equity fund, whose sole owner is the Chinese government. The chairman is Li Rongrong, born in 1944 and trained as an engineer, who began his career in 1963 as a factory worker in a plant he eventually came to manage. In 1986, he was appointed vice chairman of the Wuxi Municipal Economic Commission in Jiangsu province, and from that position he took on increasingly important responsibilities, including secretary general and then vice chairman of the State Economic and Trade Commission.

At the first SASAC working conference in August 2003, Li Rongrong identified five priority sectors for future development: (1) national security, (2) monopolies for natural resources, (3) provision of key public goods and services, (4) critical resources, and (5) core enterprises and high-tech industries.

Within those five divisions there were originally 196 central enterprises, many of which controlled dozens of subsidiaries. In 2003, the 196 central industries were consolidated to 191, and in 2007 they were further reduced to 161. At the 2003 conference, Li Rongrong also announced that China would create 30 to 50 large corporations with international competitive power before 2010. These will be companies on the scale of Microsoft, Motorola, GE, General Motors, and Pfizer.

Under SASAC, it is clear that China's economy is being transformed in a way that will form a pattern of development for the next generation or so. A cluster of state-owned enterprises (SOEs) will remain under the tight control of the central government. They include what the Chinese call the "lifeline" sectors: oil, coal, petrochemicals, metallurgy, power, telecommunications, defense, ocean shipping, air transport, defense, coal, scientific instruments, and related industries. In these industries the government maintains absolute control.

In 2003, China also announced that foreign investment would be permitted in banking, telecommunications, education, medical services, auto industries, civilian satellites, large-equipment manufacturing, and large-scale integrated circuits. While foreigners can own a minority position, the Chinese make the major decisions. In this way, the foreigners get a toehold in China and China gets their capital and expert help in becoming world-class competitors.

Under Li Rongrong's direction, these state-owned industries are making sharp gains in productivity and overall production. In mid-December 2006, Li reported that their sales were up 21 percent over the same period in 2005 and profits were up 19 percent. They paid 23 percent more taxes to the central government. Thirteen of China's top state-owned enterprises were on the *Forbes* 500 list of the world's top companies in 2006, versus five in 2003. The average return on SOE assets in 2006 was 10 percent. Without a doubt, China's socialist corporations are becoming efficient and globally competitive.

Equally interesting and important, Li also reported that the overall number and strength of Party members in the SOE were improving and building membership in the Party was being strengthened. Systems were being deployed to educate Party members constantly. The Communist Party is not planning to wither away in China's new economy.

A reality of China's economic transformation, however, is that hundreds of thousands of small and secondary Chinese businesses are now privately owned and operated. This gives the impression to outsiders that China is privatizing its economy. It also masks the growing competence and efficiency of the state-owned enterprises, which control the nation's lifeline industries as they are being shaped into national champions, much as Japan did with many of its core industries in the early and middle 1960s.

Currently, foreign-invested companies account for more than 50 percent of China's exports and 60 percent of its imports. But that will change as China's national champions grow and become more technologically sophisticated and many of the existing foreign firms are purchased for their distribution networks or forced aside. There will come a time when China will no longer need them.

China's Price Advantage China's economy has developed to the point that it has a price advantage over foreign competitors in virtually every product it makes in almost every market in the world. In 2006, the Paul Merage School of Business at the University of California–Irvine released an important study titled *A Report of "The China Price Project."* Professor Peter Navarro identified eight factors that gave China a price advantage in global competition and calculated their relative contributions to that advantage.

1. *Low wages for high-quality work:* Chinese wages are not the lowest in the world, but the country's workers are very productive and do high-quality work. Adjusting China's wages to account for the productivity of Chinese workers, Navarro found that the cost of an hour's work by a Chinese employee is about 18 percent that of a comparable American worker. What this means, of course, is that a company can hire five Chinese workers for the same price as one American. In all, low wages constituted 39.4 percent of China's price advantage.

2. *Piracy and Counterfeiting:* China is the center of world piracy and counterfeiting. As I documented in my book *Hot Property* (2005), almost every commercial item for sale in the world, including patented, trademarked, and copyrighted materials, has been copied and sold by Chinese pirates and counterfeiters. The government regularly promises to stop such activities but makes only a token effort. Since its accession to the World Trade Organization, China has created an elaborate judicial system to deal with violations of intellectual property rights and model laws. But the system does not work well, if at all. Sophisticated Western investors realize that if they take their technology to China it will be ripped off. Japan has asked its leading technology corporations to keep their most advanced work inside Japan and not even patent it out of fear that the patent applications themselves might give away that nation's most vital technological secrets. Navarro calculates that more than 8.6 percent of the Chinese price advantage can be attributed to the piracy and counterfeiting factor.

3. *Minimal worker health and safety regulations:* The World Health Organization and International Labor Organization jointly report a
growth of workplace accidents in China. Their most recent data
show that more than 90,000 Chinese workers died in 2001 because
of work-related accidents and 69 million were so badly injured
they were absent from work for three or more days. One of the
attractions to foreign investors is the fact that they can eliminate
investments in occupational safety equipment and training in Chinese factories and escape virtually any obligation when workers are
killed or injured. Laws exist but are not enforced. Silicosis, brown-
lung disease, cancer, and toxic poisoning are common sicknesses
among Chinese workers. Navarro estimates that factory owners in
China spend a third of what their counterparts in the United States
do on health and safety. This contributes 2.4 percent to the China
price advantage.

4. *Lax environmental regulations and enforcement:* China is the world's
top polluter. More than 70 percent of its rivers are badly contaminated. Two thirds of its cities fail to meet even the minimal standards for air quality. More than 400,000 Chinese die annually
because of air pollution–related diseases. At the same time, more
than 25 percent of the Chinese population is drinking unclean
water. Companies that operate in China are not required to meet
the environmental obligations they are in Japan and the West.
Navarro calculates the absence of environmental regulations
makes up 2.4 percent of the price advantage.

5. *Export subsidies:* The government, as well as provincial and local
regimes, heavily subsidizes both domestic and foreign-based corporations in a variety of ways. The China Development Bank and
the Export-Import Bank of China provide Chinese enterprises
massive credit lines for global expansion.

   The Export-Import Bank, for instance, provided TCL, now the
world's largest television set maker, funds it needed to take over
and operate the TV production of Thomson and the mobile phone
business of Alcatel. It also finances the export operations of
Huawei Technology, a telecom network equipment maker, and the
Haier Group, which makes a variety of technology goods. Often,
state loans such as these are then forgiven. Favored companies are
given free rent, raw materials, training, and transport facilities, subsidized shipping and telecommunications, and global marketing

support. In a 2006 report to the WTO, the government of China identified seventy-eight subsidy programs for industry that are operated by the central government, which did not include the programs of the state banks and provincial and local governments.

Tax exemptions are used extensively, particularly to lure foreign companies into China. A new foreign firm is given two full years of income tax exemption and a 50 percent reduction for the next three years. Foreign companies also receive a full refund of the income tax paid on reinvestment in China for export businesses or for companies that make advanced technologies.

Overall, Professor Navarro calculates, government subsidies contribute 16.7 percent of the China price advantage.

6. *Industrial network clustering:* Think of River Rouge, where between 1917 and 1928 Henry Ford built an automobile factory in Dearborn, Michigan, on a thousand-acre site that grew to contain ninety-three buildings, docks, a hundred miles of internal railroads, an electricity plant, a glass factory, and a steel mill. Raw materials arrived on the docks, and ultimately finished automobiles were driven out of the factory. By the 1930s, more than 100,000 people worked on this large, integrated site, which contained most of its supply chain inside the complex or close by.

China has built similar complexes that specialize in the production of specific items. Huizon makes DVDs and laser diodes. Ingrid produces computers. Leila turns out bicycles. Yanbun manufactures underwear. Dozens of these clusters, involving millions of workers, now exist, and great efficiencies are achieved. Navarro estimates that such clustering adds 16 points to the China price advantage, almost as much as government subsidies do.

7. *Foreign direct investment:* China is the world's principal destination for foreign direct investment (FDI). Unlike foreign investment in the United States, where almost 96 percent of such funds are used to buy existing assets such as stocks, almost all the foreign money going into China is invested in new production facilities. Foreign technology, managerial expertise, and global distribution networks accompany these funds. Navarro concludes that FDI adds a bit more than 3 points to China's price advantage.

8. *Undervalued currency:* In *The Trap,* Sir James Goldsmith illustrated how the value of a nation's money can be manipulated to make its products cheaper in the global market and thus create an economic

advantage. In 1981, he wrote, one U.S. dollar was worth 4.25 French francs; but by 1985, the dollar had risen sharply and was worth 10 francs. Consider a product, such as a chair, that in 1981 cost the same to make in either nation. By 1985, it was twice as expensive in America as in France, simply because of the value of the currency. Then, in 1992, the dollar's value fell again to 4.8 francs, making the price of the same chair once again competitive on open markets.

In 1994, China pegged the value of its currency at eight yuan to one dollar, where it has stayed ever since. By keeping the yuan at roughly eight to one, the Chinese government makes that nation's exports far less expensive and imports far more expensive than they otherwise would be. Ironically, if China suddenly allowed the yuan to trade at five to one, the U.S. cost of living would soar with a jump in prices of the Chinese imports upon which the nation now depends. Making a trip to Wal-Mart would be like going to Neiman Marcus now.

Congress and many trade associations have been concerned since the early years of this decade about the undervaluation of the Chinese currency. Navarro, taking a very conservative approach in his calculations, estimates that the Chinese currency is undervalued by only 20 percent. Even then, the currency factor contributes 11.4 percent to the China price advantage.

A quick way to understand how China's price advantage has changed the U.S. economy is found in a story about Wal-Mart, the world's largest retail company. In the 1980s, Sam Walton, the founder, helped lead and finance a "Made in the USA" campaign, which urged consumers to buy goods produced in U.S.-based factories by American workers. Celebrities such as Bob Hope and Barbara Mandrell served as spokespersons in a national ad campaign that cost tens of millions of dollars.

Walton died in 1992, and the company changed. Visit a Wal-Mart store today, and look at the country-of-origin labels on the goods. The same is true with all other major retailers selling in the United States. The China price advantage, coupled with open access to the U.S. market, has enabled Chinese-based producers, many of them U.S.-owned, to overwhelm their American-based competitors.

The arithmetic of this trade is daunting. In 1990, China had a $10 billion goods trade surplus with the United States; by 2000, it had grown to $83 billion. In 2007, the surplus exceeded $256 billion, thus tripling in seven years. Significantly, the composition of that trade ranges from the simplest to the most complex goods the United States consumes.

Advanced Technology Trade In March 2007, Intel Corporation announced it would build a massive $2.5 billion chip factory in China and have it operational by 2010. Paul Otellini, the CEO of Intel, said at the announcement ceremony in the Great Hall of the People in Beijing that Intel's goal in China "is to support a transition from 'manufactured in China' to 'innovated in China.' " Otellini and some of the Chinese officials present also expressed their hope that the Intel operations would draw other high-tech business to Dalian, China, and nurture other supporting industries.

The Intel decision to build in China is consistent with the eleventh Five-Year Plan (2006–2010) to invigorate the nation with science and education. As part of that strategy, national, regional, and local governments provide generous subsidies to companies such as Intel. Specifically, foreign corporations may deduct from their income tax 150 percent of their research and development (R&D) expenses incurred in China, but only if such expenses have increased by 10 percent over the previous year. In addition, the Chinese provide land, training, and a host of other benefits. Altogether, Intel will receive a package of subsidies worth between $500 million and $1 billion over five years.

As transnational corporations transfer their R&D and high-tech production to China and other nations, the United States is losing its preeminent position as the world's leading producer of advanced-technology products (ATPs); that is, leading-edge technologies that require research and development and whose benefits extend into other areas and often result in new products such as improved materials, which in turn create more spin-offs. ATP production also matters greatly because the work generally requires higher-skilled, better-educated, and better-paid participants.

The Commerce Department has identified approximately 500 items out of 22,000 possibilities that it divides into ten fields and classifies as advanced-technology goods.

1. Biotechnology
2. Life sciences
3. Opto-electronics
4. Information and communications

5.   Electronics
6.   Flexible manufacturing
7.   Advanced materials
8.   Aerospace
9.   Weapons
10. Nuclear technology

For decades, the United States was the global epicenter of advanced-technology production. No longer. In 2007, the United States exported $273 billion of such goods but imported more than $369 billion. Of these imports, almost $88 billion (21 percent) came from China. Overall, the United States had a $57 billion ATP trade deficit with China in 2006, up from $11 billion in 2000.

These are the technologies and products on which the U.S. economy and national defense rely. Many of these imported ATP goods are components for most other advanced-technology products the United States still makes. Moreover, as discussed earlier, the Department of Defense's policy to use commercial technologies in military goods means that many of our most advanced weapons are dependent on ATP production from China and the nations surrounding it—the Chinese "sphere of influence."

The arithmetic of ATP trade outlines the United States' vulnerability. The nations surrounding China include Hong Kong, Indonesia, Japan, Malaysia, the Philippines, Singapore, South Korea, Taiwan, Thailand, and Vietnam. In 2007, China and these other countries were the source of $191 billion of the $369 billion of ATP goods the United States imported—almost 52 percent.

The composition of these imports is equally significant. The United States now relies on China and these other Asian states for 60 percent of opto-electronics, 77 percent of information and communications equipment, 52 percent of electronics, and 53 percent of flexible manufacturing products it imports annually. For dozens of goods—a list that grows each year—these suppliers are the only source. While U.S., Japanese, and European corporations own many of the factories, Chinese managers and workers control the actual work. Often, the top manager of the production facility is an American or European who too often cannot speak Chinese and thus can communicate with the employees only through interpreters. He or she is captive to China.

Sovereign Wealth Investment How can a government with $3 trillion of reserves and assets that are growing by $400 billion per year invest that capital in a way that will advance its long-term interests but not trigger harsh reactions by other governments? China faces that challenge.

When the next U.S. president takes office in 2009, China's foreign reserves and assets managed by its state-owned investment fund will exceed $2 trillion, rising to $3 trillion by the end of 2010 and at least $4 trillion in 2012. Even if $1 trillion of those monies are held in reserves to defend China's currency, the remaining $2 trillion to $3 trillion will be the largest investment fund in the world, far more than that of the oil-rich United Arab Emirates, which established its fund in 1976.

China's deployment of those monies is going to shift global economics at least as much as has its quick emergence as a world-class manufacturing and exporting powerhouse. Already China's likely next steps are fairly clear. In March 2007, the government announced the creation of the State Foreign Exchange Investment Corporation to invest—initially—$200 billion to $250 billion of its financial reserves in foreign resources and technology.

Beijing is in a very-high-stakes race to diversify as much of its financial reserves into other assets as quickly as it can. Western governments, particularly the United States, are urging China to adjust the value of its currency, and that pressure will only intensify. But if and when China takes such a step, it will instantly lose much of the purchasing power its financial reserves now possess—foreign goods and assets will cost more. Moreover, as the dollar continues to weaken, so too will the value of China's dollar-denominated assets. China's instant solution is to convert as much of its reserves as possible into dollar-dominated purchases of oil, minerals, raw materials, and equities before either the dollar or the Chinese currency weakens any further.

It is reasonable to assume that China will devote $2 trillion to equity investments over the next five years, which is likely a conservative estimate. Equity investment funds will give China the financial capacity to acquire 51 percent of the stock—absolute control—of companies worth $4 trillion. The total value of all U.S.-headquartered corporations listed on the New York Stock Exchange was $15.4 trillion at the beginning of 2008. Theoretically, China could buy control of about a quarter of all the companies listed. Absolute control of General Motors and its global distribution network, for instance, could be purchased for around $9 billion. Many corporations, of course, will resist. But many will take the money if the U.S. government permits the sale.

A look at the future of such sales is Lenovo's purchase of IBM's personal computer division for $1.25 billion in March 2005. The Chinese computer maker determined that the quickest way for it to become a global competitor was to acquire the IBM Personal Computing Division, which was an also-ran in the U.S. and European markets. With the purchase, Lenovo was able to access IBM's world-class customer service organization and "take advantage of IBM's powerful worldwide distribution and sales network." It also got access to IBM's warranty services, leasing, and financial arrangements. Now China's largest computer maker and the world's third largest, Lenovo had sales of more than $14.5 billion in 2007.

Unlike so many U.S. computer companies that began in someone's garage, Lenovo was created by China's Academy of Sciences, a public institution, in 1984. The academy sold stock in the company to the public in 1988. After the completion of the deal with IBM in 2005, the academy and its employees own 42.4 percent of the company's stock—which gives them effective control.

As with Lenovo, the fastest way for China's state-owned national champions to become global companies is to buy all or a majority of the stock of a well-positioned transnational corporation headquartered in Europe or the United States. (The government of Japan is unlikely to permit such control of Japanese corporations.) Over the past twenty years, the United States has blocked only one minor sale of a U.S. corporation to foreign purchasers. The Europeans consider each purchase on a case-by-case basis.

To avoid political fallout such as in 2006, when Dubai's sovereign wealth fund attempted to take over a corporation that managed several U.S. ports, the Chinese are turning to skilled Wall Street investment bankers for advice. In 2007, that government bought a $3 billion stake in the Blackstone Group, the New York–headquartered private investment fund, which has long assisted foreign corporations to purchase U.S. assets. Yet Blackstone is only one of many experienced Wall Street firms available to help China use its vast hoard of dollars to acquire U.S.-based assets.

The Chinese government has also allowed several state-owned banks to sell a small portion of their equity in public stock offerings to Western investors. Those granted such a privilege are firms with which China wishes to establish a long-term strategic relationship.

Goldman Sachs was permitted to invest $2.6 billion for 5 percent of the Industrial and Commercial Bank of China in 2005. Within six months, the value of Goldman's stock in that bank grew by almost $4 billion. Germany's largest insurer, Allianz of Munich, and American Express invested $1.24 billion together; they doubled their money in six months. Also, Bank of America doubled its investment in the China Construction Bank, and Royal Bank of Scotland Group made a quick $1 billion profit on its investment in the Bank of China.

Foreign firms can own no more than 33 percent of an investment bank in China and no more than 20 percent of a brokerage. In late 2006, the government barred any more foreign firms from buying domestic brokerages.

These favored few banks and investment firms were given a taste of the future profits to be made by working with the Chinese government. China has now put into place the relationships it needs to discreetly buy assets and stock around the world. Dozens of other eager bankers and investment groups will be seeking a similarly favored position. Equally important, most of these facilitators seem willing to assist the Chinese government in hiding its investments from the public, as is done in Saudi Arabia, Dubai, the UAE, and many other countries.

The United States is seeing state-owned Chinese corporations trying to buy significant portions of its economy. Often, these purchases will be made through private investment groups and foreign banks, whose owners are frequently undeclared. Under existing laws, the Chinese government is under no obligation to be a passive investor. If it owns corporate assets, current U.S. law and WTO trade rules allow the government to do as it wishes, including moving production and R&D to China and leaving only distribution networks in the United States. Alone among nations, the United States zealously protects the sanctity of property owned by a Marxist government.

In the 1980s, many Americans were concerned about Japanese purchases of U.S. assets, including dozens of companies that produced equipment for the production of semiconductors and other high-tech products. That surge of investment was based on a cash "bubble" created by highly inflated real estate values in Japan. Today's situation is far different. China comes to the global marketplace with a vast store of cash. This is no bubble. Moreover, the government of China is the principal, not private corporations, as was the case in Japan in the 1980s. No private company, no matter how strong, advanced, or clever, can compete against the government of China in global markets for long.

Ideally, the U.S. government would closely monitor who is buying and taking control of the nation's productive assets, but it does not. In 2006, and again in 2007, Secretary of the Treasury Henry Paulson, the former CEO of Goldman Sachs who negotiated that firm's special access in China, called for "market discipline" rather than government oversight and regulation to address the growing global hedge fund and investment business. Thus, the official position of the U.S. government is that it does not seek disclosure of who owns what in the various investment funds and hedge funds that are buying U.S. corporations and taking them private. Today, under this nondisclosure policy, China could theoretically gain control of a significant portion of the companies listed on the New York Stock Exchange and no U.S. officials would know.

Which brings us to the question of control.

Control Eamonn Fingleton, who lives in Japan and has written extensively on East Asian economics, argues (in *In the Jaws of the Dragon*) that the political ethos in China is greatly shaped by Confucius and the ideas attributed to him. The principal political significance of Confucianism, Fingleton says, is "that it enjoins the populace to obedience, loyalty, and sacrifice. As such it is every authoritarian's dream ideology." The legal standard in the Confucian world is strict laws and lax enforcement. Selective enforcement, however, is the practice. According to Fingleton, in China the government uses the law to rule the people, as opposed to the West, where the rule of law allows the people to control their government.

Selective enforcement in China means that a family can be punished for the transgressions of a member or a group of workers can be disciplined for the actions of a single worker. A company can be destroyed for the actions of a single executive. The government decides, and there is no legal recourse. Selective enforcement, he says, is a not-so-subtle form of blackmail that is ever present. The problem Fingleton identifies is this: while the United States thinks it is exporting American cultural preferences for democracy and capitalism to China, the Chinese are actually exporting to the United States their Confucian values of authoritarian governance and selective enforcement.

China's Pavlovian conditioning of U.S. investment banks and equity funds ensures that those the Chinese have chosen for special preference and access, such as Goldman Sachs, Bank of America, Blackstone, and Citigroup, are virtually guaranteed vast profits year after year. They have enormous incentives to please their real client, the Chinese government. They also know that the Chinese have long memories and will punish those who disobey their desires.

These U.S. financial institutions bring more than money; they also bring China their unique knowledge and influence within the U.S. government. As of 2007, a number of former Goldman Sachs executives held key positions in the Bush administration, including Josh Bolton as chief of staff to President Bush and Henry Paulson as secretary of the Treasury. Robert Zoellick was appointed by President Bush to be president of the World Bank. At the same time, former Goldman Sachs Chairman Robert Rubin, secretary of the Treasury in the Clinton administration and now chairman of Citicorp's executive committee, is the leading economic adviser to the Democratic Party, even as former House Democratic Majority Leader Richard Gephardt is working at Goldman Sachs on public finance issues. Peter Peterson of Blackstone is chairman of the Council on Foreign Relations, the principal foreign relations policy organization in the United States, and the Peter G. Peterson Institute for International Economics, the most influential trade policy think tank in America.

Our financial and political elites are everywhere involved with the U.S. neuron systems of economics and politics. They have the pulse of American governance and help shape what is happening in virtually all U.S.-based industries. They bring it all to China.

China has long cultivated many of America's other governing elites. In 1977, when the two nations had begun political exchanges but had not yet established formal diplomatic relations, the Central Intelligence Agency prepared an analysis of U.S.-Chinese relations, trying to anticipate how China's leaders would interact with their American counterparts. It concluded that the Beijing government would follow its traditional pattern of cultivating those who possess power inside the United States and then use them to influence U.S. policies in China's favor.

For more than three decades, Beijing has developed these special relationships with a handful of high-ranking Americans from both the public and private sectors and through them influenced the China policies of the United States. These few, many of whom are former senior federal officials, once they leave office are given special access to Chinese leaders. U.S. corporations desiring that access must rely on those privileged men and women.

These facilitators include former Secretaries of State Henry Kissinger and Alexander Haig; former ambassador to China James Sasser; and former National Security Advisors Brent Scowcroft and Sandy Berger.

Most political appointees who serve in high U.S. positions, such as in the Office of the U.S. Trade Representative, Department of Defense, White House, State Department, or Congress, are intimately acquainted with this revolving door between public service and personal wealth. They realize that the Chinese Embassy sends staff to monitor think tank sessions, congressional hearings, and public briefings. These Americans know that what they say will be reported back to Beijing, resulting in a self-imposed censorship on those who have lobbying or investment banking ambitions after leaving public service.

The Chinese have established unique political and economic relationships with ex-presidents of the United States. Former Presidents George H. W. Bush and Bill Clinton have both been paid hundreds of thousands of dollars to make speeches in China. Prescott Bush, Sr., the brother of George H. W. Bush and uncle of George W. Bush, is a partner in the largest foreign-owned golf course in China. Neil Bush, the current president's brother, is copartner in a software business with the son of a member of China's Politburo Standing Committee. After George W. Bush leaves office, he will have many opportunities to speak in China and throughout Asia and the Middle East for six-figure fees.

China can also exert some control over what the various media have to say. General Electric, which owns NBC, has more than 20,000 employees in China. ABC is building a major Disney theme park in China. Rupert Murdoch, the owner of the Fox Network and now *The Wall Street Journal*, conspicuously took broadcasts by the British Broadcasting Corporation off his satellite system after the Chinese government complained about the content of BBC programming. Murdoch and his Chinese-born wife are building a 2,000-square-meter home in Beijing's most exclusive neighborhood.

Eamonn Fingleton describes how the government of China will diminish U.S. press freedom in China, with a technique based on an ancient Chinese adage, "Kill the chicken to scare the monkey." When a Hong Kong publisher ran articles in his magazine that offended China's leaders, for example, they closed his chain of clothing stores in China. The more U.S. industrial and financial conglomerates with media holdings invest in China, the more vulnerable they will be to Chinese censorship of their U.S. reportage.

American corporations in China are particularly vulnerable to political pressure because their access to subsidies, including cheap labor, depends on not offending Chinese officials. These companies, moreover, are also expected to defend China's open access to U.S. markets. When a majority of the small and medium-sized member companies in the National Association of Manufacturers (NAM) adopted a resolution calling upon the Bush administration and Congress to take direct action against China's manipulation of its currency, the larger corporations, most of which do business in China, swatted down the resolution at a NAM board meeting.

China hires few lobbyists in Washington. Instead, it relies on the large trade associations such as the Business Roundtable, the National Association of Manufacturers, and the U.S. Chamber of Commerce to do that work for them. Working through others—that is, by shaping the policy positions of U.S. business organizations, investment bankers, the media, think tanks, and trade associations—the Chinese exert their influence without the American people or Congress ever seeing who is actually behind their acts of political ventriloquism.

To paraphrase Alan Webber's opening quote in this chapter, the world is changing and China is different. Tolerance of some market-oriented activities does not mean the nation has a market-oriented economy or is ever likely to adopt an Anglo-American-style political or economic system.

China and the other nations of East Asia are pursuing a virulent version of the mercantilism that Adam Smith warned against in *The Wealth of Nations*. Indeed, old-fashioned mercantilism is the real focus of today's Chinese economy.

The understanding of China's price advantage reveals the impossibility of confronting Asian mercantilism through the rules-based system of free trade embodied by the World Trade Organization. Chinese wages are rising, but they will remain for the foreseeable future far lower than those paid American workers. This cheap but competent labor, combined with the global mobility of technology and capital, means that China either already has or can create an unbreakable absolute global price advantage in virtually any industry, present or future.

Even if all foreign direct investment were stopped; even if the Chinese currency were adjusted to its real value; even if U.S.- and European-type health, safety, and environmental measures were imposed; even if China stopped its direct and tax subsidies; and even if all piracy and counterfeiting were eliminated, China would still have an absolute economic advantage because of the high efficiencies derived from clustering its production, the low cost of its labor, and government subsidies.

Under the WTO's existing free-trade rules and China's price advantage, "the trap" is unbreakable. Other policies are required.

Two

CORPORATISM

The consumer advocate and three-time presidential candidate Ralph Nader sent the CEOs of the 100 largest U.S.-based corporations a letter in 1997 requesting that they open their next annual shareholder meeting with the Pledge of Allegiance to the U.S. flag. The reaction by America's corporate elite was telling.

The CEOs of Bristol-Myers, Coca-Cola, and AT&T said they would consider the idea but never did anything. The CEOs of Allstate, Hewlett-Packard, and Boeing said such an action would be "inappropriate at a business meeting," even though most unions open their meetings by reciting the Pledge.

Caterpillar, Dayton-Hudson, and Kodak said it would be a waste of shareholders' time, though the Pledge takes less than twenty seconds to recite. 3M and Anheuser-Busch replied that their meeting included many international employees, shareholders, and visitors who might be embarrassed to watch in silence as Americans recited the Pledge.

The Ford Motor Company said it did not believe the concept of "corporate allegiance" is possible. Delta, Arco, and Amoco just said no. Boeing's CEO was already on record as saying he hoped the world would soon think of Boeing as a global corporation, not an American one.

Only Federated Stores liked the idea and adopted it—all the other ninety-nine corporations rejected it.

For most of these companies, a majority of their business depends on sales to American consumers. These ninety-nine U.S.-headquartered firms do hundreds of billions of dollars of business each year with America's federal, state, and local governments. Cumulatively, over the past century, these corporations have received trillions of dollars in U.S.

government subsidies, tax breaks, research grants, and development assistance. Caterpillar and Boeing, for instance, are the beneficiaries of long-term, low-interest Export-Import Bank loans that finance many of their foreign sales.

Most have factories and headquarters that were built with state and local tax-exempt bonds. All rely on low-cost, government-provided services, including police and fire protection. They also get inexpensive federal insurance to cover any losses if their foreign investments are expropriated. Some of these corporations, such as Delta Air Lines, exist because they received U.S.-granted monopoly routes, plus federal grants and loans to cover operating losses.

Yet the CEOs of these ninety-nine corporations refused to pledge their personal allegiance to the United States and the principles for which it stands—liberty and justice for all—at their annual stockholders' meetings. As with Boeing's CEO, these corporate elites view themselves as leaders of global corporations, not American ones, who owe allegiance to nothing except profits for shareholders.

As the response to Nader's letter suggests, these elites see the interests of their corporations and institutions as separate from those of the United States and its people. No longer do most corporate leaders believe, as former General Motors CEO Charles Wilson said a half century ago, "What's good for General Motors is good for the rest of America." Jack Welch, the ex-CEO of General Electric and a widely admired leader of today's transnational elites, summed up the attitude of today's CEOs as "My job is to take care of the stockholders of GE. It's the president's and Congress's job to take care of the nation."

David M. Rubenstein, founding partner of the Carlyle Group, one of the world's largest private equity funds, makes the point even plainer, noting that his and other funds concern themselves only with making money. "Virtually no investor," said Rubenstein, "has ever asked me what type of community support we've given from our various companies in our portfolio." Simply put, private enrichment above all else is the obsessive goal of most corporate leaders and financiers today.

One of the ways that GE and other corporations take care of their stockholders and make more money is by actively involving themselves in U.S. elections and aggressively shaping the policies and laws of the United States to their advantage. Equally significant, these same policies are being used to outsource many of the services our government finances.

While the outsourcing of work at the Department of Defense through no-bid contracts to firms such as Halliburton has been widely publicized, privatization of public resources and functions throughout the rest of government, such as the corporate taking of timber in the national forests and vast underpayment of royalties on oil and minerals taken from public lands, remains largely unseen and undocumented.

Modern corporatism even extends into that most sensitive of areas, national intelligence. As R. J. Hillhouse reported in *The Washington Post*, the Bush administration has outsourced key intelligence agency work, including recruiting and operating spies, creating nonofficial cover identities, and controlling the movements of CIA case officers. Private companies now do about half the CIA's clandestine work, the agency's core function, at a price of more than $42 billion a year. The Harper Index reports that the cost of an intelligence person hired by the government is $125,000 per year. The cost for the same work when outsourced to the private sector is double that—$250,000 annually. Among the private contractors are Abraxas, Booz Allen Hamilton, Lockheed Martin, and Raytheon.

Today's corporatism is fostered in part by the way we Americans finance our elections. Our present system favors rich contributors, creating an insidious money dependency for politicians. To win a Senate seat, even in a small state such as South Carolina, candidates must raise $3.5 million or more. In 2008, the price for winning the presidency will exceed $500 million. A campaign for a seat in the House of Representatives costs on average about $650,000. Corporations and special interests provide much of that money. The federal election Web site provides the detailed documentation of all contributions to all candidates for federal office (see www.fec.org). The information provided there is instructive about the state of U.S. politics.

During the 2008 congressional election cycle, the Democratic leadership of the House of Representatives assessed each of its members a quota of funds to raise to elect other Democrats. The baseline figure was $400,000. Chairmen of congressional committees and subcommittees were given even higher goals. The Republican House leadership sets even higher fund-raising quotas for their members. Today, office seekers must be either enormously wealthy, as an increasing number are, or able to secure this money from others.

Approximately 85 percent of the political funds collected are used to buy television and radio ads. The profit-making media are allowed to charge candidates money to use the publicly owned airwaves, rather than provide free use of those frequencies equally for all candidates. Congress is unwilling to publicly finance elections for the Senate and House of Representatives or to truly regulate private political contributions to candidates.

Congress allows the two main political parties to draw the boundaries of congressional districts in such a way that virtually guarantees incumbents lifetime employment, should they wish it. And it permits the parties to decide who is eligible to participate in televised presidential debates, meaning that whoever controls the two parties decides who gets to be president.

Corporate money, both domestic and foreign, dominates U.S. governance. In part, the growing foreign influence is the result of foolish fiscal and trade policies that are producing the deepening federal budget and trade deficits we are financing by borrowing from abroad and selling our assets to foreigners. The desire of foreign lenders and owners to shape the public policies that affect their property is natural, legitimate, and legal. The maxim that "foreign money comes with foreign influence" is true.

Warren Buffett, the richest man in the world, describes the present U.S. situation as one in which Americans risk turning into "a nation of sharecroppers."

A good starting point for examining the current era of corporatism is the unreported part of the health care scandal that *The Washington Post* uncovered at the Walter Reed Army Medical Center in Washington in February 2007. The *Post* published an investigative series on the grossly substandard care and conditions many wounded and recovering soldiers were subjected to at Walter Reed. We'll follow the money.

Walter Reed is the jewel in the crown of America's military health system. It treats members of Congress, Supreme Court justices, and cabinet officers. It is the most visible part of a giant organization whose mission is to provide medical services to people who are on active duty, military retirees, and their dependents, and includes 75 hospitals and 461 clinics worldwide that are staffed by 39,000 civilians and 92,000 active-duty military personnel, all under the control of the Department of Defense.

After the United States began hostilities in Afghanistan in 2002 and Iraq in 2003, Walter Reed began receiving steadily increasing numbers of wounded. *Post* reporters found that outpatient services for the wounded were in total disarray and that too few people were available to help the wounded soldiers handle red tape, monitor their living conditions, and ensure they were given the care they needed. Patients were often unkempt, and many were housed in a seedy hotel whose rooms were plagued with mold, mice, rot, and cockroaches. Even members of Congress and their spouses who visited constituents at Walter Reed were appalled and complained to those in charge but were ignored.

The Department of Defense took remedial action only after the *Post* reported on the soldiers' conditions and treatment in a series of articles that received international attention. In March 2007, the newly appointed secretary of defense, Robert Gates, fired the secretary of the Army and two generals responsible for managing Walter Reed. President Bush visited the facility, apologized to the troops, and appointed a blue-ribbon commission to investigate. Congress held hearings. Then national attention shifted to other matters, which brings us to what the radio personality Paul Harvey would describe as "the rest of the story."

The greater scandal at Walter Reed is not what happened when too few people were available to care for the injured but why the hospital was so understaffed in a time of war in the first place.

That story began during the Clinton administration, when Vice President Al Gore led an effort to "reinvent government"—that is, improve services and cut costs by forcing federal civil servants to form work teams and then bid against private contractors. In other words, outsourcing. As part of the Gore effort, the Army decided to pit civil servants against private corporations in a bidding process. The Walter Reed bid was one of 205 similar initiatives begun in 2000, the last year of the Clinton administration, by the Department of Defense. In June 2000, Walter Reed had more than 300 federal employees providing base operations and support services, including facilities management.

When George W. Bush became president, the Clinton/Gore initiative fit neatly into his management plans. The new president announced in his Fiscal Year 2002 Management Agenda that "nearly half of all federal employees perform tasks that are readily available in the commercial marketplace—tasks like data collection, administrative support, and payroll services." The Bush administration intended to bid out to the private sector up to half of the work done by federal civil servants, which it set about doing.

In 2003, the workers at Walter Reed formed a team and submitted a bid that, if successful, would allow them to keep their jobs. A private corporation named Johnson Controls World Services also made a bid. In September 2004, the Army determined that the workers at Walter Reed could perform the operations and support services at Walter Reed at a lower cost than Johnson Controls. In December 2004, the private bidder filed a protest with the Government Accountability Office, which decides such conflicts. The GAO dismissed the workers' bid. Then the private contractor filed an appeal with the Army.

As the review of bids and the initial protests were being filed, a company named IAP Worldwide Services bought Johnson Controls. Two former Halliburton executives led IAP. Both were skilled in military outsourcing and dealing with such protests as those filed by Johnson Controls.

IAP filed a second objection with the GAO on March 30, 2005, arguing that the Walter Reed workers had failed to include all the costs required for in-house performance. At this point, the Army withdrew its certification of the Walter Reed workers' bid and the GAO dismissed IAP's protest as academic since the award to the workers had already been canceled.

IAP immediately requested that it be reimbursed for the costs of filing and pursuing the protest on the ground that the Army had handled its protest inadequately. The GAO recommended that the Army reimburse IAP's costs. The Army reviewed the workers' bid and unilaterally added $7 million to their price. Then, in January 2006, the Army ruled that, given the workers' higher bid, IAP had won the contract.

Not surprisingly, the workers felt cheated, and ten days later they filed a protest arguing that the Army's recalculation was wrong and also that the law required the bidding process to be concluded within thirty months, a deadline that had long since passed. The American Federation of Government Employees (AFGE) funded the workers' legal costs, and Alan D. King, deputy garrison commander of the Walter Reed Medical Center, submitted the protest on their behalf.

The Army and IAP did not deal with the substance of the workers' protest. Amazingly, the GAO agreed that the workers' boss, King, had no standing and dismissed the workers' challenge altogether. The GAO refused to examine whether the Army's recalculation was valid or whether the workers could do the job better or for less cost. Instead, it used a legal loophole to allow the Army to give IAP the Walter Reed contract.

The GAO decision was made in February 2006, and IAP entered into a five-year, $120 million agreement to operate and maintain the 219 buildings and facilities at Walter Reed. A year later, on February 5, 2007, the private company began the work. But in that one-year interim, 250 of the 300 federal employees quit, retired, or found other jobs. Most believed they would not be hired by the new contractor, and if they were their pay and benefits would be reduced. Meanwhile, the number of wounded soldiers being admitted to Walter Reed continued to rise and the quality of care continued to fall.

In retrospect, the Army's hierarchy seemed absolutely determined to outsource the work, even as it disregarded pleas for help from hospital administrators to handle the increasing numbers of injured soldiers being admitted.

As the scandal unfolded in the pages of *The Washington Post,* IAP caught the attention of Representative Marcy Kaptur (D-Ohio), a member of the House Appropriations Subcommittee on Defense, who wanted to know whether politics had played any role in the Army's reversal of the workers' bid and the extraordinary delays in making the changeover. She directed the committee's investigators to examine what had happened, asking "Was the outsourcing a matter of favoritism with people with the right connections?" She also told her fellow members on the subcommittee that IAP's corporate connections "look like a Republican parking lot."

Her questions were fair. Among the members of the IAP board are Dan Quayle, the former vice president and senator and personal friend of President George W. Bush. The board also included a former vice chief of staff of the U.S. Air Force, a former commander in chief of the U.S. European Command and NATO Supreme Allied Command, and a former commandant of the U.S. Marine Corps. Clearly, IAP has a board of directors with powerful connections in the Department of Defense. While this is common in companies that deal in military affairs, IAP is also a major contractor in dozens of other federal agencies. Its activities illuminate the modern nexus between corporate globalization, politics, and government.

What Kaptur learned is that the U.S. government uses IAP to outsource more than $1.2 billion of federal work annually, up from $220 million in 2000. By the middle of 2007, IAP had a contract with the Army to construct and maintain power plants in Iraq, Kuwait, Kyrgyzstan, Qatar, Turkmenistan, and the UAE. It also provides operational support at six U.S. Army bases, six Air Force bases, and four Navy and Marine Corps stations.

These contracts are only part of the services IAP provides the U.S. government. It also operates facilities and provides staff for NASA, the Department of the Interior, and the Department of Energy. At the U.S. Patent and Trademark Office (USPTO), which is part of the Commerce Department, IAP staff opens and sorts the mail, collects fees that come with patent applications, assembles the patent applications into a file, operates the file room, enters data, and provides USPTO's customer and information support services.

At the U.S. Treasury, IAP hires supplemental staff for the Federal Deposit Insurance Corporation and maintains the Internal Revenue Service facilities in six major U.S. cities, including Washington, D.C. And these are only a few of its government contracts.

And who owns IAP?

IAP is owned by Cerberus Capital Management, one of the world's largest private investment firms, with headquarters in New York and offices in London, Germany, Tokyo, and Taipei. According to Cerberus, it has control of or significant minority interest in companies that generate more than $60 billion of annual revenue. In 2007, Cerberus bought the Chrysler Corporation. It also owns Pitney Bowes Capital Services, GMAC, a Japanese bank, and dozens of other ventures, including several U.S. defense contractors.

Quayle and other executives at IAP and Cerberus are politically active in Washington. In January 2006, *USA Today* published an in-depth report on the Cerberus-related contributions to Representative Jerry Lewis (R-Calif.), then chairman of the House Appropriations Committee. Lewis has championed hundreds of millions of appropriations dollars for a naval project in which a Cerberus subsidiary is a major contractor. Cerberus in turn has raised hundreds of thousands of dollars of campaign funds for Lewis, which helped him secure his chairman's position.

The New York Times reports that Lewis was the target of a federal investigation by one of the nine U.S. attorneys dismissed by the Justice Department after the 2006 midterm elections. Lewis told *USA Today* in 2006 that Cerberus fund-raising efforts helped him win the House Appropriations Committee chairmanship, but he insisted he had done nothing wrong.

The chairman of Cerberus is John Snow, a former secretary of the Treasury. In 2001, Secretary of Defense Donald Rumsfeld's disclosure forms stated that he was an investor in Cerberus.

The Walter Reed bid-off is unique because some public information exists about that deal. Between 2003 and 2006 the Bush administration conducted 1,243 bid-offs involving more than 46,000 federal workers; yet little information is available about most of these competitions and their outcomes.

The point of the Walter Reed story is that a great deal of the federal government's work is being outsourced to well-connected corporations, including IAP, Halliburton, Lockheed, Boeing, General Electric, and dozens of others. This corporatism, moreover, is not limited to traditional commercial services, such as accounting. Jeremy Scahill describes in his book *Blackwater* how the Department of Defense is outsourcing even military functions—privatizing war.

As with so many recent federal outsourcing contracts, the beneficiaries have close political ties inside the Bush administration. Blackwater is owned and managed by Erik Prince, whom Scahill describes as a charismatic ultraconservative who has close political ties to President George W. Bush.

In Iraq and other combat areas, private security firms such as Blackwater Corporation protect the top generals and civilians, something that in the recent past would have been simply unthinkable and an insult to the armed services. Based on State Department data, Scahill estimates that from 2004 to 2007, $5.6 billion was spent for such private security services.

The cost of private security is far greater than the cost of the Army's soldiers. Scahill testified before Congress in May 2007 that some contract warriors make in a month what active-duty soldiers make in a year. Consequently, one of the Army's major personnel problems is that soldiers who have finished their term of service are not reenlisting but going to work for companies such as Blackwater.

The main reason private firms are being used so extensively is that the Army is stretched thin and President Bush and the Congress are unwilling to reinstate the draft. Thus, reserve units and National Guard forces that are normally not involved in such warfare are being used extensively. But they are not enough. The Army has been unable to retain its high personnel standards and still meet its recruitment goals. Consequently, it has lowered its thresholds, recruited foreigners who seek citizenship through military service, hired 126,000 contract employees in Iraq to perform work normally done by soldiers, and let contracts to private security firms such as Blackwater to provide specialized functions, such as executive security. The United States now has as many contract employees at work in Iraq as it does military personnel.

The massive outsourcing and privatizing of U.S. military services are not just a consequence of the Iraq War. They are the result of a policy that took hold earlier. Scahill reports that between 1994 and 2002, the Department of Defense issued more than 3,000 contracts to U.S.-based firms worth more than $300 billion.

The Bush administration greatly accelerated military outsourcing and privatization. Thus, military contracts have allowed Blackwater to grow from a tiny start-up in 1997 to a corporation that as of 2007 had its own 7,300-acre military base, a fleet of twenty-three transport aircraft, and some 2,300 privately employed troops deployed in nine countries. Blackwater, Triple Canopy, and DynCorp International, plus military companies from other nations, constitute a shadow force that neither the American people nor Congress knows much about.

The most intriguing aspect about the recent increase of federal employment of private corporations is what we do not know about the 1,243 bid-offs between federal workers and private contractors that occurred between 2003 and 2006. Today, we are not aware of which companies received contracts, which agencies were involved, under what terms, and for what purposes. We know only that OMB reports that twenty federal departments and agencies have conducted such contests.

The Bush administration has gone to extraordinary lengths to hide information about its activities from Congress and the voters, including data from previous administrations. Immediately after President Bush took office, White House Counsel Alberto Gonzales requested that the National Archives, the repository of official documents, postpone the planned release of materials from the Reagan-Bush administration.

The Presidential Records Act of 1978 provided that the National Archives would store and control a former president's papers for a twelve-year grace period before any releases would be made. On November 1, 2001, President Bush issued Executive Order 13233, which effectively overturned the 1978 act. The order mandated that the release of any such papers required the permission of both the former and the sitting presidents. His order also provides that the U.S. government pay the legal costs any former president incurs in the assertion of that privilege.

In addition to sealing presidential papers, the Bush administration sharply narrowed what information citizens could secure under Freedom of Information Act requests and put barriers, such as high fees and long delays, in the way of those seeking information.

The Federal Advisory Committee Act, whose objective is to identify for the American public those on advisory boards, has been ignored, allowing secret advisers to operate without any public knowledge. The most famous of these was the membership and work of Vice President Dick Cheney's Energy Task Force. The next chapter will examine another such example that involves the work of the presidents of the United States and Mexico and the prime minister of Canada to further integrate the economies and populations of the three nations.

In the first three years of the Bush administration, the average number of decisions to classify information rose by 50 percent over the prior five years. In its first three years, it classified more than 19 million documents per year, a 95 percent increase over President Clinton's last four years in office (1997–2000).

Perhaps most significant, the Bush administration has even limited Congress's access to federal records, preventing its basic oversight of the executive branch. The administration has also restricted the Government Accountability Office's access to records it needs to prepare audits and investigations of federal expenditures. This extraordinary expansion of government secrecy has created an environment in which unfettered corporatism can flourish unnoticed and unchallenged, which is one of the intents of such secrecy.

Since 2001, the Bush administration has sponsored three initiatives to shift work traditionally performed by government to private corporations. Privatizing Social Security was one, and outsourcing work at the Department of Defense, which I have discussed, is another. Both those efforts have received massive attention from the media and other interested parties.

By contrast, the third corporatism initiative has been virtually unnoticed by the national media. The U.S. Department of Transportation is aggressively trying to shift the financing, construction, and operation of America's busiest highways, including the interstate highways, to privately operated toll road corporations. This is a historic shift of public policy.

The two principal corporations involved in this conversion of freeways to toll roads are foreign-based companies. One is Cintra, a Spanish corporation; the other is Macquarie Infrastructure Group, an Australian company. Often working together on joint projects, these two transnationals are trying to change the way America finances its highways and do so in a way that will yield massive profits for both them and their U.S. partners. The business model used by both corporations is to offer state and local elected officials, who are averse to enacting new taxes, large fees, often in the billions of dollars, in exchange for 50- to 100-year leases on prime public facilities that they can convert into toll operations. Literally hundreds of billions of dollars of public assets are involved. The properties these two companies want most are the high-traffic portions of the Interstate High-way System, which they want to convert to toll roads. As the following two stories illustrate, the globalization of America's roads and bridges is well under way.

The 46,000-mile Interstate Highway System is the largest public works project ever constructed. It is part of a national system of more than 4 mil-lion miles of roads, fewer than 6,000 miles of which require tolls.

The interstate system was conceived in 1938, during the second Franklin D. Roosevelt administration, authorized by Congress in 1944, and built beginning in President Dwight D. Eisenhower's first term (1955). One of the principal stumbling blocks faced by Eisenhower was figuring out how to pay for this system.

Interestingly, Eisenhower's strongest ally on the highway project in the U.S. Senate and one of the principal architects of the pay-as-you-go system to build it was a former investment banker named Prescott Bush (R-Conn.), a grandfather of President George W. Bush. Largely completed in less than fifteen years, the interstate system was paid for as it was built and thus is owned debt-free by the American people.

But as with many legacies, monies are constantly required to maintain and refresh the existing system and expand it for a growing population. The Bush administration's remedy for financing these ongoing needs is not to increase federal and state gas taxes, the traditional method of fund-ing road construction, which have not been adjusted for inflation since 1982, but to lease these public facilities to private corporations for a period of a half century or more.

The name for the administration's program is public-private partner-ships (PPP). Under PPP, states and cities are now being urged by the Department of Transportation (DOT) to convert existing highways to pri-vately owned and operated toll roads, including the interstates, and to allow private corporations to plan, finance, build, and operate most new roads the United States will need.

The shift from pay-as-you-go public roads to private toll highways is a nondebated, unexamined historic change of national policy that has mul-tiple ramifications. For generations, the policy of the national and state governments has been to build a first-rate road system that keeps the cost of highway transportation as low as possible. America is a big nation, and holding down the costs of transport makes it more economically competitive and gives taxpayers and their families an inexpensive way to travel for work and pleasure.

Under PPP, just the opposite philosophy exists. Road tolls are set at market rates—that is, to maximize profits for the private operator. In many cities and regions where public highways are the only means of transport, toll rates could be raised to very high levels. With such rates possible, and with rates set by the private company, many corporations are willing to pay massive up-front concession fees to control and operate these transport monopolies for up to fifty to a hundred years.

These initial fees, which are often in the billions of dollars, allow today's antitax politicians to finance other public programs, such as schools, without having to ask voters for tax increases. They are able to keep their "no-new-tax" pledges by effectively selling debt-free public assets. In many of these deals, a part of the toll profits is to be shared with the state government concerned, sometimes outside the normal budget and legislative processes. Often the money goes into a governor's discretionary fund.

Imagine having your credit card charged a new fee of $250 to $300 per month for tolls to commute to work by car. The Department of Transportation is making this a reality that millions of American commuters will soon have to confront. Ironically, commuters in Washington, D.C., and the surrounding region are already experiencing this form of "highway corporatism," with several toll roads now proposed or operating in the region.

The political lexicon of such road financing was changed in 1982, when the Reagan administration proposed raising the federal gas tax by five cents. The principal opposition was from Republican senators, who were divided as to whether the nickel add-on was a tax increase or a user fee. In the 1982 lame-duck session of Congress, GOP Senate leaders decided it was a user fee and not a tax. Only then did they approve it.

Today, raising a user fee is considered a tax increase, which it really always has been. For those officials who are ideologically opposed to tax raises, the innocuous-sounding "public-private partnership" is a perfect solution. It provides politicians a new way of raising massive amounts of money without the necessity of their raising taxes, and when toll rates must be raised the private contractor does it, thereby allowing politicians to remain tax "pure" with their constituents. They also receive the upfront fees to dispense, which to many officials is like "free" money.

Indiana's experience illustrates how PPP works. The Indiana Toll Road runs east–west for 157 miles across the northern part of the state. The four-lane divided highway was built in the early 1950s and officially dedicated in

September 1956. A public toll road commission collected tolls and ran the operation until 1981, when the state took control. The promise made to taxpayers in the 1950s was that the road would become a freeway when the bonds issued to pay for it were paid, but Indiana chose to continue collecting tolls, though at a low rate, which it used to pay for the road's operation and maintenance. The state's policy was good roads at the lowest possible cost.

Because the Indiana Toll Road is a major east–west artery, traffic on it is heavy. PPP advocates realized that if a politically acceptable way could be devised to increase those tolls, substantial additional revenues could be collected from the road. In 2004, the newly elected Indiana governor, Mitch Daniels (R), also understood that potential.

Daniels had been political director for President Ronald Reagan; headed the Hudson Institute, a conservative think tank; and served as George W. Bush's first director of the Office of Management and Budget, where he helped design and refine the PPP concept with Federal Highway Administrator Mary Peters and her general counsel, David James Gribbin, IV.

Daniels resigned from OMB in 2003 and ran for governor in 2004 on a promise to bring to the state private capital, " 'other people's money' that no Hoosier need be taxed for, to build the great projects we cannot afford, bringing with them countless thousands of new jobs and a more prosperous future for our children."

Early in his administration, Daniels moved to lease the Indiana Toll Road under a PPP agreement, and in mid-2005 the state put together a bid package with the assistance of the investment bank Goldman Sachs and the Federal Highway Administration. The state then bid out the project and chose a winner "in the fastest bid process in the history of such transactions."

The process took 117 days, and the winner was the Australian/Spanish consortium made up of the Macquarie Infrastructure Group and Cintra. Six months after the announcement of the deal, the private operators took control and paid the state of Indiana $3.85 billion for their concession to maintain, operate, and collect tolls on the turnpike for seventy-five years. To make the arrangement politically acceptable to Indianans, Daniels distributed approximately $250 million to the counties surrounding the toll road and promised to build dozens of other projects throughout the state with part of the monies.

The governor also agreed to raise the tolls sharply before the private operators took charge, after which they could make further increases if they wished. Under Daniels's deal, tolls immediately rose from 3 cents to 5 cents per mile on passenger vehicles and from 9 cents to 11 cents per mile on commercial vehicles.

But that was just the start. By 2009, the toll for commercial vehicles will be 20 cents per mile, more than double that in 2006. After 2010 and for the next seventy years, Macquarie/Cintra will be allowed to raise the tolls at a rate greater than 2 percent of an amount equal to an increase in the Consumer Price Index or the nominal gross domestic product per capita growth.

Macquarie/Cintra will recoup its $3.85 billion investment over the first fifteen years of the contract. For the remaining sixty years, the corporations refuse to say how much profit they anticipate making.

Once the deal was announced in January 2006, Daniels sent approval legislation to the state legislature. The state of Indiana paid Goldman Sachs $20 million for financial advice and millions more to specialized law and accounting firms. Daniels, however, withheld from legislators the analysis and recommendations made by Goldman Sachs and the other advisers. Using information that was available, however, such as toll collection data, the legislators calculated that they were being asked to sell a state asset for $3.85 billion that would produce $121 billion of revenues under this new "market value" model.

Opponents also objected that the agreement precluded the state from building or improving any roads ten miles on either side of the toll road because of a "noncompete" clause. If such roads diverted traffic from the toll road, the state obligated itself to pay the private consortium for its losses. Consequently, the foreign consortium now effectively controls development on a 20-by-157-mile swath across northern Indiana, more than 2 million acres.

As the tolls increased in 2006 and 2007, Daniels's deal became progressively more unpopular, but there is nothing the people of Indiana can do. Their road is now leased to a foreign concessionaire until the year 2084 under a tight contract that will be difficult, if not impossible, to break.

The leasing of the Indiana Toll Road is instructive in many ways. The first is that although such vital arteries have been operated with low tolls as part of a strategy to keep transport costs down, existing roads (free or toll) can be used to raise enormous amounts of money if tolls are priced at "market value"; that is, what the market will bear.

The second is that existing toll roads can be converted to immediate cash quickly if a governor and legislature are willing to sell or lease them because those roads are now operating under a policy of "good roads at a low cost." But under a private operator using a "whatever the market will bear" model, massive amounts of monies can be generated. Selling state assets to pay for current consumption is attractive to politicians who seek office on a "no-new-taxes" pledge.

Indiana's experience also reveals the wisdom of Shakespeare's admonition in *Macbeth:* "If it were done when 'tis done, then 'twere well it were done quickly." Unless quickly enacted without sufficient public examination, such arrangements wither when put into the sunshine where voters can examine them. Act in haste and repent in leisure.

The money Daniels raised in his scheme is to be spent within ten years, while the state has turned over control of a major highway and accepted constraints on the development of a portion of the state for seventy-five years. By then, of course, Daniels will be long gone and the problems will be those of his successors.

If Daniels's actions constitute an example of corporatism done with political skill, Texas Governor Rick Perry's (R) attempt to do the same, but on a Texas-size scale, reveals corporatism done grandly, arrogantly, slowly, and badly.

James Richard "Rick" Perry, a sheep rancher from Paint Creek, Texas, is the first graduate of Texas A&M University to be elected governor of that state. Born in 1950, Perry served in the Air Force after graduating from college. At the age of twenty-eight, he was elected as a Democrat to the State Board of Education. In 1982, as that term of office was ending, he was elected to the first of three terms as a state representative.

In 1989, Perry switched political parties, and in 1990 he won the race for commissioner of agriculture, defeating the incumbent. In 1999, he became lieutenant governor, and when President-elect George W. Bush resigned as governor in December 2000, Rick Perry became the forty-seventh governor of Texas.

Perry is a self-defined fiscal ultraconservative whose tenure as governor has been marked by three actions: cutting taxes, calling three special legislative sessions to redraw congressional district lines in a way that favors Republicans, and corporatizing Texas highways.

The challenge faced by office seekers who run on a "Read my lips: no new taxes" platform, as Perry did, is that a growing economy and an expanding population create demands for public services whose costs rise over time. President George H. W. Bush, who made the "Read my lips" pledge famous in his 1988 acceptance of the GOP nomination, ultimately resolved the conflict between his promise and the need for additional funds—by increasing taxes. President George W. Bush has "solved" the same "No new taxes" problem by borrowing massively from the central banks of China, Japan, South Korea, and Taiwan. Neither solution by either Bush has proved politically popular.

Perry, as are other governors and elected officials, is keeping his "No new taxes" pledge by leasing and selling public facilities, notably highways.

In January 2002, he instructed the Texas Department of Transportation (TxDOT) to outline his vision for a vast new system of privately financed highways, rails, and utility right of ways throughout Texas. In June 2002, he introduced his privatization program, the Trans Texas Corridor (TTC), with the following description:

> *The Trans Texas Corridor is an all-Texas transportation network of corridors up to 1,200 feet wide. The corridor will include separate toll ways for passenger vehicles and trucks, high-speed passenger rail, high-speed freight rail, commuter rail, and a dedicated utility zone. The concept includes separate lanes for passenger vehicles (three lanes in each direction) and trucks (two lanes in each direction): one for high-speed rail between cities, one for high-speed freight rail, and one for commuter and freight rail. The third component of the corridor would be a protected network of safe and reliable utility lines for water, petroleum, natural gas, electricity, and data.*

The TTC would be more than 4,000 miles in length, cost between $145 and $184 billion, and be financed by a combination of state funding, local toll segments, and exclusive development agreements with private corporations that would be solicited by requests-for-proposals or from unsolicited private proposals to the state. The Texas corridors would exceed any transportation project anywhere else in the world.

What Perry omitted in his announcement was the fact that for each mile of the TTC, the state would be required to take 145 acres of privately owned farm and ranch land. Collectively the state would take more than a half-million acres of land on which to build these roads. Neither did Perry make it known that two of the corridors would connect to a new system of toll roads and railroads built in Mexico that would speed the movement of freight from three deepwater ports in southwest Mexico being built by Wal-Mart and Chinese interests. One of those routes goes from Brownsville, Texas, on the border with Mexico, through San Antonio and up through Austin and Dallas to the Oklahoma border. The other route stretches from Laredo to Houston and on to Texarkana.

Later, TTC advocates explained their ultimate intent is to use these corridors to speed the flow of imported goods from Mexico and Asia into the central and eastern parts of the United States. In recent years, these two routes have become popularly known as the "NAFTA Superhighway," named after the North American Free Trade Agreement. Interestingly, advocates of this giant transportation corridor now try to avoid having it linked in any way with NAFTA, which has become increasingly unpopular. In testimony before Congress, U.S. Department of Transportation officials have claimed that there is no proposed NAFTA Superhighway. This is torturing entirely innocent words. The official name of this highway, as defined by the Congress and used by DOT, is National Highway System High Priority Corridors 18, 23, and 3. (For this book, the parts of that system in Texas will be called the "TTC" and the connecting roads in other states, the "NAFTA Superhighway.")

When Perry introduced his plan in 2002, most legislators and community officials ignored him because of the many legal and financial barriers sure to be in the plan's path. Taking more than 500,000 acres of land in Texas through the process of eminent domain seemed impossible, they thought, as was raising the required enormous amounts of money. And the idea of securing environmental approval for such a project appeared to be the ultimate barrier.

In his 2002 plan, Perry identified ten changes in Texas law that he wanted from the state legislature. One was new authority for TxDOT to acquire private property through quick condemnations. Other changes were authority to enter into agreements with private organizations to develop all types of transportation projects anywhere in Texas, create trust funds outside the state treasury for toll revenues, assign ownership of toll revenues to corporate developers, allow the issuance of bonds to finance the TTC, and remove all restrictions on the number of projects that could be undertaken. Also, if the TTC would not involve any federal monies, he wanted an exemption from federal environmental laws. In short, the governor hoped for a free rein.

But first, the Texas Constitution had to be changed. In the 2002 election, the governor had an amendment placed on the ballot. Proposition 15 read, "The constitutional amendment creating the Texas Mobility Fund and authorizing grants and loans of money and issuance of obligations for financing the construction, reconstruction, acquisition, operation, and expansion of state highways, turnpikes, toll roads, toll bridges, and other mobility projects." The apparent purpose of the amendment was to create a supplemental fund to finance highways. The tricky part was the last four words: "and other mobility projects." Governor Perry and TxDOT have subsequently justified their massive highway toll plan with those four little words, claiming that the people of Texas knowingly ratified the Trans Texas Corridor when they approved Proposition 15.

That argument, however, did not emerge until after the 2003 session of the legislature, when implementing language was slipped into law. In June 2003, as the session was drawing to a close, after redrawing the Texas congressional district boundaries, State Representative Mike Krusee (R), a longtime Perry ally who chaired the House Transportation Committee, introduced a transportation bill that zipped through the legislature on a vote of 146–0 in the Texas House and 31–0 in the Senate. Few legislators read the particulars, and Krusee emphasized to the media that this was a law that would crack down on drunk drivers and repeat offenders, plus provide some monies for the governor's proposed Corridor program. The act was commonly referred to as the "Driver Responsibility Law."

Krusee tricked his exhausted legislative colleagues. House Bill 3588 was substantially more than a drunk drivers' bill. At its core, it provided that "to the maximum extent practical and economical, TxDOT shall encourage the participation of private parties in the planning, design, construction, and operation of facilities" for the proposed TTC. With only a few members of the Texas Legislature in the know, both houses authorized the governor and TxDOT to privatize the Texas Highway System.

The bill they passed was revolutionary in nature. It gave TxDOT new powers, called "quick take," that allowed the state to swiftly take possession of private property. Under the quick-take provisions, TxDOT is empowered to file a "declaration of taking" with the local clerk of the court, serve a copy on each person owning an interest in the condemned property, file evidence that the declaration of taking has been filed with the owners, and then immediately assume possession of the property. If the property is a homestead, TxDOT must wait ninety days after the date of service to gain possession. In both instances, the condemnation price will be determined later.

The legislation also allowed TxDOT to convert any existing state road, or portion of a road, into a tollway. TxDOT was also authorized to take options on property or buy it outright and get possession of it before a final decision is made on routes. The legislation authorized the establishment of multicounty Regional Authorities that would build and operate local toll roads and would have the same quick-take powers as TxDOT. In all instances, the governor would appoint the chairpersons of those regional authorities.

Immediately after the legislature adjourned in 2003, TxDOT identified ten priority toll road projects with a collective value of $20 billion. It also concluded that Texas law firms lacked the experience and expertise required for so complex and massive a project, and consequently TxDOT outsourced the legal work to Nossaman Guthner Knox Elliott LLP, a California-based firm that specializes in infrastructure projects. The Nossaman firm has what legal publications describe as seven "Super Lawyers," all of whom worked on the Texas project. In early 2007, the firm was also doing the legal work for infrastructure projects with a value of $40 billion in twenty-five other states. TxDOT refuses to release the cost of Nossaman's services, but the TTC chairman informally told reporters in early 2007 that it had already spent $30 million at a billing rate in excess of $500 per hour. For that money, the California law firm did TxDOT's procurement and financing strategies for the TTC and all the related legal work—a massive job by any measure.

On August 20, 2003, barely two months after H.B. 3588 was enacted, TxDOT convened a preproposal conference at its Austin headquarters with its staff and private contractors. Among those in attendance were Phillip Russell, the director of the Texas Turnpike Authority; Robert Nichols, a TTC commissioner; John Bourne, the TTC Corridor engineer; Jack Ingram, the TxDOT general counsel; other aides to senior TxDOT officials; and Geoffrey S. Yarema, the lead lawyer from Nossaman.

Russell opened the meeting with a few words about H.B. 3588: "By all accounts it's probably the most revolutionary transportation legislation that's come out of anywhere in the last 40 or 50 years," Russell said, "probably all the way back to the Interstate years and perhaps beyond." The legislation, he pointed out, "gives us all of the authority and all of the power we need on a state level to move forward on the Trans Texas Corridor, plus some."

Russell repeatedly emphasized that the ideas they were discussing that day were confidential, as were the proposals. He announced that the TTC had already issued a request for proposal on July 25, 2003—less than thirty days after H.B. 3588 was enacted—for the first phase of work, which would include sections of the North-Texas-to-Mexico road along Interstate I-35.

He told the group the governor wanted a developer selected and a contract in place by the next year.

Yarema's briefing included an observation that the "form of contract that will come out of this, while new, has domestic and international precedence." "It would require," he also noted, "special approval from the Federal Highway Administration (FHWA)," which, he assured TxDOT, he had "every confidence that we'll be able to achieve." Yarema is a longtime friend of Federal Highway Administrator Mary Peters and thus could make that assurance with some confidence.

As Yarema noted, TxDOT and the U.S. Department of Transportation were forging a new model for the building and operation of U.S. roads. As part of that, the Nossaman team developed a training course for TxDOT personnel that explained the "dollars and sense" of toll roads, as well as the provisions in the new legislation that authorized something called "comprehensive development agreements" (CDAs). A CDA differs greatly from the traditional low-price procurement and pay-as-you-go financing that TxDOT had used for decades. Under the new authority given TxDOT, the process was changed from one that relies on the lowest bid for the same work to a "best value" selection. The state now had the power to consider subjective factors when awarding a bid, such as the qualifications and experience of key personnel, innovation, and technical approach.

An unstated side effect of the new CDA process was that it also allowed political factors to be considered. TxDOT could make an agreement with a single company or group to design, develop, construct, finance, acquire, operate, and maintain facilities such as turnpikes, highways, freight or passenger rail systems, and public utilities.

The new legislation also authorized two procurement methods. In the more traditional arrangement, TxDOT could initiate procurements by issuing a request for proposal, developing a short list of bidders and selecting the one that offered the "best value." In the other method, a developer could submit an unsolicited proposal. If TxDOT found it meritorious, it could solicit competing proposals, select the one with the best value, and award a contract.

In effect, the state of Texas put a "For lease" sign on all state roads. If a private corporation thought a road could generate enough traffic to make collecting tolls profitable, TxDOT could lease it for fifty years in exchange for an up-front concession fee, plus a portion of the tolls. If a developer identified a new route that might generate large toll revenues, TxDOT could authorize the project, use its quick-take powers to buy the land, and then give a private corporation a fifty-year lease to design, finance, build, operate, and profit from a new toll road.

Regardless of which approach TxDOT uses, it requires an up-front fee to be paid to the state by the toll operator and a part of the future tolls. In effect, TTC is as much about financing state government by selling highway concessions and collecting tolls as it is about providing good roads.

The Nossaman team's work was made easier because the Bush administration, as well as Governor Perry, opposed any increases in highway taxes, even to offset inflation, preferring instead to sell toll road concessions and convert U.S. freeways to privately operated facilities. In this process the Nossaman lawyers are key advisers to the leadership of the Federal Highway Administration and the Department of Transportation, the parts of the federal government responsible for America's roads and highways. It is a significant relationship.

From 2001 to 2005, Mary Peters headed FHWA. Prior to that job, she worked for fifteen years at the Arizona Department of Transportation, where she was named director in 1998. Smart and competent, Peters is an aggressively outspoken toll road advocate.

Equally significant, during the first administration of President George W. Bush, the FHWA general counsel was David James Gribbin, IV, also a devoted toll road advocate. Gribbin's family has long been involved in Republican politics. His father, David James Gribbin, III, was the top congressional aide to then-Representative Dick Cheney (R-Wy.) and later assistant secretary of defense when Cheney was secretary of defense. During the 1990s, the younger Gribbin was national field director for the Christian Coalition, where he worked with coalition president Ralph Reed and its founder, Pat Robertson. Prior to joining FHWA, Gribbin was the Washington director of government affairs of Koch Industries, where he led that corporation's advocacy for the privatization of public roads. A lawyer and skilled advocate, Gribbin was an ideal choice for an administration that wanted to lease U.S. roads to private corporations.

The Federal Highway Administration's Peters and Gribbin worked closely with Governor Perry, TxDOT, and the Nossaman firm in putting together the Texas toll road programs. In March 2004, Peters even designated part of the Interstate 35 bypass that runs southeast of Fort Worth as a special experimental project and then waived many of the usual federal environmental and bidding restrictions so that TxDOT could speed up the project. The use of "experimental" projects is the Transportation Department's favored way of skipping compliance with existing laws.

The big problem that Perry, TxDOT, Krusee, Peters, and their lawyers faced is that as the people of Texas began to learn just how revolutionary and potentially costly to them the Perry plan was, they also came to oppose it. Voters were shocked to learn that a round trip by automobile between Austin and Dallas on a publicly owned road that had been free would soon cost $40 for tolls and that the state intended to use its powers of eminent domain to take more than 500,000 acres of Texas farm and ranch land. The state's ability to seize farms and ranches seemed "communist" to many landowners. In earlier times, people had been shot for making such land grabs.

What seems to have particularly galled many Texans is the idea that existing roads, paid for and owned by the people, would be converted into toll highways operated by private corporations from Spain and Australia. In fact, Texans were more than galled; the more they learned, the more they became outraged, unable to believe what the governor and legislature were preparing to do.

Among the first to act were David and Linda Stall of Fayetteville, which is between Austin and Houston. David Stall is a fourth-generation public servant and for twenty-one years was a police officer and arson investigator. His second career is as a professional city manager. Linda Stall is a community organizer and issues activist.

David first became aware of the Perry highway privatization plan in 2002, when the mayor of Columbus, Texas, where he was working as city manager, gave him a letter from TxDOT describing the TTC. He shared it with Linda, and they agreed that it seemed a political fantasy.

In February 2003, Michael Behrens, the TxDOT director, returned to his hometown of La Grange and gave a luncheon speech to the Chamber of Commerce. The Stalls attended and obtained a copy of the executive summary of the TTC that Behrens distributed. They were horrified.

Linda called TxDOT headquarters in Austin and asked for copies of the bigger plan. TxDOT sent her several boxes of the full plan, entitled "Crossroads of the Americas: Trans Texas Corridor Plan," in which Governor Perry identified his proposed actions step by step. It remains the guiding document for the TTC.

Perry based his plan on the assumption that Texans oppose raising taxes to offset inflation. He refuses, however, to ask them directly by putting the question to a vote. He also declaims on the rising congestion on Texas roads and argues that Texas lacks the money to build the new roads that are required. Toll roads are the only solution he offers.

The Texas State Auditor's Office examined Perry's TxDOT's assertion that the state faced an $86 billion funding gap between the estimated funding needed to achieve a desired level of mobility by 2030 and the anticipated traditional available funding. The auditors concluded that the TxDOT calculations "may not be reliable for making policy and/or funding decisions." If the state would index its gas taxes for inflation and return to TxDOT the monies that had been diverted elsewhere, selling or leasing Texas roads would be unnecessary. The problem is that former Governor Bush and his successor, Perry, diverted more than $15 billion from TxDOT into the general budget, where it was used to finance other programs. By channeling TxDOT's monies to finance general government, Perry was able to keep his "No new taxes" political pledge, lower spending on new construction, and build a political demand for toll roads. Of the money TxDOT does receive, more than 85 percent is spent for maintenance. The national average is 52 percent. This means, of course, that a substantial portion of the money collected through gas and other taxes is being diverted to nonroad uses.

As a career public servant familiar with the laws and rules of Texas, David Stall says he was particularly offended by the high-handed manner in which the governor was proceeding. There was no transparency, no participation by other public planning entities, no involvement of local governments, and worst of all no participation by the public.

In the spring of 2003, Linda Stall pulled transcripts from the Internet of TxDOT hearings and started collecting information about the TTC. She found that House Bill 3588, authorizing the TTC, imposed the requirement on TxDOT to hold a hearing in every county through which a TTC corridor would go.

Although the first corridor, from Brownsville through San Antonio and Dallas to Oklahoma, touched only a few of the 254 counties in Texas, TxDOT lawyers decided that if they held an early hearing in all of the state's counties they could dispose of the "individual county public meeting" requirement quickly for all future roads and before any political resistance could be mounted. Accordingly, TxDOT regional personnel were instructed to hold 254 public meetings during the month of February 2004, which they did. Often, public notice of the meetings was given only a day or two beforehand and was published in a small font in local newspapers alongside TxDOT's requests for gravel and other materials. Many of the meetings throughout the 254 counties in Texas had no attendees other than TxDOT employees.

TxDOT did all it could to hold down public attendance at these meetings, and it succeeded in all but two counties. When Linda Stall learned of the meeting in Columbus County, where her husband was working, she went to the Lions Club, Chamber of Commerce, and other local organizations, urging people to attend. Twenty-five people came, including the Stalls. The presentation consisted of a taped DVD message from the governor and the distribution of the executive summary of the TTC report. The local TxDOT employees knew little about the Perry plan and could not answer questions.

After that meeting, the Stalls decided to create a Web site where information about TTC could be shared with the people of Texas. It is www .corridorwatch.org.

A week after the meeting in Columbus County, TxDOT scheduled a session for Fayette County, where the Stalls live. TxDOT set the date for Ash Wednesday; in a county with a population that is overwhelmingly Catholic, TxDOT expected that few people would attend. With a week's notice, Linda Stall went to various local organizations and stirred up enough interest that more than eighty residents flooded the meeting at the local TxDOT office, which could handle only sixty. Once again, TxDOT personnel could not answer the public's questions.

Among those unable to get a seat that evening was Judge Ed Janecka, who stood along a wall during the presentation. He interrupted the meeting, introduced himself, and told the presenters that this did not count as a public meeting. Under Texas law, Janecka pointed out, all parties who wish to attend must be accommodated. Plus, he said, people were not getting answers to their questions.

The plainspoken Janecka told the TxDOT staff, "If this is the governor's plan, I'd like to have the governor come down and explain it to us." He told the staff he would arrange a meeting space big enough and he wanted TxDOT to send people who knew enough about TTC that they could answer questions. With that, everyone went home.

Three weeks later, a second meeting was held in La Grange, at the Knights of Columbus Hall. This time more than seven hundred people attended and TxDOT sent its senior people. David and Linda Stall distributed a handout they had prepared. On one side, they described what TTC was and the purpose of these public hearings, and they urged people to let TxDOT know their opinions. On the back side of the handout they warned the audience not to allow TxDOT to slip around their questions with "weasel words," such as "probably, likely, expect, anticipate, confident, assume, opinion, maybe, could, and future." Always ask, the Stalls advised, "Does the law permit or prohibit TxDOT (or the concessionaire) to do that?"

During the TxDOT presentations, the Stalls heard snickering from the audience and finally a burst of applause and a couple of shouts of "Bingo!" Many in the audience, which included many bingo players, were checking off each time a "weasel word" was used. All the words on the Stalls' list were said.

In spite of the levity, hard questions were asked. Local newspapers reported afterward that the overwhelming majority of those in attendance had decided they wanted the TTC canceled. The Stalls decided they had to engage the Texas political system if they were to make progress against the TTC. So they began attending political meetings in their area.

In August, the Stalls were delegates to the 2004 Republican State Convention in San Antonio, where they urged the Platform Committee to include in their recommendations a plank that called for the repeal of the Trans Texas Corridor. The convention adopted it. The repeal plank was adopted in 2004 and again in 2006 because, as the platform states, of issues concerning confiscation of private land and questions about state and national sovereignty.

In June 2006, the Texas Democratic Party also agreed on a party platform that called for the repeal of the TTC. That same month, the Texas Libertarian Party adopted a similar platform.

By November 2004, the Stalls had identified many others who were also working to stop TxDOT from tolling Texas freeways, and they organized a conference of activists that was held in Austin. Among those attending were Sol Costello, who had created a campaign in Austin, and Terri Hall, who had done the same in San Antonio. Linda Curtis of Independent Texans, who was organizing political opposition against legislators who had supported the bill, was there, as was "Sputnik," the head of the Texas Motorcycle Rights Association, who had inspired the opposition of motorcycle owners. Chris Hammel, a retired banker, organized farmers and landowners from the Blackland region in central Texas who would stand to lose 50,000 acres to the I-35 corridor also attended.

As the attendees shared information, what had been a concern of a few isolated people soon became a movement involving all political parties and all parts of the state.

Meanwhile, undeterred by this growing public opposition, TxDOT reviewed the conceptual and detailed proposals for phase one that had been submitted by three teams of developers. In December 2004, it awarded the project to a business group called Cintra-Zachry.

Zachry is one of the largest construction corporations in Texas and its owners are longtime political supporters of Rick Perry and George W. Bush. The Cintra-Zachry team included sixteen other firms, including JP Morgan Securities and PricewaterhouseCoopers. The team's law firm is Bracewell & Giuliani LLP, of which former New York Mayor Rudolph Giuliani is a name partner. The 400-lawyer firm is a legal and political powerhouse in Texas. Giuliani's affiliation with the firm helped him both raise $2.2 million in campaign funds during the first three months of 2007 and secure Governor Perry's early endorsement in the 2008 race for president.

Giuliani's involvement with Macquarie goes far beyond the TTC and legal work done by his law firm. In March 2007, he sold Giuliani Capital Advisors to the Macquarie Group for an undisclosed sale price. Various financial analysts have estimated the price tag at between $70 million and $100 million, of which Giuliani Partners was reported to have received 70 percent. Giuliani Capital Advisors, a "boutique" investment bank that Giuliani had bought from Ernst & Young in 2004, was reported to have had revenues of about $48 million in 2005 and a loss of about $1.4 million that year.

Giuliani's sale to the Macquarie Bank immediately generated political questions. Linda Curtis, the chairperson of Independent Texans, asked whether such a small firm with a net loss was really worth $70 million to $100 million. Her point was that Macquarie cannot contribute to U.S. political campaigns, but candidates can spend their own money. A generous price for Giuliani Capital would allow the candidate to legally use monies not otherwise available. And Macquarie would gain a useful, pro-toll road friend in the White House, should Giuliani win the presidency.

Mary Peters and David Gribbin of the Federal Highway Administration resigned at the end of President Bush's first term. Peters went to work for HDR, Inc., a large engineering firm with an extensive PPP practice. Gribbin became chief Washington lobbyist for the Macquarie Infrastructure Group, where his job was to promote public-private partnerships (PPP) such as those he had helped create at FHWA.

In March 2005, Cintra-Zachry and TxDOT signed the first TTC Comprehensive Development Agreement (CDA). When the media and groups such as the Stalls' asked for copies of the agreement, Governor Perry refused, claiming much of the information was confidential. *The Houston*

Post sued the governor and a Texas judge ruled that the information must be shared with the public. Cintra-Zachry lawyers challenged the order and delayed the release of information for a year. When Perry finally released part of the agreement, almost two hundred pages of financial details were missing.

Because TTC-35, the portion of the Trans Texas Corridor that runs south–north from San Antonio through Austin and Dallas to Oklahoma, uses some federal funds, environmental hearings were required in the counties along the route. TxDOT held them in the summer of 2006. More than 14,000 people attended. William H. Molina, a filmmaker, recorded the hearings and created the documentary "Truth Be Tolled," which shows Texans at those hearings who are stunned, angry, and desperate not to have their farms and ranches taken from them. It also reveals the clear indifference of TxDOT officials, who would sometimes drag out their presentations until late in the evening so people would leave or not ask questions or make statements. Most attendees, however, remained and had their say.

In September 2006, a first edit of the film was shown throughout the state, drawing large audiences. The documentary was awarded first prize at Houston's 2007 film festival.

Not surprisingly, the TTC became the principal issue in the 2006 Texas elections. A major question was the vast amount of political money that had been spent to amend the Texas Constitution and rewrite state laws to make the TTC and other toll roads possible. One "good government" group identified more than $2.7 million of such expenditures that had been made in the three years before 2006. Governor Perry won reelection with only 38 percent of the vote, largely because the opposition vote was divided among the Democratic candidate, an independent, and Kinky Friedman, a musician and author. Opponents of the TTC came together after the election and mounted a lobbying effort with the legislature to enact a two-year moratorium on TTC activities, which they thought would kill the project.

Before the legislature went into session in 2007, the Macquarie organization bought a chain of forty-two small Texas newspapers along the route of the I-35 corridor. Most had been strongly opposed to the TTC. Macquarie said it would not influence the papers' editorial opinions on the TTC.

When the legislature convened in January 2007, many bills were introduced to impose a moratorium on the TTC and other toll roads being planned by numerous Texas regional transportation authorities. Emotions were high. In March 2007, the Senate held its first hearing on the TTC and more than nine hundred people came to testify. So many wanted to speak in opposition that a line was formed and each person was given only three minutes to speak.

By the end of the day, hundreds of potential witnesses had not been heard and were forced to submit their views by mail. The next day almost five thousand TTC opponents held a march to the Capitol steps, where speakers expressed their outrage at what their government was planning to do. As prospects for the enactment of a moratorium brightened, the governor rushed into a deal with Cintra to allow the Spanish corporation to lease a partially finished state highway in Dallas, convert it to a toll road, and pay the state $2.8 billion for the rights.

Perry's panicky move angered many Texans, including Jere Thompson, Jr., a former chairman of the North Texas Toll Authority (NTTA), an old and experienced toll organization, which TxDOT excluded from bidding on the Dallas project. He sent a letter to *The Dallas Morning News* claiming that if the NTTA had been allowed to bid using the same assumptions as had Cintra, the state would have received $3.5 billion more money.

The resulting political uproar forced Perry to reverse himself and ask for a NTTA bid, which he got. In a further twist, the U.S. Department of Transportation threatened the state that it might be forced to withhold future federal highway funds from Texas if the Cintra bid were rejected. U.S. Senator Kay Bailey Hutchison (R-Tex.) contacted DOT and received assurances that such a cutoff would not happen.

The NTTA bid included a $2.5 billion up-front payment to TxDOT, a total of another $833 billion to TxDOT in forty-nine annual payments, and $1.3 billion of profits that NTTA promised would be reinvested in Texas roads. The Cintra bid included a $2.1 billion up-front concession and $700 billion to TxDOT over the next forty-nine years. In the end, the NTTA bid of $3.3 billion plus the reinvestment of the $1.3 billion in profits in Texas won out over the Cintra bid of $2.8 billion.

Although the NTTA bid gave Texas $1.8 billion more benefits, the Federal Highway Administration administrator, J. Richard Capka, wrote TxDOT a letter admonishing the agency for conducting a bidding process that was unfair to Cintra. He implied that he feared that the award to NTTA might discourage private investors from bidding on future projects. Capka also wrote TxDOT that the FHWA would impose additional oversight on Texas for two years to ensure that public entities were not again allowed to bid against private firms on road projects in that state. He warned that if it happened again Texas might lose funds under the Federal-Aid Highway Program. Apparently, the fact that TxDOT had initially excluded the NTTA from the initial bidding on the project was of no concern. The Bush administration's preference for private tolling shines through in Capka's letter to TxDOT, even when the state gets a better deal elsewhere.

In 2006, Norman Mineta, the long-serving secretary of transportation, retired and Bush appointed Mary Peters to be his replacement. In January 2007, the president announced that D. J. Gribbin, IV, would become general counsel for the department.

Once back in government office, both Peters and Gribbin have made the expansion of the public-private partnership program their top priority. To speed PPP projects into being, the Department of Transportation is doing an analysis of all state constitutions and all state laws on contracting. DOT is creating a package of model legislation that every governor and state legislature can use to speed conversion of their freeways to tollways.

The principal resistance to tolling U.S. roads comes from Congress. James Oberstar (D-Minn.), chairman of the House Committee on Transportation and Infrastructure, and Peter A. DeFazio (D-Oreg.), chairman of the Subcommittee on Highways and Transit, sent a letter dated May 10, 2007, to all the governors and the USDOT that warned, "We write to strongly discourage you from entering into public-private partnership ('PPP') agreements. . . . The Committee will work to undo any state PPP agreements that do not fully protect the public interest and the integrity of the national system." The Department of Transportation has ignored that congressional warning.

In the 2007 session of the Texas Legislature, tens of thousands of angry voters bombarded their legislators with demands for a moratorium on the TTC. Both sides of the issue deployed all the usual political and legislative tricks in order to get their way. But the demands from voters were, at least temporarily, irresistible.

In May 2007, the Texas House voted 139–1 for a TTC moratorium. Representative Mike Krusee voted nay. The vote in the Senate was 27–4. Since a veto by the governor requires a two-thirds majority in each house to be overridden, the moratorium legislation seemed veto-proof.

The governor, however, warned that if the legislature overrode his veto, he would hold it in special session in Austin for as long as it took to get his way; his project supporters also bombarded the legislators with their reasons, lures, and threats. When thus confronted by the governor and his allies, "the legislators," according to one Austin political writer, "crumbled as easily as a piece of tin foil."

Perry vetoed the moratorium bill. Neither the Texas Senate nor House attempted to override. Instead they adopted a weak compromise bill that would slow construction on parts of the TTC, limit any toll agreements to fifty years, give greater public access to TxDOT contracts, prohibit financial advisers from rushing through a revolving door between working for the state and TTC private contractors, require the state auditor to verify traffic and revenue estimates of concessions, and prohibit gifts to authority directors.

The legislation signed into law, though weak, is important because it put an overwhelming majority of legislators into the public record, repeatedly, saying that it was their intent to halt any TTC construction contract from being signed until the legislature returned two years later. The governor's office assured the leadership of both houses that none would be. More important, the highly visible political fight alerted millions of Texans to Perry's and TxDOT's plans.

After the legislature adjourned, Perry and TxDOT acted as though the legislative session had not happened. The Texas Highway Commission authorized TxDOT to move forward on eighty toll road projects across the state. David Stall wrote Corridor Watch members in early August 2007 that TxDOT had resumed its "headlong rush to use every available loophole, exception, and remaining authority to build toll roads and grant toll road concessions just as fast as possible."

Once the legislators had left Austin, Perry also vetoed several other pieces of legislation that would have constrained TxDOT's tolling agenda. One bill would have reduced the potential abuse of TxDOT's eminent domain powers by ensuring limited uses for private properties seized and providing for just compensation. Another bill that Perry vetoed released TxDOT from any requirement to study the upgrading of existing routes before seizing property for new corridors. Another would have required the Texas attorney general to determine if TxDOT's authority was limited in any way by NAFTA or any other trade agreement.

Old-fashioned public blackmail was TxDOT's next maneuver. In August 2007, the Highway Commission announced that the state would stop all new highway construction. Instead, highway monies would be used for maintenance of existing facilities. If Texas communities wanted new roads to relieve congestion, Perry announced, the communities would be required to either raise local taxes or accept toll roads.

What perplexed many Texans is how the state government could be short of funds when the governor was making tax cuts based on a $14 billion budget surplus. In an attempt to lower outrage among Texas voters, TxDOT diverted $9 million into a statewide ad campaign promoting the benefits of toll roads, a use of public monies that was soon contested in the Texas courts.

In late August 2007, San Antonio radio station WOAI obtained a copy of a TxDOT report titled "Forward Momentum: A Report to the 110th Congress, 1st Session," which identified several actions Perry had asked the U.S. Congress and the Bush administration to take that would speed the tolling of Texas roads. Foremost of these was a recommendation to reverse existing law, which generally prohibits imposing tolls on interstate highways that federal funds have been used to build.

While he was House majority leader, Tom DeLay (R-Tex.) had gotten Congress to enact a provision that allowed the U.S. Department of Transportation to authorize a few "pilot" toll projects on existing interstates. Perry wanted the law changed so states could toll all parts of all interstates. Additionally, he requested Congress to exempt private investors in toll road projects, such as the Cintra and Macquarie consortiums, from federal income taxation.

Perhaps Perry's boldest request was that Texas be allowed to buy back or reimburse the federal government for the state's share of federal investment in its interstate highways. Texas could then take these highways and lease them to private operators for fifty years or more. Under existing U.S. Department of Transportation rules on real estate sales, TxDOT would also keep such repayments for use on other Texas highway projects.

Transportation Secretary Peters and her general counsel, Gribbin, are moving aggressively to convert a large portion of U.S. freeways to tollways before they return to private life. By the winter of 2007, the FHWA had privatization projects under way in twenty-five states. Large foreign and domestic corporations, including banks from around the world, are scrambling to capitalize on these projects. Also, President Bush has appointed the pro-TTC Texas State Representative Krusee, TxDOT lawyer Geoffrey S. Yarema, and other TTC consultants to the U.S. Department of Transportation's National Surface Transportation Infrastructure Financing Commission, where they will offer the next president and Congress recommendations on how to finance future U.S. highways.

The PPP is a sly form of taxation for which politicians need not take responsibility but that can generate tens of billions of dollars in revenues, including campaign contributions. Maybe the existing U.S. model of highway financing is obsolete and the nation no longer wants good roads at the lowest price. Perhaps the United States would be better served by the toll policies used in Europe and Japan. Maybe it does not matter if our governors put our roads and bridges under control of foreign companies for a half century or longer and leave massive unfunded liabilities for their successors.

One thing is certain, however: this is corporatism in its most basic form. How America should deal with it is one of the thorniest issues the Bush administration will bestow upon the next president and Congress.

Three

ELITISM

In a provocative piece for *The National Interest,* Harvard professor Samuel P. Huntington quoted Sir Walter Scott's "The Lay of the Last Minstrel," which asks:

> *Breathes there the man with soul so dead,*
> *Who never to himself hath said,*
> *"This is my own, my native land!"*
> *Whose heart hath ne'er within him burn'd,*
> *As home his footsteps he hath turn'd,*
> *From wandering on a foreign strand!*

Huntington concludes, "A contemporary answer to Scott's question is: Yes, dead souls are a small but growing part of America's business, professional, intellectual, and academic elites. Possessing in Scott's words, 'titles, power and pelf,' they also have decreasing ties with the American nation."

These elites have, according to Huntington, "little need for national loyalty, view national boundaries as obstacles that thankfully are vanishing and see national governments as residues from the past whose only useful function is to facilitate the elite's global operations."

Huntington estimates that these elites worldwide numbered approximately 20 million people in 2000, of whom 4 million were Americans. Of them, he notes, "Someone whose loyalties, identities, and involvement are purely national is less likely to rise to the top in business, academia, the media, and professions than someone who transcends those limits. Outside politics, those who stay home, stay behind."

The paradox is that the elites' "attitudes and behavior contrast with the overwhelming patriotism and nationalistic identification of the rest of the American public." An extraordinary 96 to 98 percent of Americans in the late 1990s said they were "very proud" or "quite proud" of their country, a count that included more than 13 million naturalized citizens. In 2007, despite much negative feeling caused by the war in Iraq, Americans were still overwhelmingly proud of their country.

These elites, including many from abroad, control a large number of the corporations, media, think tanks, law firms, and banks that shape U.S. policies. And now, as in the early 1930s, when corporations dominated U.S. governance, the only counterbalance to these elites is the federal government, which itself is controlled by a handful of people, many of them themselves drawn from the elites and virtually all of whom are intractably enthralled by the laissez-faire ideology of globalism. As Huntington notes, the U.S. government has become an "unrepresentative democracy"— a nation whose leaders are selected through free and fair elections but pass laws "contrary to the views of the American people."

Elite control has radically shifted U.S. global economic policy over the past quarter century. As Barry C. Lynn notes, the Truman and Eisenhower administrations confronted the Cold War by fostering industrial interdependence with America's allies, with security the foremost goal of these policies. Lynn writes that such security was "pursued through locking former enemies and traditional allies into complex webs of industry from which it became ever harder to escape and through the creation of multinational-scale systems of production and research that increased the efficiency of the West in its industrial rivalry with the Soviet Union."

The succession of presidents from Eisenhower through Reagan never allowed other nations to manipulate these webs in a way that made the United States dependent on them for technologies or goods essential to America's security or economy. Yet the elites who have dominated the administrations of Presidents George H. W. Bush, Bill Clinton, and George W. Bush have actively pursued policies that have pushed the United States into that dependency trap.

The growing U.S. dependence on other nations for everything from food to energy to advanced technologies is one of the many consequences of rule by those dead souls. This system of governance is not only open to foreign political money but aggressively seeks it.

The most fundamental questions, of course, are who are these elites and how do they operate?

The United States now has a permanent governing class that moves almost effortlessly among public office, Wall Street financial firms, transnational corporations, law firms, elite think tanks, and lobbying concerns. One example of this permanence is that a Bush or Clinton has been atop or near the top of the federal government since 1981. As control of government shifts back and forth from one faction to another, the influential jobs in the executive branch are filled by their appointees, most of whom permanently live and work in Washington, D.C. This coterie of insiders exerts a perpetual influence over our national policies. Their careers are not a conspiracy. Rather, they reflect the ossification of our politics and a resulting system of governance that is increasingly unaffected by elections, retaining in power these insiders, who each year become more and more distant from those they supposedly represent and serve.

As a longtime Washington political insider, Jock Nash, notes, "The safest job in America today is being a member of Congress." Unfortunately, his joke is our reality. Once elected, most members of Congress are able to raise so much campaign money that they can retain their office until they tire of the work or find something better. Each election cycle, fewer than 40 out of 435 House incumbents face a real electoral challenge, creating a permanent unrepresentative government.

In our money-driven system of electoral politics, foreign interests have numerous opportunities to participate. Campaign contributions are one way. The easiest and most effective way for such interests to influence U.S. policies, however, is to hire lobbyists and advisers who were previously members of Congress, congressional staffers, or senior officials in the executive branch. In the revolving-door world of Washington, many of the ex-officials who work as lobbyists will eventually move back into high public positions.

In my book *Agents of Influence* (1990), I identified two hundred former high-ranking U.S. officials (half Republicans and half Democrats) who left top federal positions between 1980 and 1990, registered with the U.S. Justice Department as foreign agents, and then lobbied Congress and the federal agencies on behalf of foreign governments and corporations.

That list included fifteen former assistants to the president, a White House press secretary, a chief of staff to the vice president, a chairman and a vice chairman of the International Trade Commission, three deputy secretaries of commerce, three assistant secretaries of commerce, a U.S. trade representative, two deputy U.S. trade representatives, six senators, ten representatives, twelve senior Senate staff, five senior House staff, five retired generals, and 125 other equally high-ranking ex-officials from the State Department, Central Intelligence Agency, and Department of Defense.

Washington's revolving door became a major political issue in the 1992 presidential campaign when the political independent Ross Perot announced that if elected he would impose strict postemployment standards on all federal officials. Perot lost, but soon after Bill Clinton won that presidential election, *The Washington Post* reported that Ronald Brown, Clinton's secretary of commerce–designee and the chief Washington lobbyist for Japan's electronics industry, would be hosting a preinauguration private dinner for his Japanese clients and the president-elect.

In the resulting political furor Brown canceled the dinner, but the media quickly focused on the lobbying backgrounds of other Clinton appointees. They discovered that Mickey Kantor, the president's designee for U.S. Trade representative, represented the Suzuki Motor Corporation. The deputy national security advisor was to be Samuel R. "Sandy" Berger, who worked for the Toyota Motor Corporation. Stuart E. Eizenstat, ambassador-designate to the European Community, advised Hitachi. The appointee for under secretary of state for economic affairs was Joan Spero, also a consultant to Toyota. The assistant secretary of state for economic affairs was to be Daniel Tarullo, a registered foreign agent for Komatsu, the giant Japanese construction equipment maker.

Once this information became public, several members of Congress announced their intention to explore those lobbying relationships during the confirmation process. Several announced that once Congress convened, they would introduce tough new ethics laws for post–U.S. government employment. As inauguration day approached, the issue gained political momentum.

At noon on January 20, 1993, Bill Clinton became president of the United States. After the ceremony, Clinton and congressional leaders went into the Capitol for the traditional reception and luncheon. Before the event began, however, the new president was guided to a side room, where aides presented several important documents for his signature. One of those was Executive Order 12834, titled "Ethics Commitments by Executive Branch Appointees," which Clinton signed into law.

This Executive Order required every senior appointee in every executive agency of the U.S. government appointed on or after January 20, 1993, to sign an ethics contract that read:

1. I will not, within five years after the termination of my employment as a senior appointee in any executive agency in which I am appointed to serve, lobby any officer or employee of that agency.

2. I will not, at any time after the termination of my employment in the United States Government, engage in any activity on behalf of any foreign government or foreign political party which, if undertaken on January 20, 1993, would require me to register under the Foreign Agents Registration Act of 1938, as amended.

3. I will not within five years after termination of my personal and substantial participation in a trade negotiation, represent, aid or advise any foreign government, foreign political party or foreign business entity with the intent to influence a decision of any officer or employee of any executive agency, in carrying out his or her official duties.

With a stroke of his pen, Clinton put into U.S. law an ethics code for the executive branch that was by far the strictest, most comprehensive, most inclusive, and most detailed that any president had ever adopted.

Once the details of the Executive Order became known, the controversy over Clinton's appointments died down almost instantly since, once out of office, the appointees were legally bound to wait five years before lobbying their former agencies or becoming agents of influence. Over the next eight years, every policy-level appointee of the Clinton administration signed the federal ethics contract.

On the morning of January 20, 2001, just before the inauguration of President George W. Bush, the White House media director issued a press alert announcing that Clinton had pardoned 140 people, including his brother, drug dealers, stock swindlers, two brothers from Arkansas imprisoned for rolling back odometers on used cars, and a fugitive commodities broker named Marc Rich, whose ex-wife had contributed hundreds of thousands of dollars to the political campaigns of both Bill and Hillary Clinton, and a middleman in Saddam Hussein's Oil-for-Food scandal.

Unnoticed in the media's coverage of the pardons was Clinton's issuance of Executive Order 13184, which provided, in its entirety:

Executive Order 12834 of January 20, 1993, "Ethics Commitments by Executive Branch Appointees," is hereby revoked, effective at noon Janu-

ary 20, 2001. Employees and former employees subject to the commitments in
Executive Order 12834 will not be subject to those commitments after the
effective date of this order.

With a second stroke of his pen, Clinton canceled the thousands of
ethics contracts signed during his administration, thereby allowing all of
his appointees to rejoin Washington's lobbying industry instantly.

Absent his revocation, Clinton's ethics code would automatically have
been law for Bush's appointees. Revoking the order would have been a
most difficult step for the new president, given the negative publicity such
an action surely would have created. Bush never reinstated the 1993 Executive Order, and the postgovernment employment of both Clinton and
Bush administration appointees has been regulated by the loophole-
ridden ethics laws of the past, which in effect means that there has been no
regulation.

Lobbying is a growth business in Washington. Between 1998 and 2007,
more than 33,000 people registered as lobbyists at the Senate Office of
Public Records. It is a $10-billion-a-year industry, more than a fifth of
which goes for salaries. (See the Appendix for a partial listing of the postgovernment employment of these officials.)

Jeffrey H. Birnbaum, a *Washington Post* journalist who reports on lobbying, attributes this boom to three factors: the rapid growth in the federal
government, GOP control of the White House and Congress (until 2007),
and "the wide acceptance among corporations that they need to hire professional lobbyists to secure their share of the federal benefits." As Birnbaum notes, lobbying in the 1990s was heavily reactive, trying to fend off
regulations and government proposals. After the 2000 election, lobbying has focused on ways to cut taxes, get contracts, and make money off
government.

There is also a fourth factor: the expanded efforts by foreign governments and corporations to shape U.S. policies and expenditures to their
advantage.

Data produced by the Center for Public Integrity, a nonprofit organization that monitors lobbying, reveal that between 1998 and 2004 companies
headquartered in seventy-eight countries spent more than $620 million
for the lobbying work of 550 Washington, D.C., firms and 3,800 lobbyists,

including a hundred former members of Congress who are working as foreign agents. For instance, British Petroleum (BP) spent more than $33 million during that six-year period trying to influence U.S. legislation on the environment and the Superfund, plus attempting to persuade Congress to open the Arctic National Wildlife Refuge to oil drilling. Sixteen foreign defense contractors used their Washington lobbying muscle to secure $16.4 billion in Defense Department contracts, a third of which were awarded without competition. Examples of such corporatism seem limitless.

The lure of these lobbying dollars has sharply changed the nature and concept of public service in Washington. Between 1998 and 2004, half the members of Congress who left office went to work in Washington as lobbyists. More than 250 former members were working as domestic and foreign lobbyists at the end of 2005, a postemployment shift that would have been politically unthinkable as recently as three decades ago. Today, the brass ring of public office, whether elected or appointed, is the opportunity it creates to become a rich lobbyist in the future.

Increasingly, many such political appointees, deeply embedded in the policy-making process, are deliberately shaping U.S. policies, regulatory decisions, and administrative actions for the benefit of corporate and foreign interests—that is, future clients. A position of public power is often a stepping-stone to a future career as a lobbyist.

One particularly disturbing example of such careerism concerns the CIA station chief in a nation who left office and became an "adviser" for that nation at a fee of $50,000 per month, a move that raises obvious questions about which, if any, U.S. intelligence he may have shared with his new employers. Equally significant, many former U.S. ambassadors have become "advisers" and lobbyists for the governments where they once represented the United States. Saudi Arabia and China are notable for the number of former U.S. ambassadors who have gone on their payrolls after leaving office. The idea of lifetime public service that President John F. Kennedy promoted is rapidly becoming a quaint notion as the generation he inspired to action exits public life.

In part, the diminished appeal of lifetime service is caused by the extraordinary growth in the differential between public and private sector salaries. People who now take government jobs sacrifice more money than they would have when Kennedy and Johnson were president, and they are always aware of what they are giving up. Also, the civil servant protections that existed for decades have been weakened significantly, beginning with

Jimmy Carter's "reforms" in the late 1970s. Simply put, the people we need to staff the senior professional and administrative jobs in the federal government can find more secure, better-paying, and more rewarding work elsewhere.

Lobbying is one area where talented and well-connected people now go. Washington's political class, moreover, now accepts foreign-paid lobbying as a normal state of affairs. As the number of foreign-controlled corporations in the United States expands, most of their lobbyists are no longer required to register as foreign agents, only as domestic lobbyists like those employed by U.S. corporations. Also, the line between being a foreign-controlled or a domestically controlled company has virtually disappeared in Washington. The ownership and leadership of foreign corporations, many of which are actually state-owned, have interests that are not the same as those of the United States and its people.

The principal change in foreign lobbying over the past fifteen years is how greatly it has expanded. Between 1998 and 2005, corporations and governments from the United Kingdom, Germany, and Switzerland spent more money lobbying in Washington than did the Japanese, who for many years had maintained the largest foreign political presence in the United States. It is not that the Japanese spent any less but that the others spent more.

Simply put, policy in Washington is for sale. And those who ignore this reality sacrifice much of the influence they may have on policy debates and the decisions Congress and the president make.

Thus, immigrants and companies from India have formed the U.S. India Political Action Committee (USINPAC). It deals with issues that these new Americans face in the United States. It also tries to influence decisions such as U.S. positions on India's nuclear program and aid for India. As part of that lobbying, USINPAC persuaded members of the House to form the Congressional Caucus on India and Indian Americans, which now includes 173 representatives. In 2004, Senators Hillary Clinton (D-N.Y.) and John Cornyn (R-Tex.) organized a bipartisan thirty-five-member Friends of India Caucus in the Senate, the first foreign country–focused caucus in that body. In her bid for president, Indian Americans are major donors to Senator Clinton's campaign. One prominent fund raiser promised to raise $5 million from the Indian-American community for her campaign. In June 2007, she collected about $2 million at an "Indian Americans for Hillary" event in New York City.

Of all nations, China has expanded its political influence in Washington the most over the past fifteen years. Chinese diplomats are almost omnipresent at congressional hearings, think tank briefings, and public policy events, meeting those in power and collecting information. Yet the principal way the government of China exerts its influence is through U.S.-headquartered corporations and banks that do business inside China and the diplomacy involved with the State Department's efforts to control the atomic programs of North Korea and Iran.

Many foreign governments and the institutions they finance now practice what is known as long-term lobbying; that is, activities that shape Americans' basic thinking about those countries. The name for this used to be "propagandizing," and, in all fairness, the United States has long spent massive amounts of time and money doing the same thing around the world.

What is so odd about this long-term lobbying is that our leaders allow other governments to dominate what U.S. colleges and universities teach about those countries' history, culture, and vital bilateral policy issues. Today, for instance, Japan's government, corporations, and foundations finance an estimated 95 percent of the intellectual work performed on U.S.-Japan issues by American universities. The same is true at think tanks where U.S.-Japan issues are considered. The Japanese also provide elementary and secondary education programs used in thousands of U.S. public schools. China dominates U.S.-China studies, Korea influences the substance of U.S.-Korea studies, India controls U.S.-India studies, and European nations fund U.S.-European studies. Nations affected by U.S. policies are financing, and thus influencing, America's immediate and long-term thinking about those policies.

America's open system of politics and governance is ill equipped to cope with globalization and the foreign political influence that comes with it. While this vulnerability has many sources, three are pivotal. First, a political environment in Washington that openly tolerates the buying and selling of influence, even to the point of larceny, has developed. Second, national governance has devolved over the past decade into boss-run machine rule whose leaders rely on ever-increasing infusions of campaign cash to retain power, creating a political system in which national interests are openly exchanged for campaign dollars. Third and most significant, much of that cash is coming from corporations and foreign interests that are without allegiance to the United States, do not identify with the nation's principles or its people, yet are allowed to participate actively in the U.S. political process.

. . .

Ethics standards on Capitol Hill are even weaker than in the executive branch. The Senate and House of Representatives separately set and administer their standards, and, not surprisingly, most members are unwilling to limit their pre- or post-office activities, thus creating a vacuum with almost limitless opportunities for corruption and influence peddling.

The root of today's collapse of ethics in the House of Representatives can be traced to the tactics that ignited the so-called Gingrich Revolution, the Republican takeover of that body in 1995. When the leaders of this "revolution," Newt Gingrich (R-Ga.), Tom DeLay (R-Tex.), and Richard Armey (R-Tex.), entered Congress two decades earlier, a relative state of political comity existed between Democrats and Republicans. These three members, however, rejected interparty cooperation and adopted the politics of personal attack, similar to what George H. W. Bush and his political adviser Lee Atwater had inflicted on their Democratic opponent in the 1988 presidential election, with tactics such as the infamous "Willie Horton" advertisement that portrayed Democrats as soft on crime.

By 1987, Gingrich's strategy to gain political power, both in his own party and in the House of Representatives, centered on impeaching Speaker of the House Jim Wright (D-Tex.) for supposed ethics violations, including sales of a vanity book. Charges were brought. A proud man, Wright resigned in June 1989, becoming the first Speaker to quit because of ethics violations. In fairness to Gingrich and his allies, the Democrats had greatly abused their power in the pre-1995 era before the Republicans took control.

Setting aside the merits of either party's leadership, Gingrich's takedown of Wright ignited an ethics war in the House that raged for seven years. Democrats filed eighty-four separate ethics charges against Gingrich; ironically, one claimed that a $4 million book deal was nothing less than bribery from the media baron Rupert Murdoch. By the end of 1996, the House ethics war had scarred so many members in both parties that legislative work had slowed to a virtual halt.

In February 1997, the leaders of both parties appointed an ethics review task force and gave it a mandate to review the House ethics system. Both parties then declared a temporary moratorium on ethics investigations until the working group's recommendations were available. Seven months later, the task force recommended that the House exclude media accounts as a basis for ethics complaints, largely because many prior filings had resulted from stories published by newspapers such as *The Wall Street Journal*, *The New York Times*, and *The Washington Post*.

The task force also recommended changing House ethics rules to prohibit citizens and "good government" organizations, such as Common Cause, from filing complaints. With these changes, only members could file complaints about other members, and the leaders of both parties agreed that their members would not do so. Thus, after taking from American voters the right to file a protest against ethical violations by their elected representatives, the House began a seven-year "policing holiday."

The ethics truce held until June 2004, when Representative Chris Bell (D-Tex.), a freshman member who had lost his primary race because of redistricting and thus would not be returning to Congress, filed a 187-page ethics complaint against then–Majority Leader DeLay accusing him of "bribery, extortion, fraud, money laundering, and the abuse of power" concerning DeLay's redistricting efforts in Texas. The House Ethics Committee reacted with an "Alice in Wonderland" ruling that acquitted DeLay of any wrongdoing but scolded Bell for having personally signed the complaint and transmitting it to the committee. Eventually, Texas legal officials disagreed with the committee's conclusion and DeLay was indicted for violations of that state's campaign laws. He then resigned from Congress.

In spite of all this, since the Democrats took control of Congress in January 2007, only minor reforms have been approved, such as prohibition of the purchase of meals by lobbyists and better disclosure of the bundling of campaign contributions. Ironically, the meals prohibition actually works to the advantage of the well-financed special interests that exert their influence primarily through campaign contributions. For those without such deep pockets, one of the few opportunities to get the undivided attention of a member of Congress had been during a breakfast, lunch, or dinner, when the merits of an issue could be discussed for the price of a meal.

Consequently, an ethics truce once again exists in Congress, making its members a ruling elite that has granted itself the privilege of public unaccountability, unlimited by any meaningful system of ethical constraints.

Today, America's financial leaders, as they always have, sit among the top of our national elites. The newest variation in their changing role in the economy is the rise of hedge and equity funds. They trade stocks and take large positions in corporations, where they often mount takeovers and conduct restructuring. As of 2008, hedge fund managers had almost $3 trillion under management, most of which comes from pension funds, insurance companies, and wealthy investors.

Such investment funds are organizations, such as the Blackstone Group and Cerberus, that raise massive amounts of equity from institutions and individuals, borrow even greater sums from banks and other lending institutions, and then buy corporations and operate them as private entities.

The political power of these elites is reflected in their ability to persuade Congress and a succession of presidents to leave untouched a loophole that taxes their multimillion-dollar earnings at a much lower rate than what most Americans pay. These managers charge a base fee of 2 percent of the value of the investment, plus 20 to 50 percent of profits. Their profits can be enormous. In 2005, the top ten hedge and investment fund managers were paid more than $7 billion. The top performer was a Texan, T. Boone Pickens, who was paid $1.5 billion for a year's work. In 2006, James Simons of East Setaucket, New York, took the top spot with a paycheck of $1.8 billion.

But unlike other service providers, such as high-earning accountants and lawyers, who are taxed at a 35 percent rate, hedge fund managers pay a tax of only 15 percent on what they earn. When the Blackstone Group sold equity to the public in 2007, the partners were able to structure the deal so they were taxed less than 5 percent on $3.7 billion of the stock they sold.

Paradoxically, Peter Peterson—the multibillionaire cofounder of this firm and a major beneficiary of this tax loophole—is arguably the nation's most visible advocate for "shared sacrifice" by the American people when it comes to paying taxes as a means of strengthening the U.S. economy. Ironic, for sure.

As these funds have taken private trillions of dollars of corporate assets, they have also been able to persuade Congress and presidents to exempt them from reporting to the public even basic information about their activities. Thus, these giant funds, which own thousands of companies and exert a major influence in the world economy, operate in almost total secrecy. They offer foreign governments and corporations the opportunity to buy into major parts of the U.S. economy without oversight.

At the same time, these funds and institutional investors are changing the nature of investment in a way that undercuts the capacity of U.S. companies to meet the global competition they face. These funds' and investors' myopic focus on quick results and fast profits is diverting capital from investment in long-term productive purposes to short-term speculation. It is crippling American companies.

If U.S. business is to take a longer-term focus, it requires an economic environment that permits and encourages long-term action. The creation of such an environment hinges on a reduction in the demands of investors for immediate returns, regardless of future consequences.

Today, control of America's major corporations, particularly those listed on the New York Stock Exchange (NYSE), is essentially in the hands of institutions: public and private pension funds, insurance corporations, foundations, investment companies, hedge funds, educational endowments, trust funds, and banks. This is of great consequence because individuals and institutions generally invest in the stock market for sharply different reasons; individuals are looking largely for long-term performance while institutions are pursuing primarily short-term profits. Just at the moment when U.S. business needs to be making long-term investments to meet global competition, the owners—institutions—are pressing for quick results.

Institutions now hold so much equity and are such a powerful presence in stock markets that most corporations are at the mercy of their demands. The raw economic power of institutional investors can be measured in two ways: their stock holdings and their willingness to get rid of stocks that fail to produce quick earnings.

As to the power of ownership, institutional stock holdings have risen rapidly over the past three decades. In 1980, U.S.-based institutional investors held 37 percent of all U.S. equities, rising to 51 percent in 2000. The Conference Board reports that as of 2005, institutions owned more than two thirds of the stock of America's 1,000 largest corporations.

The biggest impact of this ownership comes through the accelerating pace of their transactions. In 1953, when institutions controlled about 15 percent of the equities listed on the NYSE, their trades constituted a quarter of stock market transactions. Today, institutional trades constitute well over 90 percent.

Because institutions own such a large share of all stock and trade that stock so zealously, there has been a sharp increase in the turnover rate of the NYSE (the pace at which the total value of stocks listed on the exchange is traded). In 1970, the turnover rate was less than 20 percent a year. Then investors bought a stock and waited for the company's growth. By 1990, the rate was 46 percent. At the 1970s pace, it took five years for the entire value of the stock market to turn over; by 1990, it took slightly more than two years. By the end of the decade, the turnover rate was 103 percent. The turnover of the entire value of the New York Stock Exchange in less than twelve months means that massive amounts of capital are being used for speculation rather than investment.

In the speculative, short-term-oriented equity markets that now exist, few U.S. firms have sufficient assets and profits to conduct long-term research and development and make other commitments that global competitiveness requires. Most companies are obliged to focus their efforts and resources on results that can bolster the price of their stock each quarter. By ceding the future to the present, institutional investors have greatly reduced the capability of U.S. corporations to cope with foreign competitors whose actions are shaped by long-term perspectives, particularly state-owned enterprises, such as those in China, that do not face such short-term pressures.

The secrecy surrounding the actions of hedge and equity fund managers is not unique to that industry. America's ruling elites almost always exhibit little desire to inform, let alone involve, the American people in policy making or in the actions they are taking, even actions with profound consequences for the public's future.

A glaring example of such disregard is the trilateral negotiations among the governments of Mexico, the United States, and Canada on an initiative called the Security and Prosperity Partnership of North America (SPP). The goal of the SPP is to deeply integrate the economic and political systems of the three nations. The work is being accomplished in secret, and only a handful of political and business elites are being allowed to participate. The media, of course, are excluded, as is the U.S. Congress.

The SPP had its formal origin on February 16, 2001, less than one month after George W. Bush became the forty-third president of the United States. The newly inaugurated president flew to Rancho San Cristobal in Guanajuato, Mexico, where he met with Mexican President Vicente Fox to discuss a North American "Partnership for Prosperity." The two presidents named their initiative the "Guanajuato Proposal."

In their joint news release the two presidents announced their intention to:

1. Work with Canada to "consolidate a North American economic community."
2. Negotiate short- and long-term agreements that will lead to a new approach to dealing with migration and labor issues between the two countries.
3. Immediately implement the North American Free Trade Agree-

ment (NAFTA) provision that gives Mexican trucks and drivers full access to U.S. highways.

4. Devise a trilateral approach to development of North America's energy resources.
5. Jointly support extension of NAFTA to include all of the Americas—the Free Trade Area of the Americas.

Before work could be launched on this project, however, terrorists attacked the United States on September 11, 2001, and the Guanajuato Proposal faded into the background of policy priorities during Bush's first term.

In retrospect, the Guanajuato Proposal was about more than the objectives stated in the news release. It was a carefully planned and staged move to develop an agenda of actions that would deepen the economic and political integration of the United States, Mexico, and Canada. It was to be NAFTA II.

By 2004, with the effort stalled, the question that SPP advocates faced was how to reignite the trilateral negotiations at the highest levels of the three governments. Their solution was to form a private, trilateral study group whose recommendations would then be taken to the heads of the three governments. Thus, on October 15, 2004, the New York–based Council on Foreign Relations (CFR) announced the creation of a trilateral task force that would issue recommendations on creating a North American Community. The Archer Daniels Midland Company, Merrill Lynch, and Yves-André Istel, vice chairman of the Rothschild Group, provided the financial support for the task force's work.

Mexico was represented on the trilateral task force by the Consejo Mexicano de Asuntos Internacionales (COMEXI) and Canada by the Canadian Council of Chief Executives (CCCE), those nations' premier business associations. Each nation had ten panelists. Those from the United States were:

1. Nelson W. Cunningham, a managing partner for Kissinger McLarty Associates and member of the Council of the Americas. He was special adviser to President Clinton for Latin American Affairs, and he was an adviser to the presidential campaign of Senator John Kerry.
2. Richard A. Falkenrath, a visiting fellow at the Brookings Institution, who was special assistant to President George W. Bush and

senior director for policy and plans at the White House Office of Homeland Security.

3. Gordon D. Giffin, a senior partner at McKenna Long & Aldridge, who was U.S. ambassador to Canada (1997–2001); a director of the Canadian National Railway Company, the Canadian Imperial Bank of Commerce, and Canadian Natural Resources, Ltd.; and a member of the advisory board of the Canadian American Business Council.

4. Carla A. Hills, chairman and CEO of Hills & Company, who was the U.S. trade representative (1989–1993), negotiated NAFTA, and subsequently served as a consultant and adviser to President Clinton during the NAFTA ratification process (1994).

5. Gary C. Hufbauer, a fellow at the Peter G. Peterson Institute for International Economics and author of several reports and books that supported the creation of NAFTA.

6. James R. Jones, CEO of ManattJones Global Strategies and a former member of Congress from Oklahoma; a director of Anheuser-Busch, Kansas City Southern Railroad, KeySpan Corporation, Grupo Modelo, and San Luis Corporation; chairman of the World Affairs Councils of America; and chairman of the U.S.-Mexico Business Commission, a standing committee of the Council of the Americas.

7. Doris M. Meissner, a senior fellow at the Migration Policy Institute, who was the commissioner of the U.S. Immigration and Naturalization Service (INS) during the Clinton administration (1993–2000).

8. Thomas M. T. Niles, vice chairman of the United States Council for International Business, who served as U.S. ambassador to Canada (1985–1989) and ambassador to the European Union (1989–1991).

9. Robert A. Pastor, the director of the Center for North American Studies and vice president of international affairs and professor of international relations at American University. He is the author of *Toward a North American Community: Lessons from the Old World to the New.*

10. Jeffrey J. Scott, a senior fellow at the Institute for International Studies and formerly a trade negotiator. He is the author of *NAFTA: Achievements and Challenges.*

The U.S. cochairman of the task force was William F. Weld, a financier, author of three novels, former governor of Massachusetts (1991–1997), and a strong NAFTA advocate.

Each of the U.S. panelists had been intimately involved with the creation of NAFTA, and each for many years had written, spoken, and worked diligently to deepen the political and economic integration of the United States, Mexico, and Canada. Moreover, the panel was equally divided between Republican and Democratic elites and included people who were advising both candidates for president in 2004. The panelists from Mexico and Canada came from prominent elites in their nations, which guaranteed a favorable reception from those governments.

As the U.S. panelists knew, NAFTA is more than about trade and investment. It is also a trilateral agreement on intellectual property rights, immigration, transportation, regulatory standards, food safety, and energy, among many other measures. Most important, NAFTA advocates, such as Professor Pastor, view it as the first step in a longer-term initiative to tightly integrate the economies and political institutions of the three countries, leading to the creation of a North American Community.

By ratifying NAFTA in 1993, the U.S. Congress also authorized the executive branch to participate in more than two dozen trilateral committees and working groups whose purpose is to harmonize the three nations' national policies and regulations on a wide range of issues, including trade in agriculture and goods, setting standards for telecommunications, integrating the North American automotive industry, land transport, rules of origin, and food safety, among many other issues. Under this pact, sharing of natural resources is envisioned. Already, Canada is obligated to share almost two thirds of its petroleum production with the two other nations.

Many Canadians fear that NAFTA will eventually be used to force their country to divide its vast store of water with the United States and Mexico. Certainly, the authority to do so exists in that pact. If the giant, half-mile-wide supercorridor from Mexico to Canada discussed in the previous chapter is completed, the means of transporting that water on a massive scale could be built. NAFTA also authorized the creation of a new trilateral judicial process, outside each nation's judicial system, whose decisions on trade disputes are binding on the three nations.

The Council on Foreign Relations task force released its report, *Building a North American Community,* on May 17, 2005. It contained six major recommendations for the heads of state of the three nations:

1. Create new institutions to sustain a North American Community including an annual summit meeting by the three national leaders.

The report also recommended creation of a permanent North American Advisory Council to prepare and monitor follow-up actions on decisions made at those summits.

2. Establish a common security perimeter for North America, harmonization of entry and exit procedures, joint inspection of container traffic, and the full sharing of data on travel by foreign nationals, thereby "diminishing the need for the current intensity of the governments' physical control of cross-border traffic, travel, and trade within North America."

3. Adopt a common external tariff for the three countries and strengthen the NAFTA dispute resolution panels by creating a permanent roster of trade judges.

4. Establish a North American Investment Fund to stimulate economic growth in Mexico.

5. Create a North American energy and natural resource security strategy that would allow more U.S. investment in Mexican and Canadian energy development.

6. Deepen educational ties among the three nations.

The task force gave further definition to its recommendations in a news release that called for (1) full labor mobility among the three nations, (2) a common security perimeter by 2010, (3) a North American border pass with biometric identifiers, (4) a unified border action plan and expanded border customs facilities, (5) a single economic space in North America, (6) a common external tariff, (6) the seamless movement of goods within North America, (7) a North American energy strategy, (8) a review of the economic sectors that NAFTA excluded in 1993, (9) expanded temporary worker programs, (10) establishment of a North American Investment Fund to build infrastructure in Mexico, (11) institutionalization of the trilateral partnership, (12) establishment of a permanent tribunal for trade and investment disputes, (13) convening an annual North American summit meeting of the three leaders to monitor progress, and (14) establishment of a Trinational Competition Commission.

The CFR study was complemented by a study sponsored by the Council of the Americas (COA), which examined the same issues. The COA is an advocacy organization composed of almost two hundred members from finance, communications, manufacturing, mining, pharmaceuticals, and service sectors whose literature says it "form[s] a unique collaborative network that supports efforts to conduct business successfully in Latin America." In April 2005, the COA released its report *A Strategy for Building Competitiveness Within North America.* James R. Jones, a former U.S. ambassador to Mexico, led the COA study and was also a member of the CFR's trilateral task force.

Not surprisingly, the COA report included many of the same recommendations as that of the CFR, including the creation of a "robust, enforceable temporary worker program," creation of a development fund for Mexico, expanded border and energy security, and regulatory harmonization with the United States.

On March 23, 2005, the president of the United States, the prime minister of Canada, and the president of Mexico met in Waco, Texas, near Bush's ranch in Crawford, where they jointly announced the creation of the Security and Prosperity Partnership of North America (SPP). Their joint press release said the three countries "would develop common border-security strategies, pursue regulatory cooperation, and promote sector cooperation in energy, transportation, financial services, technology, and other areas."

Work began immediately. Trilateral Prosperity Working Groups (cabinet-level and high-level corporate) were created in 2005 to develop an integrated North American strategy for twenty industries, including steel, automobiles, and e-commerce.

The U.S. teams were exclusionary. In the fall of 2005, the Department of Commerce organized a summit in Washington to discuss the nation's competitiveness challenge. Representatives from Merck, Lockheed Martin, the National Association of Manufacturers, the Business Roundtable, and other businesses met with senior officials of the Bush administration to share views. The meeting was invitation-only, and among those not invited were all Democrats in Congress, labor unions, environmental groups, and consumer organizations.

On March 30–31, 2006, a year after the Waco meeting, President Bush, Prime Minister Stephen Harper, and President Fox met in Cancún to review progress on the SPP and identify the next steps in its development. As part of that session, the three heads of state met privately with fifteen business leaders (five from each country), after which they adopted the recommendation presented by the Council on Foreign Relations to create a North American Competitiveness Council (NACC) composed of senior business leaders from the three nations. The leaders gave the NACC a mandate to devise concrete recommendations on issues of immediate importance, "as well as strategic medium- and long-term advice to security and prosperity ministers and to the Leaders."

In an unusual move, Bush asked the U.S. Chamber of Commerce and the Council of the Americas to choose the American delegates to the new trilateral organization and also requested that those two business associations serve as the U.S. secretariat. These delegates meet annually with ministers from the three nations to provide recommendations and set priorities for the three governments on how to advance their global competitiveness. The SPP thus represents the ultimate outsourcing of a vital government function: two corporate associations pick which companies will advise the U.S. government on its economic development actions and priorities.

As with the competitiveness summit, all noncorporate groups with major stakes in the development of the North American economy were totally excluded as delegates. The U.S. participants chosen by the chamber and the COA were:

- Campbell Soup Company
- Chevron
- Ford Motor
- FedEx
- General Electric
- General Motors
- Kansas City Southern
- Lockheed Martin
- Merck
- Mittal Steel
- New York Life Insurance
- Procter & Gamble
- UPS
- Wal-Mart
- Whirlpool

Whereas the original design of the NACC was to have ten companies from each country, so many corporations wanted to be delegates that the U.S. secretariat put fifteen on its delegation, though only ten can formally participate in the meetings. Of these fifteen, each has major economic interests in the three countries. Ford is shifting much of its U.S. production to Mexico. Kansas City Southern owns major railroads in Mexico. Wal-

Mart is heavily invested in Mexico, where it is also financing the construction of deepwater ports that will help it speed the flow of Asian imports to the U.S. market. Mittal Steel, owned by a corporation headquartered in India, is deeply involved in creating a unified North American steel industry.

In September 2006, the U.S. section of the North American Competitiveness Council (NACC) announced its recommendations for the first cycle of NACC work. In February 2007, the NACC released its initial recommendation, "Enhancing Competitiveness in Canada, Mexico, and the United States: Private-Sector Priorities for the Security and Prosperity Partnership of North America (SPP)." The fifty-eight-page report included fifty recommendations for the three heads of state.

The report notes that in many fields the standards of the three nations vary widely. What was omitted is that U.S. standards are among the highest in the world and Mexico's are among the lowest. The solution proposed by the council was that the three countries harmonize their regulations around international standards, which are often lower than those in the United States. Lowering food and other safety standards, a goal many of the concerned corporations cannot get in open debate in Congress, was to be secured through the guise of creating trilateral uniformity.

The council also wanted the United States to change its requirement of inspecting freight cars in the United States every thousand miles to accepting inspections performed in Mexico. With that, railcars would be loaded in Mexico, inspected in Mexico, and then sent into the U.S. market. The council told the three national leaders that this one change would "improve rail security, velocity, and fluidity at international border crossings and thus expand capacity, trade, and economic growth." No questions were raised about the issue of rampant corruption in Mexico, from policy makers down to rail inspectors.

As to food safety, the council pointed out that the discretionary food fortification limits are different in the United States and Canada, which "limits the access to fortified foods, such as breakfast cereals or other products fortified with vitamins and minerals in the case of Canada." The United States rejects most fortification of meat and poultry products. The report concludes, "The ability to market products that are fortified with vitamins and minerals in all three North American countries would allow businesses to use the same labels throughout the region. This would result in significant cost savings for the industry."

The council also concluded that duplicate food audits, stiff sanitary requirements, phytosanitary regulations, diverse standards on nutrition and allergens, health claim regulations, and packaging requirements are really veiled trade protectionism. It also opposed country-of-origin labeling for foods sold in North America.

In mid-August 2007, Prime Minister Harper, President Bush, and President Felipe Calderón met in Montebello, Canada, a small town a few miles from Quebec, under tight security provided by Canadian and U.S. forces. A twenty-five-mile approach limit kept tens of thousands of protestors away from the conference site. On August 21, 2007, the three heads of state released a joint statement announcing their continued commitment to multilateral trade liberalization, sustainable energy, secure borders, and improved emergency management preparedness. They also put forth a seven-page list of future actions and work under way. The three heads of state accepted the NACC's recommendations.

While the reportage by Canada's national media gave great attention to the protests and tight security, the substance of the sessions received little coverage. Likewise, the national media in the United States largely ignored the summit. *The New York Times* published a 625-word story on August 21, 2007, titled "Bush's Talks with Neighbors Are Overshadowed by Storm"—a hurricane that had hit Mexico. It also noted that protestors had been doused with pepper spray and tear gas and that the 2008 summit would be held in the United States. In sum, the national media of the three countries missed the real story.

Although many of the NACC's recommendations are quite specific, such as those on food safety, others are so broad that they give the three governments great latitude as to how the recommendations can be implemented. This vagueness is disturbing. In Mexico and Canada, the heads of state have great constitutional powers; but in the United States, the Constitution divides those powers among the three branches of government. Yet the SPP is being pursued in the United States as though the president has full authority to implement the various corporate recommendations. Indeed, in the three years since the SPP initiative was begun, Congress has not held a single hearing on this extraordinary effort to integrate the economies and policy-making machinery of the three countries.

Among the criticisms made of the SPP, one of the most potent is that the U.S. executive branch lacks the legal authority to integrate the U.S. economy and political system with those of Mexico and Canada. Consequently, the Bush administration attempted an end run around Congress in June 2007 by persuading some friendly members of Congress to slip a special provision into Section 413 of the Kennedy-McCain Immigration Act (S.1639), entitled "Bilateral Efforts with Mexico to Reduce Migration Pressures and Costs." After enumerating eight "whereas" provisions, that section said:

> • *The Partnership for Prosperity is a bilateral initiative launched jointly by the President of the United States and the President of Mexico in 2001, which aims to boost the social and economic standards of Mexican citizens, particularly in regions where economic growth has lagged and immigration increased.*
> • *The Presidents of Mexico and the United States and the Prime Minister of Canada, at their trilateral summit on March 23, 2005, agreed to promote economic growth, competitiveness and quality of life in the agreement on Security and Prosperity Partnership of North America.*
> SENSE OF CONGRESS REGARDING PARTNERSHIP FOR PROSPERITY. *It is the sense of Congress that the United States and Mexico should accelerate the implementation of the Partnership for Prosperity to help generate economic growth and improve the standard of living in Mexico, which will lead to reduced migration.*

The Senate rejected the Kennedy-McCain immigration bill, and thus the administration did not get its de facto authorization to pursue, let alone accelerate, its trilateral harmonization agenda. Nonetheless, the SPP continues to be implemented and expanded, out of sight of the U.S. Congress and the American people.

The SPP is elitism, "unrepresentative governance," and globalism mixed together in their rawest forms. The executive branch proceeds to change laws, regulations, and procedures secretly with two other governments with no involvement of the legislative branch, which does not conduct even minimal oversight. The media are excluded from meetings yet accept spoon-fed information that is tangential to what is actually happening. Only favored corporations are allowed to participate in the construction of a North American economic agenda, including perhaps the creation of a North American Union.

Ironically, this elite-driven, corporate-controlled, unfettered attempt to integrate the North American economy provides the next president and Congress the institutional and political means to renegotiate the North American Free Trade Agreement, as discussed in the final one-third of this book.

II

The Path to Globalism

Four

PARADISE:
CREATED AND LOST

Globalism is nothing new. The late 1800s and early 1900s were the first great era of global economic integration. Indeed, the entwining of national economies in the half century before World War I, as a share of world economic output, has been matched only recently.

By 1914, technologies such as the multimessage telegraph and the telephone had tightly tied the world together as never before. The fastest ways to send a message before the introduction of the telegraph in 1844, for example, were the same as 2,200 years earlier, in the time of Alexander the Great: a pigeon, a ship, a reflector, or someone on a horse. By the late 1870s, however, domestic and international telegraph lines could simultaneously transmit sixteen messages over a single copper wire, eight going each way, each line sending and receiving up to a thousand words per minute, thus connecting nations that had been geographically isolated. In 1914, newspaper readers in Berlin, London, and Paris could read the same news simultaneously as readers in New York, Hong Kong, Buenos Aires, Tokyo, and Melbourne. Local market prices for commodities and finished goods were instantly available to almost anyone, anywhere.

Industrial nations in that era were assisting developing countries with massive transfers of capital, technology, and know-how. The world effectively had a single currency, one based on gold, and exchange rate fluctuations did not exist. The newly invented, fast, large, iron-hulled, steam-powered ships, coupled with the construction of national rail networks in the late nineteenth century, enabled the quick, inexpensive transport of people, food, and goods anywhere. Equally important, the Royal Navy, which kept the world's seaways open and safe for British commerce, maintained freedom of the seas for all nations.

By the summer of 1914, Germany was the best customer of Russia, Norway, Holland, Belgium, Switzerland, Italy, and Austria-Hungary. Conversely, those same nations imported more from Germany than from any other country. Great Britain sold Germany more goods than all other nations except India and bought more from Germany than from any other except the United States.

Those prewar internationalists fervently believed that the sheer power of technological progress, coupled with the momentum of global integration, would eliminate the obstacles between peoples and nations. And for more than a half century, they were right—the economies of Europe, Japan, and the Americas became so deeply intertwined that passports were not even required for most travel. It seemed possible that this economic and political amalgamation, coupled with fast communications, would so improve the lives of people everywhere and so advance the understanding of other cultures that war would become an unthinkable tool of foreign policy.

But the internationalism of that era was constructed atop fragile political systems, just as the globalism of our time sits atop a fragile financial structure. By the summer of 1914, Europe was at a political flash point, needing only a spark to flare. Technology had created sophisticated weapons whose killing power was simply unimaginable to those military and civil societies. The horrible armaments and unfettered "internationalism" of that age, however, not only failed to make war too strange or extreme even to be considered, they also increased each nation's vulnerability in war in direct proportion to its level of global integration.

Looking backward from the vantage point of 1919, John Maynard Keynes, arguably the most influential economist of the first half of the twentieth century, wrote of that pre–World War I era:

> *What an extraordinary episode in the economic progress of man that age was which came to an end in August 1914.*
>
> *The inhabitant of London could order by telephone, sipping his tea in bed, the various product of the whole earth, in such quantity as he might see fit, and reasonably expect their early delivery upon his doorstep; he could at the same moment and by the same means adventure his wealth in the national resources and new enterprises of any quarter of the world. He could secure forthwith, if he wished it, cheap and comfortable means of transit to any country or climate without passport or other formality, could dispatch his servant to the neighboring office of a bank for such supply of the precious metals as might seem convenient, and could then proceed abroad to foreign quarters, without knowl-*

edge of their religions, language, or customs, bearing coined wealth upon his
person, and would consider himself greatly aggrieved and much surprised at
the least interference. But, most important of all, he regarded this state of
affairs as normal, certain, and permanent....

  The projects and politics of militarism and imperialism, of racism and cul-
tural rivalries, of monopolies, restrictions, and exclusions, which were to play
serpent to this paradise, ... appeared to exercise no influence at all on the ordi-
nary course of social and economic life, the internationalization of which was
nearly complete in practice.

Yet war was thinkable. With what Keynes called "insane delusion and
reckless self-regard," Germany upended political and economic foundations when it led Europe into what became World War I. Decades of global
economic integration were instantly reversed, and all nations, combat-
ants and neutrals alike, suddenly learned that their unfettered, unmoni-
tored ties with other nations had enfeebled them in ways they had never
considered.

Ironically, Germany, the aggressor, was among the most vulnerable
countries because of its international linkages. When World War I broke
out in August 1914, Britain's Navy immediately blockaded the German
Imperial Fleet in its ports, forcing 734 German and Austrian merchant ves-
sels into neutral harbors around the world. As the British navy had cut off
France from its world markets and supplies in the Napoleonic Wars, it now
isolated Germany a century later. Suddenly Germany could not import
from Chile the nitrates needed to produce ammunition, nor could it import
from the Americas and Russia the beef and grain needed to feed its people.

In 1914, moreover, England was no longer the workshop of Europe; Germany was. Though the blockade eventually cut off Germany's food supplies and starved the German people into food riots, it also created an
immediate economic crisis in the British Empire. When the war began,
Britain depended on Germany for 90 percent of its optical glass; 75 percent
of its electric light glass; a majority of its semifinished steel; almost 80 percent of its textile dyes; plus most of its precision bearings, engine magne-
tos, machine tools, medical instruments, synthetic medicines, and
chemicals, among dozens of other German-made goods.

The British people were shocked to find that England was no longer
industrially self-sufficient and just how dependent they were on German
factories. Worse, the British had no substitute sources of supply for its
technological needs, not even the United States.

The British blockade, which was intensely unpopular in the United States in its early years, also revealed America's dependence on German-based factories for nearly 90 percent of its synthetic dyes; most of its optics, scientific machinery, and medical tools; and almost all of its chemical-based pharmaceuticals. Germany had dominated those industries world-wide.

As the blockade took hold, U.S. hospitals, doctors, and dentists soon exhausted their supplies of German-made "miracle" drugs. Even aspirin, a German product, was in short supply. Although many U.S. textile manu-facturers had a substantial store of German-made dyes on hand in 1914, none anticipated a long war. Soon supplies were exhausted, and prices soared.

When the United States declared war with Germany in April 1917, Amer-ican agents immediately seized more than twelve thousand German patents, almost five thousand covering chemical processes, and made them available to U.S. producers, hoping to overcome the loss of German imports. Most were useless, however, since the German owners had filed either misleading or incomplete information in their patent applications. E. I. duPont de Nemours quickly learned that some German chemical patents hid deadly traps that would produce explosions if their formulas and processes were replicated faithfully. Even by the end of the war, nei-ther Britain nor the United States had closed all the gaps created by the loss of its German-made imports.

The inability of the U.S. industrial base to supply so many vital goods startled the American people. Industrial self-sufficiency had long been U.S. policy but was not a reality when war came. Extensive congressional hearings after the war revealed that the dependence on German imports was no accident of history or economics. Rather, Germany, its banks, and its corporations—working closely together—had systematically monopo-lized global markets for dozens of technology-based goods.

Though German military leaders planned for a short war, the French and British armies held their defensive line and the struggle gradually devolved into one of attrition. By the war's end, four years later (November 1918), more than 19 million people had been killed and another 21 million wounded. The economies of Europe were shattered, the nations unable to feed their people. Russia was in a deadly civil war.

The Paris Peace Conference of 1919 lasted almost twelve months; Presi-dent Woodrow Wilson was there for almost half that time. He came to those negotiations with a high-minded, fourteen-point peace agenda that made him briefly the most popular person in the world.

Wilson, a devoted free-trade champion, tried to persuade the British and French to create a world regime in which goods and capital could flow safely and freely among nations. But Wilson was unequal to the diplomatic challenge. The other allies wanted vengeance and reparations from Germany. France hoped to cripple its old enemy so badly economically that it could never again be a military threat.

Keynes, who was the financial representative for the British Treasury at the conference, observed afterward that what he found among the delegates, including those from Britain, was a deep ignorance of "the intensely unusual, unstable, complicated, unreliable, temporary nature of the economic organization by which Western Europe has lived for the last half century."

After six months, the despondent thirty-six-year-old Keynes returned to England and wrote *The Economic Consequences of the Peace*, in which he argued that although the hope of the world was to restore the "delicate, complicated organization" in which the European people had worked and lived before the war, the harsh peace would instead "run the risk of completing the ruin which Germany began." In their zeal for vengeance and booty, the victors undermined that complicated "organization" on which all their futures depended. If Germany had been delusional in its rush to war, the victors were equally so in the peace they made. The Versailles agreement helped define the course of the forthcoming seventy-five years.

Keynes was prescient. Wilson returned to the United States, where he could sell the peace treaty neither to the American people nor to the senators who represented them.

At the same time, the enlarged production capacity the U.S. economy had developed during the war meant the country had to get access to big export markets in order to keep the factories running. But to do so, Congress had to alter the prewar policies of protectionism that had served the United States so well for so long and benefited so many.

The United States' protectionism was not some fluke or accident of national policy; it was the core foundation of development and defense strategies for almost a century and a half. Its first champion was President George Washington, who, having fought a war that he almost lost because his nation lacked the manufacturing capacity needed to supply his armies, told Congress in his first State of the Union message that the safety and the interests of a free people "require that they should promote such manufactories as tend to render them independent of others for essential, particularly military supplies."

His idealistic successors, Thomas Jefferson and James Madison, read Adam Smith's *The Wealth of Nations* and were intellectually enamored with the theory of free trade. They tinkered with the idea of imposing trade sanctions against Britain in order to weaken its mercantilist discrimination and to get the British to accept a bilateral free-trade regime. The War of 1812 shattered that fantasy.

The experience quickly converted them and their contemporaries into economic realists who finally came to understand that as long as the United States was without the means of producing the goods and weapons it needed, it was a vulnerable nation. Nothing made that more immediate than British troops' burning the White House during the War of 1812.

The policy that emerged after that war became known as the "American System" of trade. Congress imposed high protective tariffs on foreign imports, not to tax consumers but to stimulate investment in the United States and thereby enable the country to produce its own goods and provide jobs for its own workers. Under the system, the new nation grew and prospered over the next half century.

The American System was controversial. Unfettered capitalism brought with it great income inequalities and recurring financial panics. Labor was abused, and the state of the environment was irrelevant. Though Republicans unabashedly supported a nationalistic trade policy in the period 1860–1930, the Democrats vacillated between approval of free trade and wanting to provide low-cost imports to working people. The contradiction the Democrats faced was that while free trade could break the power of the protected monopolies that financed the Republicans and furnish inexpensive consumer goods, the inflow of cheaper foreign items could also devastate their own working-class constituents. For almost three quarters of a century, therefore, the Republican position prevailed among voters and in Congress.

Did the American System work? Beyond George Washington's wildest hopes. Under protectionist policies the United States evolved from a small colony with limited manufacturing capacity to the mightiest industrial power in the world.

The United States' trade isolationism, of course, was not the only reason. Other contributory factors included the development of a mass market, technology transfer, high rates of domestic capital formation, foreign investment, and a legal system that protected private property, including intellectual property.

The beginning of the end of the American System came with the election of Woodrow Wilson, who ran for office in 1912 on a platform of low tariffs and free trade. Only days after being inaugurated, Wilson summoned Congress into a special session to enact tariff reduction legislation. The result was the Underwood-Simmons Tariff Act of 1913. The problem with this legislation was that it drastically reduced U.S. tariffs unilaterally without getting, or even asking for, the lowering of foreign barriers to U.S. exports. Ironically, the bill had little effect because soon after it was enacted, World War I shut down global trade.

As soon as Warren Harding succeeded Wilson in March 1921, the new president called upon Congress to pass an emergency tariff bill, which became law barely sixty days later. The Harding legislation required reciprocal concessions as the price for reducing U.S. trade barriers, a stance that spurred two domestic political movements. One was the creation of a coalition of Republicans and industrialists who wanted the reestablishment of the nineteenth-century protectionist tariff patterns of the American System. The other group, led by Representative Cordell Hull (D-Tenn.), advocated a new system of reciprocal tariff cuts, an approach that emphasized exports.

Eventually, America got both. In 1930, Senator Reed Smoot (R-Utah) and Representative Willis Hawley (R-Oreg.) shepherded through Congress the Tariff Act of 1930, commonly known as Smoot-Hawley, which raised tariffs. Contrary to the enduring political myth, the Smoot-Hawley Tariff was not the cause of the Great Depression, which actually began nine months prior to its enactment. Neither did the law induce fierce foreign retaliation and trade wars or a spiraling decline in U.S. trade, which subsequent data have confirmed.

Nor was it the reason for the losses of office by Smoot and Hawley in the 1932 election. Hawley was beaten in the Republican primary because he refused to return to his Oregon district during the campaign to confront his challenger, a popular state official who favored the elimination of Prohibition, which Hawley opposed. The seventy-year-old Smoot was defeated in Utah by Elbert Thomas, a University of Utah political scientist who was twenty years younger. The Smoot-Hawley Act played little part in the campaign, as Thomas also campaigned on a platform of protecting Utah products, including lead, copper, and sugar, from foreign imports.

The American System was ultimately doomed in 1933 when President Roosevelt appointed Cordell Hull, a free-trade enthusiast and Congressional insider, secretary of state. He was later the 1945 recipient of the Nobel Prize for Peace, largely for his efforts to create the United Nations. Now all but forgotten, Hull had a profound influence on twentieth-century American economic policy. FDR needed Hull's support with the political barons on Capitol Hill. Beyond that, Hull was a secondary figure in the Roosevelt administration because FDR kept control of foreign policy in the White House.

Other high officials in FDR's administration deemed Hull's economic ideas, including his advocacy of free trade, eccentric. Yet it was a committed and honest position. Hull, for instance, had drafted the constitutional amendment that created the income tax—without which tariffs could never be reduced until an alternative source of federal revenues was created.

Most important, Hull also authored, championed, and first administered the Reciprocal Trade Acts enacted during the first years of the Roosevelt administration, singlehandedly changing American trade history. Hull, a sly and highly partisan politician, realized that the negotiation of concessions for foreign access for a favored few U.S. industries, notably automobiles, electric generators, and agriculture, would result in the formation of an export coalition that would provide strong political support for his policies and also political contributions for the Democratic Party. The coalition that Hull created slowly came to dominate U.S. trade policy and still provides significant political money for both parties.

Hull also persuaded Congress to delegate to the executive branch, and notably the State Department (himself), its constitutional authority to regulate global commerce through the reduction of tariffs. This was historic because Congress fiercely guarded its constitutional prerogative in that area. But in 1933, an overwhelming majority in Congress, reeling from accusations that the Smoot-Hawley Tariff had created the Great Depression, willingly, even anxiously, handed Hull their authority. Almost seventy-five years later, the executive branch still dominates the crafting of all U.S. trade agreements and reduction of tariffs, which are then sent to Congress for ratification.

Once Hull had Congress's trade negotiating authority, he created an anonymous committee of bureaucrats drawn from the departments of State, Agriculture, Treasury, Commerce, and others to coordinate U.S. trade strategy and negotiations: the Committee on Trade Agreements (CTA).

For more than two decades, the names of these members were kept secret, supposedly so industries or unions could not bribe or threaten them. Once their names were revealed, most members, like many appointees of the New Deal, were discovered to be free-trade theorists recruited from academe, a personnel practice that would be emulated by conservatives when they regained the presidency in the 1980 elections.

Under Hull, the "primary objective" of the Reciprocal Trade Agreements Program was to "reduce trade barriers rather than drive a sharp bargain ... and permit a greater increase in imports than in exports with a view to correcting the trade balance problem of the United States." In short, the United States was willing to give more than it granted in trade negotiations. The goal was to increase imports and reduce the U.S. trade surplus with other nations.

In one bargaining session after another in the 1930s, the State Department, largely unsupervised by the White House or Congress, made maximum concessions to other nations while getting minimum concessions in return. Equally significant, in the mid-1930s, the department extended trade concessions to all of America's principal trade partners, except Germany, despite those nations' flagrant discrimination against American exports. By all means possible, Hull was trying to drive down the U.S. trade surplus with other countries.

Not surprisingly, Hull in the turbulent mid-1930s soon began to use trade as an instrument of foreign policy. He made unilateral concessions to Belgium, Switzerland, Britain, Canada, Turkey, Argentina, and Venezuela, among dozens of other nations. Hull's goal was to buy goodwill and promote his vision of free trade, even though each concession cost business and jobs in some domestic U.S. industry. And these job-destroying deals were made in the midst of the Great Depression, when millions of Americans were without work.

Hull retired in 1944, but his ideology, policies, people, and Committee on Trade Agreements were deeply embedded into the structure of the U.S. government, where they eventually came to greatly influence thinking about the structure of the postwar era.

Shortly after the United States entered the Second World War, the British, Americans, and eventually forty-two other nations began discussions on how to create a postwar global economic structure and avoid the mistakes made in 1919. John Maynard Keynes led the British delegation. Harry Dexter White, a Harvard-educated economist and high Treasury Department official, represented the United States.

The irony in the situation was that Keynes, who so sharply—and correctly—had criticized the global economic structure imposed after World War I, now had a chance to devise an approach that would work. Apparently, he was not shy about his ability to do just that.

Keynes and White dominated the negotiations. The intentions of their two governments differed significantly. Roosevelt had gone to Paris with Wilson at the end of World War I and stoutly believed in the former president's Fourteen Points plan for peace, including global free trade. He abhorred colonialism and intended to use U.S. influence to end it. British Prime Minister Winston Churchill, however, intended to keep the empire, including its colonies, intact.

Thus, Keynes came to the negotiations with a double mission: to establish a global order that could function as well as the one that had been destroyed in August 1914 and to preserve the British trading bloc. White's mission was different. He was there to create a sound institutional structure for world trade but also to open wide Britain's preferred trade with its Commonwealth to American exports and investments.

Keynes was the superior negotiator, but White had the leverage created by the expanding U.S. economy, on which Britain increasingly depended.

In July 1944, more than seven hundred delegates from forty-four nations convened for three weeks in Bretton Woods, New Hampshire, to hammer out the final details of a new global economic order. Remarkably, the result, called the Bretton Woods Agreement, put into place a structure that worked well for almost a quarter century after the end of World War II. Keynes and White had done well.

The agreement called for the creation of three new global institutions. One was the International Monetary Fund (IMF), whose initial mission was to maintain stable currencies based on the price of gold. The second was the establishment of what is now known as the World Bank, which would lend monies to help rebuild the war-torn economies of the belligerents. Its first loan in 1947 was $250 million to help France. The third new body was to be the International Trade Organization (ITO), which would set and enforce global trade rules. The U.S. Senate in 1948, however, refused to ratify the treaty creating the ITO, thereby delaying its birth until 1994 as the World Trade Organization.

The architects of the Bretton Woods Agreement made two key assumptions. The first was that more trade was a key to creating world prosperity and forestalling wars. The second was that the best way to expand trade was through the creation of an Anglo-American system of rules-based capitalism. The fact that trade might be expanded by other institutional models was ignored. Thus, no accommodations were made for the communist, socialist, mixed, and Japanese approaches to trade, which in retrospect was an omission of historic proportions.

Absent the ITO, the United States and Britain nonetheless initiated trade negotiations in Geneva in 1947, not to create a treaty but to make a contract between nations. Faced with the Soviet Union's rejection of Bretton Woods, the United States was anxious to jump-start global trade negotiations. Indeed, America was willing to make virtually any deal, regardless of how "thin" the agreement might be, to get what became the General Agreement on Tariffs and Trade (GATT) in 1947. By contrast, Britain wanted concessions for its textile and manufacturing industries, plus the retention of its empire preference system. Britain got its concessions and kept its preference system, and the United States got its "thin" agreement.

The 1947 pact established both a pattern and an expectation of concessions from the United States in future trade agreements. The United States accepted the responsibility of continuing and strengthening global trade negotiations; other nations would participate as long as America conceded more than it got in return. With that, trade negotiations became a tool of U.S. foreign policy and a form of aid to other nations.

By the 1950s, the State Department had negotiated dozens of trade pacts, yet none was being monitored or enforced. In 1958, the Chamber of Commerce asked the department for a description of which countries had given concessions for U.S. exports and which products were eligible, as well as the tariff levels for those exports. The department could not supply an answer, for it had not kept a list, let alone monitored the agreements that had been negotiated.

In negotiations with Japan during this period, the State Department went an extra step. In 1953, it provided several third-party nations with concessions in the U.S. market for their imports in exchange for their acceptance of exports from Japan. The third-party beneficiaries were Canada, Denmark, Finland, Italy, Norway, and Sweden. While State representatives testified before Congress that the United States benefited greatly from these deals, historic trade data reveal that U.S. exports to Japan rose by 95 percent in the period 1954–1960. During the same period, Japanese exports to the United States expanded by more than 300 percent.

The real reason for the deals was the State Department's true mission: securing a foreign policy advantage in Japan. Once the occupation of Japan ended, the United States wanted to control Japan's military and foreign policy, plus use its territories for American military bases. The granting of special trade rights in the U.S. market, even if it meant the loss of American industries and jobs, was the price.

The trade concessions given the Japanese and other nations in the 1950s were so blatant that when John F. Kennedy became president he canceled the State Department's authority to negotiate trade matters and created the Office of the Special Trade Negotiator within the White House, where it would be under his direct control.

By the time of the Kennedy administration, however, Europe and Japan were once again major global economic powers with substantial financial reserves. While they were willing to subordinate their economic interests to those of the United States as long as the United States provided security against the Soviet Union, détente eventually removed the rationale for such policies.

Equally significant, the value of the dollar began to decline in the 1960s, when Congress refused to raise taxes to pay for the Vietnam War and Great Society programs. Inflation increased, the United States began to run trade deficits, and other nations redeemed their dollar reserves for gold. The old Bretton Woods system was failing.

By 1971, the United States was experiencing a financial hemorrhage as its gold stocks were depleted to pay for rising trade deficits. In August 1971, the administration of President Richard Nixon closed the Treasury's gold window, thus making the dollar nonconvertible to gold. Within less than twenty-four months, currencies were floating against one another in uncontrolled world financial markets.

With that, the Bretton Woods system ended. The IMF remained in place and subsequently helped dozens of nations in financial crisis. The World Bank shifted its focus to providing loans to poor and developing nations.

The two decades after the collapse of the Bretton Woods system were a tumultuous time. The stability created at Bretton Woods was gone, and policies of globalization were yet to come. It was an in-between time. An argumentative, libertarian economist from the University of Chicago soon filled that policy vacuum. Milton Friedman is his name.

Five

FRIEDMAN I (MILTON)

A major intellectual impetus for today's U.S. economic policy came from Milton Friedman, possibly the most influential economist of the second half of the twentieth century.

Friedman, a champion of laissez-faire capitalism, counseled Barry Goldwater in his 1964 race for president and later advised Richard Nixon and Ronald Reagan as well. He was awarded the Nobel Prize in Economics in 1976. Over the years, Friedman advocated abolishing the Food and Drug Administration, the Securities and Exchange Commission, the Federal Reserve, Social Security, and Medicare. He also argued for eliminating farm support, import inspections, student aid, tariffs, import quotas, managed exchange rates, regulation of airlines and telephones, the national parks, and progressive taxation.

For a man who worked at the Labor Department in the 1930s, helped devise the Internal Revenue Service's tax-withholding system, and was in almost constant disagreement with fellow economists, even those who agreed with him, Friedman evolved into what a colleague described in *The New York Times* as a "charismatic economist," which is almost an oxymoron.

Friedman's greatest influence came in the late 1970s and early 1980s, when he inspired the regulatory economic and trade policies of the Reagan administration and set the stage under Presidents George H. W. Bush and Bill Clinton for the creation of the North American Free Trade Agreement (NAFTA) and the World Trade Organization (WTO), which undergird today's globalization.

While the story of the shift from the old, pre-1930s nationalistic "American System" of trade to today's globalism, as inspired by Friedman, can begin in many places, let's begin by imagining a vivid color photograph of

Marilyn Monroe, wearing tight Levi's denim jeans with rolled-up cuffs, looking backward over her shoulder while sipping a Coca-Cola.

Monroe's image was the essence of post–World War II America—sassy, confident, and glamorous. Coke was America's representative to the world, and Levi's were more than a good pair of pants, they were a statement about egalitarianism and personal freedom. They were work clothes for the masses and leisure dress for movie stars, models, tycoons, and even presidents. Slipping into a pair of Levi's was about as "American" as it got. Still is.

While a pair of Levi's is, indeed, an extraordinary product, the company that makes them and the family that owns it are even more exceptional. For more than a century, Levi Strauss & Co. and its owners have personified the American ideal: doing well for oneself while doing good for others. Yet this company's experience with globalization also illustrates how increasingly difficult "doing well while doing good" has become in America. It reveals, in its starkest form, the dangers of globalization for the economy, companies of all sizes, and American workers.

The choice faced by Levi Strauss is the same one faced by tens of thousands of other U.S. firms that wanted to remain in the country. Their choice is whether to keep work and jobs in the United States and risk bankruptcy or to abandon American workers and outsource their jobs to penny-wage nations and prosper.

Even the most devoted and patriotic companies in the United States cannot break this trap alone. Consider the story of Levi Strauss.

The story begins before the Civil War, when the sons and daughters of Hirsch Strauss, a Jewish dry goods peddler from Bremen, Germany, emigrated to the United States. America was a wondrous place for the Strauss family. In Bremen, laws prohibited Jewish families from buying land and restricted how they could make a living. In the United States, opportunities for Jews were almost unlimited.

After working several months in New York, Levi Strauss, the youngest brother, moved to Louisville, Kentucky, where he joined his sister Fanny and brother-in-law David Stern, another immigrant peddler. In 1853, David, Fanny, and Levi moved to San Francisco, where the California Gold Rush was in its full vigor. The three were among tens of thousands of other fortune seekers drawn by the Gold Rush. A blanket that sold for $5 in New York sold for $40 in the mining camps.

Sales-trained in the streets of Germany and New York City, the brothers-in-law were shrewd merchants who understood their customers' needs.

Besides creating a San Francisco store, they hired sales representatives who went into the mining camps with goods loaded on pack mules and wagons.

Work clothes were one of the company's most popular products. Before 1873, though, Strauss's work clothing was little different from that offered by other stores. What eventually differentiated the Strauss pants was the rivets that securely bound the pockets and fly—an innovation in work clothing that originated not with Levi Strauss but a tailor from Riga, Latvia, who had Americanized his name to Jacob Davis. Davis lacked the money to apply for a patent, so he sent a letter to Strauss, offering to share the patent if Strauss would fund the patent application. Strauss always claimed the birthday of the "blue jean" was the day the rivet patent (no. 139,121) was issued: May 20, 1873. Davis eventually sold his part ownership of the patent to Strauss and became the company's head tailor, a job he held until he retired decades later.

Indeed, the riveted pants sold as quickly as they could be made. In the first six months, the company turned out 20,000 pairs. There were three sizes. Customers were advised to put on a pair that was their closest fit and then jump into a pond or bathtub; as the denim dried, it would shrink to fit the owner's body.

Today, a century and a half later, some hard-core devotees still fit their Levi's that same old-fashioned way. One complaint from cowboys in the early years, however, was that the crotch rivets became very hot when the wearer got too close to a campfire, which could be very personal and very painful. In 1941, Walter Haas, then CEO of the company and a son-in-law of Levi Strauss's nephew, had that experience when he sat too close to a campfire. The next day: good-bye fly rivets.

The company thrived as a fairly small manufacturer of household goods and denim work clothes until the end of World War II, when it began to transform itself into a national manufacturer of jeans and sportswear. The drive to make over the corporation was presided over by Walter Haas's two sons, Walter, Jr., and Peter.

During the war, Levi's were declared an essential commodity that only defense workers could buy, a scarcity that increased their popularity. The war also changed American fashion standards. Whereas men had once worn suits for virtually any nonwork event, the war generation had become accustomed to pants without cuffs, sports jackets without ties, and unfussy clothes. A pair of Levi's was a perfect choice for both work and casual wear.

Hollywood also played a big part in popularizing the company's pants. Levi's were chic, though most Americans would have termed it differently then—"cool." Marlon Brando wore Levi's with turned-up cuffs in the 1954 classic *The Wild One,* as did James Dean the following year in *East of Eden* and *Rebel Without a Cause.* Marilyn Monroe wore them daily.

During their forty-year tenure, the Haas brothers shrewdly used the charisma surrounding their denim goods to transform the family company into America's largest apparel maker. In 1971, Levi Strauss had $405 million in annual sales and 20,000 employees. By 1996, it had $7 billion in annual sales, operated eighty-five facilities in forty-nine countries and employed more than 36,000.

The success of Levi Strauss, however, was defined not simply by its size, profitability, employment, growth, fame, or quality of its products; the Haas brothers operated the company in a way that made it one of the most respected corporations in the world. It established practices that other businesses then emulated. Long before most others, Levi Strauss provided its workers with pensions, paid vacations, stock purchase plans, and profit sharing.

The company also pioneered social policies such as racially integrated facilities. After Peter Haas joined the family business in 1945, his father assigned him to oversee construction of a new factory in Vallejo, California, a city with a large population of African Americans. Haas integrated the crews that constructed the plant and later the personnel who operated it. As the company expanded into the southern United States in the 1950s, its factories were integrated. The Levi Strauss factories were integrated long before the Civil Rights Act of 1964 became law.

The company's history is filled with examples of social pioneering. In 1982, it became the first major corporation to promote AIDS awareness and education, and it subsequently awarded more than $26 million in grants to combat the HIV epidemic. In 1991, it was the first multinational corporation to develop a comprehensive ethical code for conduct for contractors operating with the company. In 1992, it became the first *Fortune* 500 corporation to provide health care benefits to partners of employees.

The company was also a national leader in what became known as the "stakeholders" debate, which flared into national attention in the fall of 1970 after *The New York Times* published an article by Milton Friedman, who ridiculed corporate executives' doing anything other than increasing profits and value for their shareholders. Friedman argued that any money that corporate executives gave for social programs did not belong to them but to their corporate owners, the shareholders. Under the Friedman doctrine,

> *There is one and only one social responsibility of business—to use its resources and engage in activities designed to increase its profits so long as it stays within the rules of the game, which is to say, engaged in open and free competition without deception and fraud.*

If the U.S. government wanted companies to take some action unrelated to making profits, such as not polluting the environment or providing a safe workplace, Friedman felt it was government's responsibility to change the rules. What Friedman urged was a return to the laissez-faire capitalism of the nineteenth century, bound only by the laws that government imposed and the prevailing ethics.

The Haas brothers viewed the issue quite differently. To them, Levi Strauss had responsibilities that extended beyond simply maximizing profits for its stockholders. Employees were one set of stakeholders. Suppliers and business partners were two others. So too were the communities in which the company operated, as well as the nation itself.

Most important, customers were also major stakeholders. Customers paid a premium to buy Levi's, and many wore them to make their own statement about social issues. The company, for instance, refused to operate in South Africa during the apartheid era. Only after Nelson Mandela was freed from prison and elected president did Levi Strauss establish a facility there. By wearing Levi's, many customers visibly registered their support of the company's social and economic activism.

Karl Schoenberg wrote in *Levi's Children,* "The core ethical conviction of five generations of the Strauss-Stern-Haas family [is] the belief that true success in business involves more than just seeking profits."

Many businesspeople of that era shared the Haases' social beliefs. Under the leadership of Irving Shapiro, the CEO of DuPont, Reginald Jones, the CEO of General Electric, and Henry Ford of the Ford Motor Company, the Business Roundtable, an association of CEOs from America's two hundred most powerful corporations, issued a formal statement in 1981 on corporate responsibility practices. It mirrored the positions pioneered by Levi Strauss. The CEOs were concerned that their companies not be seen or treated as amoral organizations, indifferent to the needs of all but their stockholders.

As the stakeholder debate raged in the 1970s, Levi Strauss was selling all the goods it could make. The company needed more factories, some of which would be located in countries where demand was exploding, and it required additional capital to finance those new facilities. In 1971, the family firm was converted into a public corporation in order to raise that money.

The most unusual feature of the Levi Strauss stock sale was the prospectus sent to potential investors warning that the company's management considered social responsibility "an essential part of business that should be considered a long-term investment in the corporation's future but which might affect short-term profits."

In 1981, the newly elected Reagan administration brought to Washington a major change in expectations about the role of corporations in society. President Reagan, an economics major in college, greatly admired the work of Friedman and staffed much of his administration with the conservative economist's disciples. Administration insiders even wore ties embossed with an image of Adam Smith, the Scottish laissez-faire economist.

When Reagan was inaugurated, the "stakeholders" debate ended and the "Friedman Doctrine" became the guiding ideology of the U.S. government for almost three decades. Greed became fashionable.

The doctrine was introduced at a delicate moment in U.S. history. One of the administration's first challenges was to bring down the inflation created by the oil shocks of the 1970s. The surest path was to cut jobs by the millions. By 1982, monthly U.S. unemployment rates were at double-digit levels, the highest since the Great Depression.

Simultaneously, Reagan's Treasury Department and the Federal Reserve allowed the dollar to increase in value against other currencies by almost 50 percent; their goal was to encourage more imports and higher U.S. unemployment levels. In effect, this policy made Levi's sold outside the United States 50 percent more expensive than they had been. It also cut in half the price of jeans imported from other nations, such as South Korea. Soon the United States had a mounting trade deficit as foreign-made goods began to replace those produced domestically. U.S. factories began to lay off workers, who in turn had less to spend, which helped reduce inflation.

As these policies took hold, many U.S. producers shifted their production to low-wage developing nations such as Honduras and Indonesia. Although Levi Strauss, of all U.S. apparel makers, was best positioned financially to outsource its manufacturing, the company remained stead-fastly loyal to its American workers and communities. As recently as 1990, its American workers manufactured more than 90 percent of the Levi's pants sold in the United States. Such loyalty, however, came at a steep price: the company began not to meet Wall Street's expectations.

In the early 1980s, one of the dangers faced by a well-run corporation with low debt, such as Levi Strauss, was a hostile takeover, of which there were many. The path for these corporate assaults was cleared in 1982, when the U.S. Supreme Court (*Edgar v. Mite*) struck down state anti-takeover laws as unconstitutional. By then the Securities and Exchange Commission (SEC) was controlled by Friedman's laissez-faire disciples, and the Court agreed with their argument that whoever was willing to pay stockholders the highest price should be allowed to take control of a public corporation.

Wall Street firms quickly created a complex structure of investors (for-eign and domestic), lawyers, and public relations specialists to help corpo-rate raiders, such as T. Boone Pickens, Carl Icahn, and Ivan Boesky, take over targeted companies. To defend against such assaults, other Wall Street teams were formed.

Investment banks that had long, honorably, and profitably served their corporate clients quickly divided themselves into two units: one did nor-mal investment banking, while the other did mergers, acquisitions, and takeovers. After that, most CEOs had to assume that their bankers might be giving their most privileged information to prospective raiders as an inducement to mount a raid, which, of course, is what sometimes happened.

The famed trial lawyer Clarence Darrow once observed that if a gunman entered a crowded courtroom of a hundred people and shot only one, the reaction of the remaining ninety-nine, even though all were unharmed, would be changed. Similarly, the takeovers of the 1980s radically affected decisions made by the CEOs of most U.S. publicly held corporations who wished to avoid hostile assaults. They loaded their balance sheets with debt, bought back stock, devised accounting tricks to improve their reported earnings, fired workers to cut costs, put into place "golden para-chutes" that would give themselves big bonuses if fired, and reduced essential long-term investments, such as research and development.

In the process, billions of dollars of corporate assets were diverted from productive investment to nonproductive defensive measures. The vulner-ability of publicly held corporations to such attacks, and the related diver-sion of resources, lasted for almost six years, ending in 1988, when state governments, particularly Delaware, where many large businesses are incorporated, enacted security laws that were constitutional and that made hostile takeovers difficult, if not impossible.

Even as the oil shock was creating an inflationary spiral in the late 1970s and early 1980s, it set into motion an even more destructive long-term dynamic. Much of the money paid to oil-producing nations returned for safekeeping in major U.S. banks such as Chase Manhattan, Citibank, Chemical Bank, and Bank of America. The banks put these hundreds of billions of petrodollar deposits to work as loans, eagerly offering high-interest financing to countries such as Argentina, Brazil, Mexico, Nigeria, Ivory Coast, and the Philippines—nations whose leaders stole part of the proceeds, wasted part, and invested the rest in the intended developments.

Forgetting how nations had defaulted on loans during economic crises in the 1800s and the 1930s, during the Depression, Walter Wriston, the chairman of Citibank, considered America's leading banker, proclaimed in the late 1970s that lending to governments was safe because sovereign nations do not default.

Wriston's error became frighteningly obvious on August 20, 1982, when Mexico announced that it was broke and was suspending payments on its principal obligations. After what became known as the "Mexican Week-end," fourteen other nations made similar announcements. By the end of 1982, more than forty nations in Eastern Europe, South America, and Asia were in arrears on their debt payments. Henry Kaufman, who was then the chief economist at Salomon Brothers, calculated that world debt, including that of the Communist nations, had exploded from $3.6 trillion in 1971 to $14.3 trillion in 1981. The growth of that debt had proven to be far beyond the management capacity of America's bankers.

The Federal Reserve and U.S. Treasury were soon scrambling to prevent major U.S. financial institutions, including Wriston's Citibank, from collapsing. By the end of the 1980s, developing nations had defaulted on more than $1.3 trillion of debt, much of which was owed to U.S. banks. A Washington Post Book Company study revealed that more than a thousand U.S. banks were technically bankrupt by 1992.

Various remedies were proposed, but by the 1990s what became known as the "Washington Consensus" eventually dominated. It was not really a consensus but rather what Moisés Naim, the editor of *Foreign Policy*, termed in a 1999 article "the views of an influential majority of academics and high level staff of the IMF, the World Bank and the U.S. Treasury, think tanks, and assorted editorialists."

Among the prescriptions advocated by this influential group was for the United States, working through the World Bank and International Monetary Fund, to withhold financial aid to developing nations until they agreed to take the following actions:

1. Privatize every publicly owned industry, public utility, public ports, government-owned mines, and any other revenue-generating function controlled by government.
2. Deregulate the private sector, permit unrestricted direct foreign investment, and strengthen property rights.
3. Cut domestic spending and raise taxes to the point where the government's budget was balanced or in surplus, while redirecting public expenditures to education, health care, and infrastructure.
4. Produce more exports than imports through a variety of steps that would increase the global competitiveness of local products, including cutting wages and benefits and becoming a low-wage, low-cost export platform for foreign companies.
5. Adopt a laissez-faire, free-trade policy.

The goal was to transform developing nations into market-oriented regimes with economies resembling that of the United States. The offer of aid usually came when the financially distressed nation had few if any alternatives. Then, a carrot was held out: if this harsh economic agenda were adopted, the country would be given expanded access to the rich U.S. market, making the country attractive for direct foreign investment in factories and other productive activities.

To make the carrot real, advocates of the Washington Consensus also championed changing U.S. trade laws in a way that would encourage the relocation of American manufacturing facilities to foreign countries and then allow those companies to import their products into the U.S. market duty-free. By using low-wage labor in countries with fewer environmental, health, social, and worker safety regulations than in the United States, companies could sharply increase their profitability, and the expanded economic activity in the developing nations could generate local taxes that those governments could use to pay their U.S. loans. Many banks refused to loan money to medium and small U.S. manufacturers unless their plans included the movement of plants and jobs to low-cost foreign locations.

The banks' demands, of course, meant that millions of American workers who held these soon-to-be-outsourced jobs would lose them.

Returning to the Levi Strauss story, by the mid-1980s, the laissez-faire policies of the U.S. government were whipsawing the company between the values of its founding family (and still majority shareholders) and an unsympathetic Wall Street. Social responsibility was passé, the Friedman doctrine dominated U.S. policy making, and Levi Strauss was considered an unattractive investment by most of Wall Street, making it a takeover target.

In 1985, in order to keep corporate raiders at bay and rather than concentrate on short-term profits above all else, 203 members of the extended Strauss-Stern-Haas family organized the largest stock buyback in U.S. corporate history. It cost the family almost $1.6 billion to buy back the company, but once done they could operate, again, as they wished and do so privately. Or so they thought.

What the family and their advisers did not consider in 1985—indeed, could not have known—was that American trade officials were negotiating with many developing nations to eliminate all quotas on their export of apparels and textiles into the United States. In exchange, these countries were being asked to accept tough, U.S.-style intellectual property protections for patents, copyrights, trademarks, and trade secrets. A deal was eventually struck in 1994. U.S. import quotas on apparel were to be eliminated in phases between 1995 and 2005, after which none would exist. In this trade arrangement, Levi Strauss and its American factory workers would be pitted against the penny-wage labor of the developing world.

Even as this new global trade pact was being negotiated in Geneva (1986–1994), transnational U.S. businesses were lobbying President George H. W. Bush to create the North American Free Trade Agreement (NAFTA), a pact among the United States, Mexico, and Canada that would allow companies to use low-wage Mexican labor and import their products into the United States duty-free. They were greatly aided by Carlos Salinas de Gortari, the president of Mexico and one of the world's most articulate and charming recruiters of foreign investment. From one of Mexico's traditional ruling families, Salinas held a doctorate in economics from Harvard University and was intimately acquainted with influential U.S. business and political leaders.

He was also a devoted neoconservative who fervently believed that the programs of the Washington Consensus to change Mexico into a United States–like market economy were the proper course of action. Thus, Salinas began his six-year tenure by privatizing Mexico's inefficient state industries, including copper mines, railroads, a national television network, manufacturing companies, and banks, and soliciting direct foreign investment. Not surprisingly, he quickly became a political favorite of the Bush administration, the editorial board of *The Wall Street Journal*, and those who favored the Washington Consensus.

Salinas went to Washington in June 1990 to explore the proposed North American trade pact with President George H. W. Bush. As he conceived the proposed agreement, most of Mexico would be opened to foreign investment. In turn, Mexico would be rewarded with a preferential trade relationship with the United States and Canada.

What Salinas did not say but Bush and most U.S. trade experts knew was that most of the Mexican state industries were being sold at a fraction of their value to Salinas's political supporters, fifteen of whom quickly became multibillionaires. The control of key Mexican assets, therefore, would remain in Mexican hands.

President Bush agreed to the historic pact. Negotiations on NAFTA with Mexico and Canada began in June 1991 and were concluded in August 1992, just before the GOP presidential nomination convention. The three governments jointly released a public relations handout that described the pact in general terms, but the details remained a secret.

Democratic presidential candidate Bill Clinton announced his support for NAFTA on September 4, 1992, subject to the successful negotiation of three-sided agreements on labor standards, environmental protection, and Mexican import surges. Barely three weeks before the election, representatives of the three nations initialed what was reported to be a 1,100-page agreement, whose details were again not released to the American public. On December 18, 1992, the pact was officially signed, although the public was still not given access to the text. Finally, on the afternoon of January 20, 1993, President Clinton's inauguration day, the U.S. Government Printing Office made available the full text of the agreement, for $40 a copy. A national radio talk-show host reprinted the agreement and made it available for a lower price. He sold more than 25,000 copies.

Readers quickly realized that the NAFTA agreement was a sharp departure from prior U.S. trade pacts, which dealt primarily with tariffs and quotas. Indeed, this was the world's first "globalism" trade treaty. Among other provisions, the three governments agreed to:

- Create a new North American regime of U.S.-style protections for intellectual property (patents, trademarks, copyrights, trade secrets).

- Create a new judicial forum in which private companies could pursue claims against host nations for breaches of NAFTA obligations.

- Eliminate sovereign immunity as a defense.

- Create judicial panels that would consist of trade experts appointed by the governments, work outside each country's judicial system, operate in secret, and have the authority to impose fines on any of the three governments, while no appeal of their decisions could be taken to national courts, including the U.S. Supreme Court.

- Alter U.S. immigration laws to allow professionals in sixty-seven categories to take jobs anywhere in the three participating nations and relocate themselves and their families anywhere they wished in the three nations.

- Allow Mexican nationals to own up to 100 percent of farms, forests, and other real estate in the United States, while restricting U.S. citizens' ownership to 49 percent of such properties in Mexico.

- Eliminate U.S. duties on imports of vehicles produced in Mexico and Canada, while allowing those nations to keep their local-content laws requiring that a certain percentage of any vehicles sold there must be made there.

- Exempt from the pact certain Mexican services and Canada's entertainment industries.

- Cut back nontariff barriers to trade in Mexico, while eliminating Mexican restrictions that required foreign firms to purchase components made in Mexico.

At its core, NAFTA was less a trade pact than a political, immigration, and investment agreement. It institutionalized two elements of the Washington Consensus.

First, it made Mexico safe for foreign investors by prohibiting state expropriation except under extraordinary circumstances and, even then, guaranteeing investors fair compensation, quickly paid.

Second, the United States bound itself to accept an unlimited amount of goods and services produced in Mexico with virtually zero import duties. In effect, NAFTA converted Mexico into a manufacturing platform that could serve the U.S. market duty-free.

Equally important, NAFTA was conceived as a new laissez-faire template that the U.S. government would try to impose on all of South America as the Free Trade Agreement of the Americas. For U.S. corporations, this meant an expanding pool of penny-wage foreign labor. To almost all economists and editorialists, it translated into an increase in trade and the creation of more and better jobs that would establish greater well-being for all involved. A majority of Americans, however, were against it.

Before NAFTA could become law, Congress had to ratify it. During the presidential campaign of 1992, George Bush and Bill Clinton supported NAFTA, while Ross Perot, the independent candidate, opposed it. During the third presidential debate, Perot famously told his two opponents:

You implement that NAFTA—the Mexican trade agreement where you pay people one dollar an hour, have no health care, no retirement, no pollution controls—and you are going to hear a giant sucking sound of jobs being pulled out of this country.

Clinton won the presidency, but NAFTA, as a treaty, could not take effect until the Senate ratified it. The U.S. Constitution requires that a treaty be ratified in the Senate by a two-thirds majority of the senators present, a stiff standard for a controversial proposal such as this one. However, in 1989, the Bush administration had persuaded Congress to consider any trade agreement it negotiated not as a treaty but under the looser standards of an Executive Agreement, which requires only simple majority approval in both the House of Representatives and Senate.

To further lubricate the path to ratification, the Bush administration also persuaded Congress to consider the NAFTA agreement under a unique set of procedures called "fast-track rules." The NAFTA legislation had priority for consideration over other bills, thereby guaranteeing that a vote would be taken. The fast-track rules also limited congressional debate, prohibited any amendments, mandated an up-or-down vote, and barred a filibuster—one of the Senate's most sacred privileges.

The stakes in the NAFTA battle were high politically and economically because the pact would be replicated elsewhere. If NAFTA were ratified, moreover, the ongoing General Agreement on Tariffs and Trade (GATT) negotiations would surely be concluded and a powerful new international body, the World Trade Organization (WTO), would be created, putting U.S.

workers into direct competition with those of Asia, Africa, and Latin America. If NAFTA were defeated, however, there would be no WTO and the United States would be forced to rethink its global trade strategy.

By July 1993, NAFTA faced substantial opposition in Congress and from voters across the nation. In mid-September, despite intensified efforts, the pro-NAFTA forces were losing congressional support. At that point, Clinton did what presidents sometimes do in such circumstances: he met with recalcitrant House members and asked what they wanted in exchange for their votes. He then set about buying a victory, vote by vote, project by project, promise by promise. Interestingly, Clinton, in his 957-page auto-biography, devotes only one paragraph to NAFTA and that hard-fought ratification struggle.

One Oklahoma member of the House of Representatives, who was on the board of the National Rifle Association (NRA), swapped his vote for a promise that Clinton would go duck hunting with him as a visible gesture of support for the NRA. Representative Esteban Torres (D-Calif.) wanted funding for a development bank that would finance environmental proj-ects on the U.S.-Mexico border. Another member was looking for an Air Force contract for a constituent. The Florida delegation asked for assur-ances, in writing, that Mexican winter tomato imports would not over-whelm Florida tomato producers. Members from Louisiana and other sugar-producing states asked that the sugar trade be totally exempted from NAFTA.

Fifteen votes swung on the sugar issue alone. To lock them up, the U.S., Canadian, and Mexican governments did something extraordinary: they reopened negotiations in mid-October 1993, and a sugar exemption was attached to the pact.

In the days leading up to the NAFTA vote in Congress, hundreds of thousands of Americans contacted their representatives by letter, e-mail, fax, and telephone. Thousands went to the capital, to their representatives' offices, and asked them to vote no on NAFTA. By early November 1993, opponents were overwhelming the Capitol switchboard with calls. Vice President Gore debated Ross Perot on television's *The Larry King Show*, which devolved into a personal attack on Perot by Gore. Corporate propo-nents were also walking the halls of Congress, holding private dinners and contributing heavily to campaign funds.

On November 17, 1993, the House of Representatives voted 234 for and 200 against. Three days later, the Senate approved NAFTA by 61 to 38. As its advocates had anticipated, NAFTA failed to get the 67 votes that would have been needed to ratify a treaty, but it did gain enough votes to approve an Executive Agreement. A few days later, President Clinton signed the legislation into law.

Two days after Christmas 1993 and five weeks after the NAFTA vote, Clinton got out of bed very early and went duck hunting at a plantation on Taylor's Island, Maryland, in 16-degree weather. Representative Bill Brewster (R-Okla.) was one of his companions. Pictures of the two in their hunting gear, holding their shotguns, later appeared on a cover of the NRA's magazine; the President kept that promise, and Brewster got his magazine cover.

The pledge to Florida tomato growers was never kept. The Department of Agriculture exempted Mexican tomato imports from grading standards imposed on Florida growers; in addition, despite a promise to inspect the Mexican imports for pesticides, fewer than 1 percent of trucks (one in a hundred) carrying Mexican produce into the United States are checked. Consequently, Mexican producers have taken more than 40 percent of the U.S. market.

Following the NAFTA ratification, the Citizens Trade Campaign (CTC), an organization created by Public Citizen, the national consumer organization, identified sixty-six specific promises corporate advocates had made to members of Congress while seeking their votes for NAFTA. The CTC can identify only seven corporate pledges that were kept.

Passage of NAFTA gave the Clinton administration and the globalization advocates the political momentum they needed to conclude the larger General Agreement on Tariffs and Trade (GATT) negotiations in Geneva and create the World Trade Organization. The WTO included many of the same provisions that NAFTA did. With the United States' ratification of those two global pacts, the institutional and legal framework for economic globalization was in place.

NAFTA was extremely unpopular among many citizens of Canada, Mexico, and the United States, a fact that the leaders of the three nations clearly knew from their polling. When Canadian Prime Minister Brian Mulroney announced his support for NAFTA in 1991, he ignited a controversy in Canada. As the 1993 Canadian elections approached, the trade pact became so contentious that Mulroney resigned as prime minister so his party could disassociate itself from NAFTA and have a chance in the October elections.

He acted too late. Mulroney's Progressive Conservative Party held a parliamentary majority of 151 out of 295 elected positions on election day in October 1993; the day after the election, only two remained in office. In the largest political upset in Canadian history, voters exterminated the Progressive Conservative Party. NAFTA was the reason.

In Mexico, where the economy was in financial shambles by late 1994, President Salinas maintained the illusion of national prosperity by borrowing heavily from abroad until he left office in early December and installed his successor, Ernesto Zedillo Ponce de León, another Harvard-trained economist, who also supported the Washington Consensus. Salinas handed Zedillo an economic catastrophe.

Only days into his tenure, the newly elected Mexican president devalued the peso from 3 to 8 per U.S. dollar and announced a moratorium on debt payments. The United States helped Mexico with a $50 billion loan, which was controversial because much of the money went back to the Wall Street banks that had recklessly loaned the Mexican government money at usurious double-digit rates. Ultimately, these firms were the ones at risk, though the U.S. Treasury has never identified which banks actually received the money.

In sum, the United States propped up the Mexican economy with expensive loans during the NAFTA and WTO negotiations, and after NAFTA and WTO were ratified, the full extent of Mexico's financial crisis was revealed to the public. In 1995, the Mexican economy contracted by 7 percent overall, manufacturing shrank by 6 percent, construction decreased by 22 percent, unemployment went into the double-digit levels, and wages fell.

Many Mexicans were outraged. Salinas went into political exile in Ireland, a nation with no extradition treaty with Mexico. His brother Raúl, a close adviser, was arrested and jailed for taking bribes and stealing more than $114 million, a massive corruption that was confirmed when most of the money was discovered in Swiss bank accounts.

In 1997, voters humbled the Institutional Revolutionary Party (PRI), which had ruled Mexico since 1929. In the 2000 election, voters rejected the PRI presidential candidate, choosing instead Vicente Fox, an executive from the opposition National Action Party (PAN).

In the United States, opponents of NAFTA took their revenge on the Democratic-controlled Congress that had ratified the pact. In the 1994 midterm elections, they held dozens of campaign rallies in districts of

NAFTA supporters. The most notable Democrat to be voted out of office was House Speaker Thomas Foley. So many Democrats were defeated in 1994 that the Republicans gained control of both houses of Congress, which they retained until the 2006 elections.

While many of the political leaders who brought globalism to the United States paid a heavy political price, many subsequently prospered in private life. Salinas was not indicted and remains a wealthy man, living outside Mexico. Mulroney became a favored board member of Canadian corporations. George H. W. Bush is a senior adviser to the Carlyle Group, a private global investment fund that manages more than $80 billion of assets, and a well-paid international speaker on the issues of globalism and other subjects.

In the period 2001–2005, the public disclosure records of Senator Hillary Clinton reveal that her husband was paid more than $40 million after he left office in 2001 for making speeches around the world, often on globalization. He also advises transnational corporations, private investment groups, and foreign governments. Al Gore won the popular vote for president in 2000 but lost the electoral count. He left public life and went onto the advisory board of Google, for which he received stock that made him a multimillionaire. In 2007, he was awarded an Oscar for a movie documentary and the Nobel Peace Prize.

Since NAFTA was adopted in 1993, the United States has replicated its provisions throughout the world. Bilateral pacts have been negotiated with Australia, Chile, Jordan, Israel, Morocco, Panama, South Korea, and Singapore. After Mexico obtained its special preferences and access to the U.S. market, more than forty African and Caribbean countries asked Congress and President Clinton for the same terms, which they received, thereby diminishing the exclusivity of Mexico's privileges.

Most important for the future, China joined the World Trade Organization in 2000 and thus received the same access to the U.S. market as any other WTO member. As China has expanded its access to North American markets, even the low-wage labor of Mexico has proven uncompetitive with the less costly Chinese workers, making Mexico itself a victim of massive outsourcing. In the thirty-two months between January 2001 and September 2003, some 500 of Mexico's 3,700 *maquiladora* factories shut down, at a cost of 218,000 jobs.

The social compact between business and American society hammered out in the middle part of the twentieth century was simple: the government would not create a national health and pension system if employers would provide those benefits to their workers. Though imperfect, the system that evolved provided such benefits to more than half the U.S. workforce by the late 1980s. Since 1974, private-sector pension plans have been governed by the Employee Retirement Income Security Act (ERISA), and pensions have been insured by the Pension Benefit Guaranty Corporation (PBGC), which as of 2006 guaranteed basic pensions to more than 44 million American workers in more than 28,000 private-sector defined-benefit plans.

But the trade deals enacted by the Clinton and Bush administrations effectively smashed that long-standing bargain with trade deals that sprang the "trap." Thousands of companies went bankrupt, and thousands more shifted their production abroad and abandoned their workers. The insurance program created to underwrite the vitality of those pensions was overwhelmed, leaving the PBGC with a massive unfunded liability of almost $19 billion by 2007. Millions of other displaced Americans have been left with no health care, no pension plans, and no adjustment assistance, including that needed for relocation. The displaced-worker training program at the Labor Department has been so underfunded over the past decade that it barely qualifies as a placebo.

Repeatedly, workers whose jobs are being transferred to other nations are asked to train their lower-priced foreign replacements brought into the United States by employers who claim, amazingly, that they are unable to find American workers. The threat held over U.S. workers is that if they do not train their foreign successors, the company will not give them any severance pay, which, along with unemployment pay for a few months, is all they get.

The Haas-Stern-Strauss family eventually saved the Levi Strauss Company by outsourcing their production. In 1999, the extended Haas-Stern-Strauss family, which again owns almost all the stock in Levi Strauss, put a new CEO into place—Philip Marineau, the first non-family member to head the company. Marineau developed an outsourcing strategy and transformed the company from a manufacturer of apparel to a designer and marketer. By 2004, Levi Strauss had closed all the company's U.S. factories, relying instead on low-wage foreign contractors to produce its clothing. In the full spirit of its history, Levi Strauss gave its fired American workers generous severance packages and even made grants to the affected communities.

Levi Strauss now operates differently from in the past, as revealed by its global sourcing and operating guidelines, which cover approximately six hundred foreign contractors in more than sixty nations. Under these guidelines, the company does business only with those that:

- Do not work their employees more than sixty hours per week
- Give their employees at least one day of seven off from work
- Refuse to use punishment or other forms of mental or physical coercion
- Employ only workers fifteen years of age and older
- Pay wages and benefits that comply with applicable laws and match the prevailing local manufacturing or finishing industry practices, which in many countries are only pennies per hour

While this may seem similar to the abusive practices of nineteenth-century America, it is actually progressive in most less-developed countries. Contractors in developing-world nations, using low-wage workers, now make 96 percent of the clothing sold in the United States. As difficult as it may be to believe, many of those contractors find the Levi Strauss guidelines too onerous.

Contrary to some political rhetoric that came out of the 2004 presidential election, Levi Strauss is not a villain for outsourcing its work. Nor are the company's CEO and board members political traitors. Rather, the company and its officers did all they could to keep their factories and jobs in the United States. Their predicament is that Washington adopted global trade policies that pitted a privately owned capitalist corporation that must pay its own way against foreign government-subsidized companies that do not.

China's predominantly state-owned textile industries operate with cheap labor and numerous subsidies of capital, fibers, natural gas, coal, equipment, and all else needed for production. They can put their finished clothing on United States retail shelves for less than what American producers, such as Levi Strauss, pay for their raw materials. No matter what else this situation may be, it is neither free trade nor fair competition.

While Levi Strauss survives, many other famous U.S. textile companies, including Cannon, Burlington, Fruit of the Loom, and Peppermill, have gone bankrupt, been consolidated, or been liquidated. Consequently, a major U.S. export to China now is used textile machinery, salvaged from the closure of 328 U.S. factories and thousands of apparel manufacturers since 1997 and sold for bargain-basement prices.

As for the fate of the displaced workers, the Department of Labor reported that during the period 1994–2004, the United States lost more than 816,000 textile and apparel jobs, most of which went to Mexico, the Caribbean, India, Turkey, Pakistan, and of course China. The department also reported that only two thirds of the workers displaced found replacement work, mostly at lower wages and with fewer benefits. The rest left the workforce.

NAFTA successfully did what its creators designed it to do: facilitate increased U.S. direct investment (FDI) in Mexico and Canada, allowing those nations to become manufacturing platforms of goods that can be imported into the United States duty- and quota-free.

Robert E. Scott, director of international studies at the Washington-based Economic Policy Institute, calculates that NAFTA cost America 879,000 jobs between 1994 and 2002. He also concludes that the trade pact indirectly diminished many other manufacturing positions that remained in the United States. Scott notes that many companies openly threatened to move their factories to Mexico if employees were not compliant about wages, benefits, and working conditions. Just the threat of relocation, he says, "suppressed real wages for production workers, weakened workers' collective bargaining powers and ability to organize unions, and reduced fringe benefits."

Yet the total effect of NAFTA goes far beyond trade with Canada and Mexico. As a template, its provisions are found in more than a dozen similar pacts, leading to staggering trade losses. Again, to provide a perspective, the United States ran a trade surplus every year during the 1960s, creating a decade-long surplus of almost $32 billion. Largely because of the oil shortages of the 1970s and rising petroleum prices, that surplus became a decade-long deficit of $87 billion in the 1970s. As the new laissez-faire policies took hold in the 1980s, the collective decade-long deficit jumped to $864 billion, and in the 1990s it exceeded $1 trillion.

In the first years of the twenty-first century, the U.S. trade deficit has soared to stratospheric levels. For the first seven years of the 2000s, the cumulative total is $4.5 trillion—the largest, fastest unilateral transfer of wealth from one nation to others in the history of the world.

·   ·   ·

In summary, Levi Strauss reversed its declining fortunes once it escaped Goldsmith's "trap" and shifted production to foreign-based contractors. In fiscal year 2006, the company did $4.19 billion of sales and produced $239 million of net income, a gain of more than 50 percent over what it had made in 2005. The company is once again prosperous. Its owner family continues to support worthy social causes, and it serves as a leader in trying to improve the condition of workers in other nations. No one knows precisely what happened to the thousands of U.S. workers the company fired in order to survive.

The Levi Strauss story makes an important point: that the best of companies, even those with a fierce loyalty to the United States and its workers, cannot survive if they retain their production in the United States, no matter how well educated, skilled, and productive the workers may be. American and global trade rules are stacked too high against them.

Milton Friedman's doctrine of unrestrained laissez-faire business practices has prevailed. Corporate profits now dominate all other considerations. As Friedman noted, if we want corporations to act differently, we must set different rules for them to obey. The questions are what those rules should be and who should set and enforce them. We'll examine those questions in chapter 9.

Six

FRIEDMAN II (THOMAS)

While Milton Friedman provided the intellectual energy for our second era of "globalization," *New York Times* foreign affairs columnist Thomas L. Friedman has helped popularize it worldwide in his writing and speeches. A three-time Pulitzer Prize winner, Friedman, whose column appears in seven hundred newspapers worldwide, has written two best-selling books on globalization, *The Lexus and the Olive Tree* and *The World Is Flat.*

Thomas Friedman is a passionate missionary for free-market economics, and his books and writings have become the modern bible of that creed. As did the advocates of pre–World War I internationalism, Friedman and his followers argue that technological advance is creating a new era of consensual and democratic market-driven worldwide production, distribution, and consumption.

As did their predecessors a century ago, these "globalists" argue that this is an unstoppable evolution, a technological determinism that will override the old obstacles to economic integration: militarism, imperialism, racism, cultural rivalries, monopolies, restrictions, and exclusions.

Friedman's metaphor for this supposedly unstoppable economic integration is "flat world." He identifies ten factors, what he terms "flatteners," that are leveling the global playing field for workers, enabling people in China, India, and other developing countries to compete on an increasingly equal footing with workers in Europe, Japan, the United States, and other developed countries.

In the order he presents them, these forces are:

1. The end of the Cold War
2. The Internet

3. Work flow innovations such as e-mail, data, and pictures
4. Software that allows the sharing of work over the Internet
5. Outsourcing of work (importing work done abroad, such as accounting and software development, via the Internet)
6. Offshoring of work (sending factories abroad and integrating their production into global distribution networks)
7. New software and techniques to better manage a global supply chain (as done, for instance, by Wal-Mart)
8. Insourcing (contracting supply-chain functions to companies such as UPS)
9. In-forming (enabling individuals to do all or most of their work by themselves)
10. Increased mobility provided by digital devices and the ubiquity of instant communications

Seven of Friedman's ten factors are technology-based, including the Internet and various accounting, software, and supply-control techniques that greatly increase work efficiency and expand the information available to anyone, anywhere. His one geopolitical factor is the end of the Cold War, which allowed hundreds of millions of people to enter the global work-force.

Outsourcing and offshoring are two of Friedman's main flatteners. Outsourcing is the contracting for all or part of work, such as a company's accounting or software development, with a company located in another nation with skilled but low-wage workers, such as India.

Friedman's operative definition of offshoring is when a company takes a factory located in Canton, Ohio, and moves it to Canton, China. "There it produces the very same product in the very same way, only with cheaper labor, lower taxes, subsidized energy, and lower health-care costs."

The power of these ten factors, he claims, is that they now work together across the globe.

Ultimately, Friedman's message is that the United States will benefit more by "sticking to the general principles of free trade, as it always has, than by trying to erect walls, which will only provoke others to do the same and impoverish us all." Although free trade is essential, he argues, alone it is insufficient. The education of every American must be upgraded, and the United States must develop a "foreign strategy of opening restricted markets all over the world." The solution, he writes, is for "America to churn out knowledgeable workers who are able to produce idea-based goods that can be sold globally and who are able to fill the knowledge jobs that will be created."

The policy implications of Friedman's books are straightforward: Remove all barriers to trade in every nation and improve the education of American workers, and the ultimate result will be more trade and more global prosperity, which will eventually create more democracy around the world and more peaceful relations among countries. Corporations that shift production to low-cost locales and send less expensive goods into developed markets are positive agents of change in a process that is unstoppable.

But Friedman's thesis and conclusions have serious flaws. First, his assumption that the U.S. economy was developed "under the principles of free trade" is simply wrong. Indeed, U.S. trade negotiations since the time of Cordell Hull have involved the piece-by-piece removal of protectionist barriers put into place between 1790 and 1930. As we have seen in earlier chapters, however, the United States rejected free-trade principles and policies until the 1930s. President Theodore Roosevelt summed up the prevailing early-twentieth-century attitude in a letter to his friend Senator Henry Cabot Lodge (R-Mass.). "I thank God," he wrote, "that I am not a free trader."

The offshoring and outsourcing that Friedman views as free trade are actually "arbitrage economics," the very antithesis of free trade. Free trade is built on the assumption that the factors of production (capital, labor, and technology) are immobile, with each nation doing that in which it has a comparative advantage.

That economic concept comes from the works of Adam Smith and David Ricardo. Modern economics began with Smith and his publication in 1776 of *The Wealth of Nations.* The Englishman David Ricardo (1772–1823), a wealthy government securities dealer, read Smith's book and was spellbound. Encouraged by his friend the philosopher John Stuart Mill, Ricardo retired at the age of forty-one so he could devote himself to the further study of economics. In 1817, he published *On the Principles of Political Economy and Taxation,* which set forth his famous theory of comparative advantage, an idea that has seduced generations of economists and politicians.

When Ricardo conceived the comparative advantage theory, agricultural production, based on climate and geography, was then the major component of the gross domestic product of most nations. Countries grew and exported, if they could, what they grew best. Manufacturing for export was just developing. In those days, capital, technology, and labor were immobile. Indeed, the idea of an Englishman building a factory elsewhere, such as France, or sending technology there was deemed too risky.

The economist Paul Craig Roberts, a key economic adviser to President Ronald Reagan, disputes the idea that Ricardo's theory can work in today's global economy. Advantage today, he argues, is created not by a nation's stock of natural resources but by the availability and mobility of capital, technology, and workers. The heart of modern trade agreements is a global guarantee that foreign capital and technology will not be expropriated by the host nation, eliminating the most important obstacle to direct foreign investment.

Unlike in Ricardo's era, capital and technologies are now totally mobile, as increasingly are high-knowledge workers. The result is a historically unique economic dynamic.

Today, dozens of nations have essentially limitless pools of labor, collectively hundreds of millions of potential workers, most of whom can be made as productive as workers in the United States or any other industrial country. When combined with imported capital and technology, low-wage labor with few benefits enables those nations to create an unbeatable "absolute advantage" based on inexpensive workers that the United States and other developed countries cannot overcome.

Even if the United States, Japan, or Europe confronts the arbitrage differential by developing even more advanced technologies, greater labor-saving approaches, or even entirely new industries, all of those advances can be transferred to the low-wage countries, wiping out any temporary gains in competitiveness.

The absolute advantage created by labor arbitrage is strengthened by the lower costs created with a lack of environmental restrictions, worker safety, and other employment benefits found in the developed world.

While Friedman's solution—more education and training—is also often advanced by others, the reality of the market is that people in worker-surplus countries will soon match any improvement of skills of people in the U.S. labor force, quickly eliminating skill or knowledge advantage. Moreover, the many transnational corporations that benefit from such arbitrage are already helping their host nations provide the improved education and training needed to maintain that advantage. As Roberts concludes, the absolute advantage that China and other nations are creating is simply unbreakable by private corporations operating in higher-wage countries. In effect, Ricardo's model of trade is as passé in today's world as are powdered wigs for men.

The modern relevance of Ricardo's model is one of today's great economic controversies. The overwhelming majority of America's policy elites, and the economists who advise them, simply will not even consider alternatives. In a 2006 CNBC interview with Tim Russert, the director of the NBC Washington bureau, Friedman described how he had recently given a speech in Minnesota and a man had stood up and asked, "Mr. Friedman, is there any free trade agreement you'd oppose?" "No, absolutely not," he'd said. "You know what, sir? I wrote a column supporting the CAFTA, the Caribbean Free Trade Initiative. I didn't even know what was in it. I just knew two words: free trade."

Russert did not challenge Friedman or follow up with any questions about the deficiencies in the Caribbean pact's labor, human rights, or environmental provisions.

Friedman's positive response to any legislation or treaty labeled as pro–free trade is neither unique nor extreme. During the closing days of the 1993 congressional debate over NAFTA, three hundred of the nation's leading economists, including two Nobel laureates, released a joint letter that urged the pact's immediate ratification. Subsequently, Delana Bennett, an enterprising journalist for a national radio network, interviewed about 150 of these economists and asked them two simple questions: Why do you support this agreement? Have you read the 1,000-page agreement you endorsed? All answered that they supported free trade and open markets. Only one of nine of them claimed actually to have read the NAFTA agreement.

Would equally distinguished lawyers sign off on a contract without reviewing it, or would any certified public accountant approve a company's books without first checking them? Why would some of America's leading economists urge the president and Congress to ratify an economic pact they had not even read? The answer, of course, is that most of them are doctrinaire free traders, as are most of America's political and opinion elite. To label a prospective international agreement as free trade, regardless of what actually is in the pact, has come to virtually guarantee an influential base of political support. Cant has replaced thought when globalization is discussed.

Modern trade agreements usually include dozens of nontrade provisions, including intellectual property rules, immigration, energy, natural resource sharing, and exemptions, plus provisions that represent second-, third-, and fourth-best compromises. Yet these pacts are presented to Congress as something that Adam Smith and David Ricardo would have blessed.

Contrary to what is presented to Congress for ratification, a simple free-trade agreement would be no longer than one sentence: "The United States and the nation of X agree that there will be no obstacles whatsoever to the flow of goods and services between our two nations." Today's 500- to 1,000-page trade agreements clearly involve many more deals and trade-offs—often second-, third-, and fourth-best choices—than a true free-trade pact would. The result is managed trade. What differs between nations is what is managed and the terms.

Prior to 1933, U.S. trade bills were about tariffs and were presented to Congress as the Tariff Bill of 1921 or the Tariff Bill of 1930, for instance. During the New Deal (1933–1944) and the years that followed, they were labeled the Reciprocal Trade Act of 1934 or whatever year they pertained to. "Reciprocal" was the operative word, as in "fair" to all parties.

Beginning with NAFTA in 1993, these agreements have been labeled "free trade." NAFTA, CAFTA, and the U.S.-Chile Free Trade Agreement are examples. The intent, of course, has been to discourage examination and opposition by positioning opponents as anti–free trade. This ploy has worked. Between the enactments of NAFTA in 1993 and the passage of CAFTA in 2006, Congress rejected not one "free-trade" pact.

Global integration in the pre–World War I era was about nations being both customers and suppliers and balanced economic relationships. The present globalization is not about such balance; it is about serving established markets from export platforms with, as Thomas Friedman observes, the cheapest labor, most subsidies, and fewest regulations. Balance and reciprocity are not operational considerations. This creates a viciously destructive downward cycle of displacement and lowered wages and benefits for workers in the established market countries.

Surprisingly, the "flat-world" model is even more destructive for most developing nations. Developing countries have two trade necessities: to earn hard currency and to provide jobs. The currencies of most poor countries are worth little to first-world manufacturers, who generally refuse to take local money for goods such as turbines, tractors, locomotives, and rails. The underdeveloped nations must export something that can earn them dollars, euros, yen, or other hard currencies, which they can then use to buy first-world goods. Apparel production is one way poor nations can both earn hard currency and create jobs. The arithmetic of the global apparel trade is perhaps the most visible example of how meaningful U.S. trade policy is to the developing world.

Apparel production is labor-intensive. To meet world demand, apparel makers need millions of workers, which developing countries have in excess. For poor nations, apparel manufacturing is one of the quickest ways to create large numbers of jobs. It is also one of the easiest, largely because the cost of entering the industry is low; sewing machines, electricity, imported fabric, workers, and rent for a work space are about all a company needs to begin production. The main challenge for developing nations is not manufacturing apparel but selling it.

In 1974, dozens of countries entered a momentous global trade pact, the Multifibre Arrangement (MFA), which opened first-world apparel markets to developing-world producers. The MFA set international import quotas that defined how much apparel each poor nation could ship into the United States and other rich markets. To spread the jobs among these countries, MFA architects structured the pact so that one or two nations could never monopolize the industry. The quotas also guaranteed a large portion of the first-world markets to their own domestic producers, which provided millions of jobs for American and European workers.

The MFA worked well for both the developing and developed world for many years. By 2003, textile and apparel production had become the major manufacturing industry in more than forty-two developing countries, creating millions of jobs for the world's poor. Equally significant, textile and apparel exports to the United States were a key component of the economies of eleven Islamic countries that are key allies in the War on Terror.

Despite the obvious success of this program, it was eliminated in the negotiations that created the World Trade Organization. Many influential American and European trade specialists opposed the MFA, despite the help it gave developing nations. They contended that the quotas raised prices for first-world consumers by prohibiting the lowest-cost producers from taking more market share. Their principal concern was that of traditional trade theorists—that is, getting the lowest prices for U.S., European, and Japanese consumers, as opposed to improving the well-being of the developing countries or providing jobs in the United States and Europe.

Surprisingly, many developing nations also opposed the quotas. Their leaders dreamed that their exports could grow far beyond their existing quotas—a hope some first-world trade negotiators slyly encouraged. Those leaders never quite realized that all their competitor nations had the same delusion.

This widespread fantasy created an opportunity for some type of global trade arrangement, and in 1994, U.S., Japanese, and European trade negotiators struck a deal with many of the leaders of the developing world. In exchange for their adopting U.S.-style intellectual property protections for patents, trademarks, copyrights, and trade secrets, the first-world countries would end all quotas on apparel imports, opening their markets to any producer from any participating nation to sell all it could.

Unlike the MFA, however, this pact did not contain safeguards to prevent one or two nations from taking the entire global market. It had two flaws. First, the agreement pitted American apparel workers against the low-wage labor of the developing world. Over the ten-year MFA quota phaseout, this resulted in the loss of almost one million U.S. jobs, almost 80 percent of which were held by American women, many of whom were minorities living at subsistence levels. The second flaw, as difficult as it may be to believe, is even more important: the arrangement did not include China, the world's principal apparel maker.

In the late 1990s, the Clinton administration remedied that situation when it negotiated China's admission to the World Trade Organization, the global body that sets and enforces international trade rules. The Clinton accession agreement, however, did not impose any restrictions on Chinese exports of apparel and textiles to the developed world. Thus, China was given full, unimpeded access to the world's textile and apparel markets in January 2005, when the MFA quotas expired.

With that, the United States unthinkingly pitted all the apparel makers in all the developing countries and all those in the United States, Japan, and Europe against the state-owned and -supported apparel makers in China. Calamity, particularly in the developing world, has been the result.

Chinese apparel and textile exports have soared, and their producers are overwhelming apparel makers in most other developing countries. The clothing manufacturers in poor countries are competing, in effect, with the Beijing government, which owns half of the country's apparel companies and subsidizes most of the rest. These public subsidies, coupled with China's rock-bottom wages, enable the Chinese to be the world's lowest-cost producer. In 2005, the Commerce Department reported that the prices of apparel produced in China were 76 percent below those of U.S. producers and 58 percent below those in the rest of the world.

China's subsidized prices are so low that its manufacturers are delivering finished goods to foreign markets for less than competitors in Turkey, Haiti, Mexico, and other developing nations must pay for their raw materials. The Beijing government, moreover, has made it clear that it will cut prices even further to expand its hold on world markets. Manufacturers paying 80 cents an hour for labor in Guatemala, El Salvador, Nicaragua, and Honduras, for instance, cannot compete with subsidized competitors paying 30 cents an hour in China, which intends to take the entire market and will pay whatever is required to do so.

A report from the National Council of Textile Organizations (NCTO) concluded that the ultimate result is that "Once China captures market share . . . no one in the world has the pricing power to seize it back." Several recent studies conclude that Chinese producers are virtually certain to control 75 percent of the U.S. apparel market and 50 percent worldwide by 2010. With this shift of production, almost 30 million apparel workers in dozens of developing nations will lose their jobs to the Chinese.

This movement of production and jobs will harm the economies of most Latin American, African, and other developing nations, all of which have limited means to create replacement positions. Turkey alone has 2 million apparel jobs that may move to China under the present WTO rules. The loss of so many jobs so quickly creates a risk of political instability and increased illegal immigration into the United States and Europe. This is "flat-world" economics in action.

Returning to Friedman's ten "flatteners," although his seven technological flat-world forces are valuable tools, ultimately they are just evolutionary advances on the telegraph, telephone, radio, and television, in addition to the systems technologies introduced in the 1940s and 1950s. Wal-Mart's logistics are impressive, but so too were those of the U.S. Army in preparation for the invasion of Europe in 1944. An electric pulse over copper lines by telegraph a century ago flowed almost as quickly as one over fiber optics does today. The point is that the United States has long been an information society.

The same new technologies Friedman extols are as capable of "rounding" the world as "flattening" it. While providing more information organized faster and delivered more quickly, these technologies also give governments the capacity to more tightly control and monitor people. Now it is possible to record, monitor, and analyze each user's every e-mail, every Internet search, every bit of information viewed and downloaded, every piece of work shared, every collaborator's identity, every item or service bought or sold electronically, every credit card transaction, everything in a company's supply chain, and every use of anyone's digital equipment wherever he or she may be.

In 2001, the Bush administration created a Department of Defense project to collect such information on every person in the United States. Once this project was made public, it caused an uproar over the potential loss of privacy and was canceled. Unfortunately, parts of it were never really discontinued. Subsequent evidence released by the Senate Intelligence Committee and news articles in *The Washington Post* and *The New York Times* revealed that much information had been collected and that it had been collected illegally.

A decade ago, one of the main arguments for China's accession to the WTO was that it would facilitate free trade and a free flow of information to the people of that country via the Internet, which would stimulate a widening demand for democracy. Consider what happened.

Prior to 2000, the U.S. Congress voted each year whether to continue China's most-favored-nation (MFN) status for trade purposes, by which the United States gave China the same best trade terms it granted to other nations, including longtime allies such as Britain and France, but only for a year at a time.

The annual vote on MFN was a bitterly contested battle in which major U.S. business organizations argued on China's behalf and opponents of China's human rights practices tried to persuade Congress to deny trade benefits until the Beijing government stopped human rights abuses. Twice during the administration of President George H. W. Bush, Congress enacted legislation to tie MFN privileges to China's improvement of its human rights record. Twice, the president vetoed that legislation.

When Bill Clinton ran for president in 1992, he promised to sign such legislation, but after he took office he persuaded congressional leaders instead to accept an Executive Order that contained the language of the vetoed legislation. As James Mann, author of *The China Fantasy*, observed, this was a cynical decision because "It is easier to abandon an executive order than a congressional statute," which is exactly what Clinton did two years later in 1994.

Under pressure from U.S. corporations and Wall Street firms that wanted more commerce with China, Clinton revoked his own executive order and broke the links between U.S. trade and China's human rights practices.

As Mann noted, since 1994 the relationship between the United States and China has been primarily economic in nature. China has become a location for American investment, and the United States has become the principal outlet for Chinese exports. Trade has soared. When Clinton broke the trade–human rights link in 1994, the trade deficit with China was $26 billion. But when he left office six years later, it was $83 billion.

Clinton's political problem was how to make palatable a deal that many critics deemed unprincipled. First, he urged U.S. corporations to adopt voluntary codes of conduct for their Chinese operations. He also expanded U.S.-financed radio programs supporting human rights that are beamed into China, and, finally, he sponsored a resolution at the United Nations condemning China's human rights practices.

By the time Clinton was in his second term, those measures were viewed as the meaningless political placebos they clearly were. Then his administration came forth with another explanation of why it was not confronting Chinese repression: more trade would automatically lead to free trade, and free trade would create a freer, more democratic China.

The way to facilitate this logic was equally simple: if more trade was the way to reform China, the fastest, easiest way to enact such a policy was to allow China, a nonmarket Communist-led country, to join the world's largest free trade group, the World Trade Organization. Consequently, in 2000, Clinton persuaded Congress to ratify China's membership in the WTO. With that, China automatically got MFN privileges *and* Congress lost its right to bargain trade rights for human rights improvements.

After China's accession to the WTO, the U.S. trade deficit with that nation tripled in six years. By 2007, China had a $250 billion annual trade surplus with the United States and was a major supplier of U.S. foods, high-technology products, consumer goods, and electronics.

Moreover, Clinton's premise that free trade would lead to more human rights was wrong. The Congressional-Executive Commission on China's 2006 Annual Report concluded that nearly every major Chinese dissident is in prison or exile. Government abuse of Catholics and Buddhists has expanded. The commission noted that Chinese officials "detained, sequestered, threatened, or exerted pressure on dozens of registered Catholic clerics to coerce them into participating in the consecration of bishops selected by the state-controlled Catholic Patriotic Association but not approved by the Holy See." The one-child policy remains in effect. China remains a one-party dictatorship. It continues to improve and expand its military forces. In sum, more trade has not produced more political freedom or democracy.

China's Internet is closely censored. Yahoo!, Microsoft, and other Internet companies have capitulated to Chinese bureaucrats and now allow the Beijing government to dictate both which computer sites the Chinese can use and the content they can access, restrictions that China enforces with thirty thousand censors. Yahoo! has publicly acknowledged that it provided the Chinese government the identity of a dissident who used the Internet to post prodemocracy messages. The man was then arrested and imprisoned for ten years.

The irony of China's acquisition of "flat-world" technologies is that it enables the government to maintain tighter control over its citizens and foreigners who go there to visit or do business.

While the collapse of the Soviet Union and the end of the Cold War brought hundreds of millions of people into an open global labor marketplace, the dozens of trade pacts put into place since 1990 have made no provisions for the protection of those workers from exploitation or human rights abuses. Nor have those agreements imposed any requirements for the abolition of child labor or slavery. The environmental damage caused by unregulated production and various polluting techniques have also been ignored in these trade pacts. Indeed, most other nations have stoutly opposed such social provisions, as have the transnational interests that lobby Congress and the president for "free-trade" pacts. For more than a decade, a majority in Congress refused to even consider any of those social provisions.

Equally significant, though the old era of internationalism was built atop a complicated and unstable political system, the current era of globalization rests on an even more unstable world financial system. The principal source of that instability is U.S. policies based on this "flat-world" economic creed.

In less than twenty-five years, the United States has gone from being the world's principal creditor to its principal debtor. When President George W. Bush's successor assumes office on January 20, 2009, the annual U.S. trade deficit will likely approach $800 billion per year, the federal budget deficit will exceed $300 billion, the national debt will exceed $10 trillion, and the country's net international financial position will be at least a negative $4 trillion.

The United States has created these imbalances by borrowing from foreign lenders on a massive scale and liquidating national assets to an equally vast degree. By 2009, foreign interests will own more than half of the federal Treasury debt, a third of corporate bonds, and a sixth of corporate assets. Professional economists across most ideological spectrums, including Alan Greenspan, Paul Volcker, Paul Krugman, and Paul Craig Roberts, agree that this imbalance foreshadows a major global economic restructuring and if handled improperly could trigger a worldwide depression. As for the "serpents" that John Maynard Keynes referred to in *The Economic Consequences of the Peace*—militarism, imperialism, racism, cultural rivalries, monopolies, restrictions, and exclusions—they are the same ones that threaten the economic and political stability of our time. They set the boundaries (visible and invisible) that define the limits of progress, change, and global economic integration.

C. E. Ayres, the founder of neoinstitutional economics, said of these inhibitors, "The history of the human race is that of a perpetual opposition by these forces, the dynamic force of technology continually making for change, and the static force of ceremony—status, mores, and legendary belief—opposing change. Most of the time and most parts of the world status (quo) has prevailed."

If Friedman's ten factors are the "flatteners," then these are the seven "rounders" that make globalization so dangerous.

Nationalism People around the world are turning to their governments for relief from the changes being created by global economic integration. Russia, for instance, is retreating from the open-market regime it first pursued after the Soviet breakup, and it is becoming more nationalistic. China, India, and Brazil, among dozens of other nations, remain intensely nationalistic. If the world economy slows, those blinkered feelings are likely to intensify and lead to greater protectionism and less economic integration.

Closer to the United States, half the voters in Mexico's 2006 presidential election supported a self-proclaimed economic nationalist who almost won on a promise to close the country's markets to foreign-produced goods and create jobs for the millions of workers displaced because of Mexico's participation in NAFTA and the United States' perfidious actions to bring China into the WTO in 2001. Once inside the global "trade club," with all its preferences, the Chinese overwhelmed Mexican producers.

When President Bush traveled to South America in 2007 on a five-nation trip, he was met at the airport in Brazil and Uruguay by thousands of protestors. Venezuelan President Hugo Chávez, who was visiting Argentina, told leftists there that Bush should "go home." In Nicaragua, Daniel Ortega, a leftist nationalist, took office as president in January 2007.

In each of these nations, governments had tried the unregulated capitalism promoted as flat-world economics and failed to better the lives of their people. Not surprisingly, the result has been a rise of nationalism throughout the world.

Ironically—or maybe more accurately, hypocritically—many of the principal advocates of global integration in the U.S. Congress are the same who support a constitutional amendment prohibiting burning the U.S. flag—the principal symbol of U.S. nationalism. To them, protecting U.S. industries and jobs are nationalism and thus bad, but protecting the flag is patriotic and thus good.

Militarism The military-industrial complex, which President Dwight D. Eisenhower warned about in his farewell presidential speech, developed, as he feared it would, with a worldwide arms race. With the end of the Cold War, the great hope was that a massive shift of national resources from the tools and programs of war to those of peace would occur. Yet the United States still devotes more than 4 percent of its GDP to military expenditures. Equally significant, the administration of President George W. Bush has adopted an aggressive policy of "preemption," whereby the United States reserves the right to attack any nation the president decides is a threat to America. The invasion of Iraq was the first such application of that policy.

China is constantly expanding and modernizing its military forces. The paradox is that as China and the United States entwine their economies, their military forces are devoting enormous planning and resources to possible conflict, much as Germany and Britain became increasingly economically integrated before World War I even as each tried to build a larger navy than the other's.

Global militarism remains a prominent force, a true serpent, and a major inhibitor to economic integration. A real danger to the United States is that under its globalist defense procurement policies, the Department of Defense increasingly relies on suppliers in locales that may be inaccessible in time of war.

Racism Racism is a major "rounder." In Japan, race consciousness is reflected in an immigration policy that gives citizenship to fewer than 11,000 foreigners a year, the overwhelming majority of whom have Japanese ancestry or are married to Japanese citizens. Equally telling, hundreds of thousands of men and women born in Japan to descendants of Chinese and Koreans forcibly brought there generations ago as indentured workers are permitted to live in Japan but are denied citizenship. Such insularity and exclusion rankle people in other Asian nations and serve as a constant reminder of Japan's insular and racist attitudes toward those from other nations and cultures. Chinese leaders have repeatedly emphasized Japan's racist attitudes to distract the attention of Chinese citizens from other internal matters.

Tribalism in Africa has resulted in racial-based genocide for decades. Anti-Semitism in the Middle East, Europe, and even South America remains a constant spark of conflict. In Europe, generations of immigrants from Asia, the Middle East, and Africa have often failed to be assimilated, resulting in racial resentment on the part of both immigrants and native Europeans. The race issue is an ageless inhibitor that is seemingly immune to "flatteners" such as increased access for all to technical advances such as computers and the Internet.

Cultural Rivalries Although people throughout the world may like the taste of Coca-Cola or Kentucky Fried Chicken, the music of Eminem, or a George Clooney movie, this does not mean that they share the attitudes, values, goals, religions, politics, and practices that Americans do. Yet a basic assumption of "flat-world" advocates is that people from other cultures either are now or will become "Americanized" once they are exposed to free-market capitalism.

The presumption of such inevitability ignores the inconvenient fact that cultural rivalry is alive and well. The same rivalry that ignited World War I with an assassination in Serbia reignited a deadly conflict that, for many of the same reasons, caused the dissolution of Yugoslavia eighty years later.

For almost a half century, China has been trying to extinguish the culture of Tibet. Conflicts over religion and nationality have killed thousands of supposedly civilized and educated people in Northern Ireland for decades. Israelis and Palestinians are divided by a cultural rivalry that repeatedly flares into war, one that would surely go nuclear if Muslim extremists could get their hands on a device.

Religion, tribes, social groups, customs, practices, ethnicity, and the moral standards that people believe in and follow are the most powerful, and often most invisible, boundaries of all. In short, culture matters.

Monopolies If there is one true maxim in economics, it is this: Perfect happiness, for a serious monopolist, is complete control of something everyone must have. Control of water, minerals, land, petroleum, and waterways, among dozens of other important resources, has repeatedly led to wars.

For thousands of years, monopolies have been a basic element of commerce. Adam Smith railed against them in *The Wealth of Nations.* Breaking the trusts was a major obsession of Theodore Roosevelt, Woodrow Wilson, Franklin Roosevelt, and Harry Truman. Much like weeds, monopolistic practices can be sheared, but they usually reemerge.

In *Hot Property* (2005), I described the conflict between the IG Farben chemical trust in Germany and Dow Chemical. In *Agents of Influence* (1990), I wrote about the battle between Zenith Corporation and the Japanese consumer electronics cartel. Both are famous examples of a large entity attempting to monopolize a worldwide industry. Many of the industries of Europe and Japan operate today through similar cartels that divide markets, set prices, and exclude nonmembers. Market-driven policies are about as attractive to these monopolies as poison is to weeds.

The real purpose of the European Union's Monopolies Commission is to ensure that no foreign cartel or industry operates without accommodating that region's own cartels. Microsoft, for example, is being forced, under threat of devastating fines, to share its source codes and reach accommodation with European software producers. The French government, acting as a stand-in for Europe, tried to force Apple to share its iPod music standards with members of the European electronics cartel and has abolished penalties for people copying and distributing music from Apple's proprietary library.

In many industries Europe and Japan have created world cartels, such as in consumer electronics, whose corporate representatives periodically meet to divide markets, agree upon production volumes, time the phase-in and phase-out of technologies, set prices, and block new entrants into the market. The practice is so common and accepted in Japan and Europe that in his autobiography the late Akio Morita, the cofounder of Sony, described in some detail the operations of the Japanese-European consumer electronics cartel, revelations that have gone virtually unnoticed by regulators. When an American firm tries to beat one of these cartels in its own market, the Europeans or Japanese dump cheap goods until the new entrant is either destroyed or, if it survives and prospers, is invited to join the cartel.

American companies competing with these foreign monopolists face a ruinous price competition that so lowers their profit margins that they cannot invest in the research and development, new facilities, and new equipment necessary to compete. If the upstart lacks the financial resources to sustain itself, cartel members usually buy up desirable pieces of the company at bankruptcy prices.

These global and domestic cartels are usually invisible but nonetheless are major "rounders" that shape global economic integration, reduce competition, and increase prices everywhere.

Ideology Charles "Chip" Bohlen, a prominent U.S. diplomat during the Cold War years, concluded his autobiography, *Witness to History*, with the observation that the only way to understand the Soviet Union is to realize that it was not a nation but an ideology. The same could be said of U.S. elite opinion about global trade; that is, that globalization is not just economic policy but rather an ideology.

Consider this story, which begins in the old Soviet Union.

On August 19, 1991, Communist hard-liners in Moscow, including the defense minister and the head of the KGB, attempted to seize control of the government. Soviet leader Mikhail Gorbachev and his family, who were on vacation at their Crimean dacha, were arrested by their own security detail. The coup d'état was broken in seventy-two hours, and Gorbachev and his family returned safely to the capital, where he held a press conference that was broadcast live to the world. One of the questions Gorbachev took from the journalists was whether the coup had raised any doubts in his mind about Marxist philosophy. He responded with a stout defense of communism. How ironic it seemed as he actively, and sincerely, defended a philosophy whose flaws had resulted in the economic and political collapse of his nation and facilitated a coup that had threatened his life and those of his entire family.

Gorbachev's response was far from unusual. Ideas can induce powerful obsessions that grip the mind and sometimes cannot be broken by other than death, particularly ideas about religion, politics, and economics, which many people view as absolutes. John Maynard Keynes wrote in *The*

General Theory, more than a half century before the Moscow coup (1936), "Practical men, who believe themselves to be quite exempt from any intellectual influences, are usually the slaves of some defunct economist."

Just as Gorbachev was mesmerized by the ideology of Marxism, our leaders are transfixed by David Ricardo's ideology of comparative advantage and the leaders of China are transfixed by the concept of one-party rule and market socialism.

Religion In Friedman's discussion of the breakup of the Soviet Union, he totally ignores the role of the Catholic Church and Pope John Paul II. They are never mentioned in his book, yet the pope was a major factor in bringing freedom to the Polish people and, ultimately, in the collapse of the Soviet Union.

Almost every religious group has at one time or another been persecuted for its beliefs. The war in Iraq has disintegrated into a religious conflict between the Shia and Sunni sects, which have been in conflict since the death of the Prophet Mohammad as to who should lead the Muslim people. Religion is a "rounder" that shows little sign of weakening as a force for the status quo.

The seven "rounders" described above will always be with us and continue to influence our political and economic world, keeping us from becoming completely integrated into one flat world.

The principal structural flaw in the flat-world view of global economics is that most other national economies, particularly the major ones, are not structured like that of the United States, nor should they be nor will they be. Countries compete in the global market using vastly different assumptions, serving different ends, which reflect fundamental differences in history, culture, national aspirations, and politics. Once upon a time, economic students studied such differences under the label of comparative economic systems. Increasingly, the fact that such differences exist is ignored under the assumption that they do not matter in a world that is flat.

The economy of Japan, for instance, involves a long-term working relationship between the major corporations and the national government. Cartels are created and monitored, and companies share information and technologies under the eyes of the government in ways that would be totally illegal in the United States. Finance, development, production, and distribution within and outside Japan by those companies are intensely competitive, but the citizens of Japan expect their government to exercise control over the companies.

The Chinese economy today is highly mercantilist. The government owns almost 60 percent of all industry. Those companies are highly subsidized through nonperforming loans, cheap energy, low-cost components, strict control of the workforce, and subsidized transport. The government operates an intellectual property system whose function is to take foreign technologies for use by Chinese companies, as opposed to protecting foreign intellectual property rights in China.

China seeks control of global resources for its future production and willingly engages in geopolitical negotiations to that purpose all over South America, Asia, and Africa. Its goal is to become the world's preeminent center of technology and manufacturing.

Satisfying consumer desires is low on the government's list of priorities. Thus, China forces savings by its people by holding down consumption, using the money saved to build a world economic superpower. The concepts of open markets and consumerism are alien to China's plans.

France, Sweden, and some other nations operate mixed economies. Some industries are privately owned; others, such as Airbus Industries, are public enterprises that are heavily subsidized. Parts of the European economy are cartelized, such as consumer electronics, and government elites have repeatedly established import and export quota arrangements with other nations. Such arrangements are acceptable to the people of those nations, whose middle-class status is far less endangered than that of Americans, who have seen so many middle-class jobs move overseas.

The Anglo-American economies of the United States, Britain, and a few other countries rely on rules that are enforced through judicial processes. Economies such as those in Japan and China are results-oriented. Those governments, working with industry, set five-year plans and aim their efforts at achieving specific results. Also, the economies of Europe, Japan, and China work well with one another because they focus on hard results rather than rule-driven processes, allowing them to achieve their respective goals without amassing the massive deficits the United States has experienced for the past twenty-five years.

For the United States, the goal of trade negotiations is to put into place a process and rules that will facilitate free trade among nations. Other countries work to secure specific results-oriented goals, such as control of specific industries. This is rules-oriented trade versus results-oriented trade.

The policy debate of which global trade approach to take—to put rules into place or aim for results—has raged for more than twenty-five years in the United States. The rules-driven free-trade advocates have won every political trade battle in Congress during that time and enacted every trade agreement proposed by the federal government. The fundamental flaw in their approach to policy is that they assume that globalization is free trade. It is not.

Ralph E. Gomory, president of the Alfred P. Sloan Foundation and former head of research at IBM, emphatically made that point in testimony before the House Committee on Science and Technology on June 12, 2007. He told Congress:

What is good for America's global corporations is no longer necessarily good for the American economy. . . . [W]hen U.S. companies build semiconductor plants and R&D facilities in Asia rather than in the U.S., then that is a shift in productive capability, and neither economic theory nor common sense assert that shift is automatically good for the U.S. even in the long run. . . . [G]lobalism is thriving today at least partly because it supports and gains support from a group that is very powerful today, the multinational corporations.

The philosophy of flat-world economics assumes that corporations and businesspeople, operating with ever-improving technologies, will overcome the obstacles and prejudices that have long plagued nations and people hoping to create open, unimpeded global markets and through that more democratic societies. Although over time the world economy will surely become "flatter" and national economies will surely become more closely entwined, a flat world remains more of an idealistic goal than a reality. The world is far more intricate and dangerous than such simple thinking allows.

America's problem is that our leaders believe the world is flat when it really is round. The next section of this book will examine what the United States can do to ensure its future sovereignty, security, and prosperity in this second age of globalization.

III

Looking Forward

Seven

SOVEREIGNTY

A central purpose of U.S. policy since the American Revolution has been to ensure that the United States remains a politically independent, self-governing sovereign state. Yet in the cause of globalism, the last three presidents and Congresses have knowingly entered into international trade agreements that have seriously eroded that independence. The World Trade Organization (WTO) administers the most economically significant of these pacts.

The WTO, which was created in 1995 and whose staff is located in Geneva, Switzerland, has 151 member countries. It provides a forum for governments to negotiate trade agreements that provide the legal rules for global commerce. It is also a place where nations can settle trade disputes with each other.

One of the claimed benefits of WTO membership is that it shields governments from lobbying by their own narrow domestic interest groups— that is, its workers, industries, and citizens. Instead, according to WTO literature, membership allows governments "to focus on trade-offs that are made in interests of everyone in the economy." By "economy," the WTO means the "world" economy. Of course, what may be best for the world may not be best for America and its people. By joining the World Trade Organization in 1994, the United States agreed:

- To ensure the conformity of U.S. laws, regulations, and administrative procedures with its obligations as provided in the WTO agreement.
- To make no reservations in respect of any provision of the agreement.

- To subject all U.S. federal, state, and local laws and practices that affect trade to international review by WTO.
- To allow any WTO member to challenge any federal, state, or local law as trade-impeding.
- That all interpretations of WTO provisions require a three-quarters majority vote and the rejection of a WTO judicial decision on a trade dispute requires a consensus vote by all members of the WTO, including the affected party nations.
- To take all trade disputes with other nations to the WTO for resolution.
- To give the WTO judicial process final jurisdiction over all trade disputes.
- That the proceedings of WTO judicial panels will be kept secret. All documents used shall remain secret. Opinions in the final report shall be secret. Votes of panelists shall be secret. No appeal procedure exists outside the WTO.
- That the WTO is empowered to enforce its ruling by imposing fines on the United States until the nation complies, deny national trading rights and authorize cross retaliation on any U.S. export, thereby allowing fines to be collected from any industry, even those not involved in the trade dispute.
- That all trade policies and practices of the United States are subject to international review by the WTO.
- That when the European Communities exercise their right to vote, they will have a number of votes equal to their number of member states.
- That the United States will have only one vote in WTO proceedings.

Because the U.S. proponents of WTO membership feared that they could not gain the two-thirds majority of votes in the Senate that the Constitution requires for ratification of a treaty, the United States joined the WTO by Executive Agreement, which required a simple majority vote in each house of Congress. As an Executive Agreement, however, the authorizing legislation provides the president authority to withdraw from membership by notifying the WTO by letter. Six months later, U.S. membership would end. The president is mandated neither to consult with other nations nor to secure approval from Congress for such a drastic step. In this, Congress granted the president a powerful negotiating tool.

Fortunately, U.S. history provides a model of how to deal with important, but dysfunctional, institutions. After Washington, Jefferson, Madison, Franklin, and others concluded that the Articles of Confederation were inadequate to the needs of the United States, they were wise enough to replace them with the Constitution. The WTO as now structured is a failing institution and requires major reform.

A principal problem is that though the WTO is the global rules-setting body and main institution for trade expansion, it is operated in an exclusionary and autocratic manner, largely by a career staff. The flawed WTO voting procedures reinforce their powers. Votes by members, for instance, carry equal weight, although participating nations may be unequally affected by WTO decisions. The vote of the tiny nation of Antigua (population 69,000), for instance, carries the same weight at the WTO as that of China (1.3 billion) or the United States (301 million). In itself, this would be insignificant were it not for the fact that WTO practice is to seek unanimity in voting, which gives the greatest power to those with the least stake. In this situation the WTO staff are the power brokers.

By joining the WTO, the United States agreed not to take unilateral, direct action against nations that violate their trade obligations to the United States or seek bilateral solutions. Instead the United States agreed to take such disputes to the WTO for resolution. This process has proven far from satisfactory. The judges in these cases are chosen by the WTO and may come from any member nation. They may be current or former trade officials or experts, and they serve on an ad hoc basis. Many are lawyers, academics, and former officials who were the principal champions of U.S. membership in the WTO. Altogether, this pool of panelists is a global club of open-market advocates. While their decisions can be of enormous consequence, the panelists are also not thoroughly examined for conflicts of interest, as are U.S. judges. In a world of high-stakes trade issues and massive corruption, such trust is naive and dangerous to U.S. interests.

Unlike in U.S. judicial proceedings, the WTO dispute settlement panels operate in total secrecy. Detailed complaints from other nations cannot be revealed to the public, affected U.S. industries and unions cannot attend deliberations, panel votes are kept anonymous, amicus briefs are classified, and the rationales for decisions are kept confidential. Dispute decisions are final, and the only appeal is to another WTO panel.

Since the founding of the WTO, the United States has been named a defendant in far more cases than any other nation. Worse, it has lost an overwhelming majority of them. In August 2007, former Deputy U.S. Trade

Representative Robert Lighthizer testified before the House Ways and Means Trade Subcommittee that the WTO had ruled against the United States in forty of forty-seven cases in which it was a defendant, which is highly significant because most of these losses have forced the United States to change its laws and administrative rules. Lighthizer told Congress, "Clearly, one of the biggest threats to our trade laws is from the dispute settlement system at the WTO. The system is fundamentally flawed, and the decisions being issued by the WTO are gutting our [fair] trade laws."

One ruling prohibited the United States from distributing the fines collected on imported goods dumped into the U.S. market back to the companies and workers victimized by such predatory trade practices. Another ruling penalized America for prohibiting Internet gambling. Yet another ruling required the United States to weaken its environmental rules to allow the import of polluting fuels from Venezuela.

Foreign governments that flagrantly disobey existing global trade rules are using the WTO to eliminate fair trade disciplines on dumping and subsidies and by extension forcing the United States to change its domestic laws to comply with WTO decisions. Repeatedly, according to Lighthizer, WTO judges have "exceeded their mandate by inventing new legal obligations that were never agreed to by the United States . . . allowing our trading partners to achieve through litigation what they could never achieve through negotiation." WTO panels and the Appellate Body are "creating new WTO obligations out of whole cloth." By this, foreign governments and global corporations have a backdoor means to change U.S. laws in secret proceedings and then impose fines on this nation if these decisions are not obeyed.

Among the least discussed and understood characteristics of the WTO is that member nations are obligated to accept the common industrial standards promulgated by the International Organization for Standards (IOS) and the standards for food, additives, residues, and contaminants set by the Codex Alimentarius Commission, a U.N. organization. Both the IOS and the Codex rely on private companies and associations to develop the standards they promulgate. The Codex deliberations, like the WTO's, are closed to the public. Companies and trade associations that have been unable to weaken standards through legislation and open rule-making processes in the United States can do so by working with other nations and helping set lower IOS and Codex standards, which are then imposed on the United States through the WTO.

The time is long past for the U.S. government to review its experiences at the World Trade Organization and think about changes that will be necessary for us to continue our membership. The incompleted Doha Round of negotiations and the massive U.S. trade deficit are compelling reasons to redefine the WTO's role overall and its relationship to U.S. trade policy making specifically.

At an absolute minimum, the United States should insist that the WTO voting structure be altered to reflect the stakes each individual nation has in global trade. If the United States has 22 percent of global trade, it should have 22 percent of the WTO votes. After some period, such as five or ten years, the stakes and votes should be recalculated and apportioned to ensure fairness among countries. The WTO charter provides for decisions being made by votes. While the consensus model was appropriate for GATT, the WTO's predecessor, because it was only a weak negotiating forum, the WTO is a global regulatory body empowered to impose substantial penalties. Apportioned voting would provide vigor and fairness to its decisions.

Also, the United States should insist on open procedures at the WTO, in its dispute panels, and in the work of the IOS and the Codex. Americans should have full transparency from any quasigovernmental body that can compel the United States to revoke any of its health, safety, environmental, or food standards or force the payment of financial penalties to other nations. As a simple criterion, the United States should refuse to participate in any panel or obey any decision unless the proceedings are open. C-Span at the WTO would be dull but useful.

All WTO panelists should be thoroughly screened for conflicts of interests, and sitting government officials should be barred from such positions. Lighthizer advised Congress that it should hold hearings on the WTO's judicial activism, form an expert body to advise Congress and U.S. trade negotiators on WTO dispute settlement decisions, and allow private lawyers to participate in dispute proceedings. When American trade lawyers represent foreign governments at the WTO, they can participate in all the proceedings. Yet the WTO prohibits attorneys representing U.S. companies and unions involved in these cases from even observing the proceedings or being given the documents. Only attorneys for the U.S. government can participate.

Finally, all WTO decisions that require changes of U.S. laws should require a simple majority vote of approval in both houses of the Congress through normal legislative procedures before the United States accepts them. Nothing would better focus the attention of foreign governments that are trying to change U.S. trade laws through judicial activism than an assured congressional scrutiny, which this would provide. Those governments would be constantly reminded that U.S. membership in the WTO is a political choice, not an unbreakable obligation.

The ultimate responsibility for the surrender of U.S. sovereignty to international bodies such as the WTO lies with the American people, who have allowed transnational interests to take control of the electoral processes and governance of their government.

The first step in restoring a more representative democracy is to confront the mindless secrecy that obscures the actions of the U.S. government at all levels. Secrecy is the archenemy of democracy. Obsessive official concealment has allowed a succession of presidents to make covert agreements with other countries on matters of great importance, including the trading away of hundreds of U.S. industries and millions of good-paying jobs for dubious ideological and foreign policy objectives. Official secrecy has allowed our leaders to put forth misinformation as a means of advancing unwise foreign and economic policies and to keep American citizens ignorant about their real intentions, actions, and mistakes.

The Bush-Cheney administration, for instance, has systematically reduced the amount of information available to the public concerning the government's operations. Although the Freedom of Information Act (FOIA) provides for public access to federal records, this administration has systematically curtailed such sharing. In October 2001, Attorney General John Ashcroft distributed throughout the federal government a policy memorandum stating that the Justice Department would defend agencies from challenges when they claimed FOIA exemptions. Justice and other agencies were urged to broaden the classification of what information is "sensitive," withhold basic information on matters such as economics and health, charge high fees for any data released, and establish administrative delays in the release process.

This administration also sought and gave exemptions to the Federal Advisory Committee Act, which requires openness and balance on all federal advisory boards. The most notable instance of the evasion of such openness was Vice President Cheney's Energy Task Force, whose membership was kept secret from Congress and the public.

This secrecy "fetish," as the *Los Angeles Times* describes it, is a reversal of policies introduced after the end of the Cold War by the Clinton-Gore administration. In 1995, President Clinton issued Executive Order 12958, which introduced a new procedure called "automatic declassification," under which classified information is routinely declassified after twenty-five years unless special action is taken by the administering agency to keep it secret. In the six-year period 1995–2000, the Clinton administration declassified more than 864 million pages of government documents. In the six-year period 2001–2006, the Bush administration declassified 282 million pages—two thirds less than its predecessor.

Equally significant, congressional access to federal records has been sharply limited since 2001. During the debate on Medicare in 2003, for instance, the Bush administration refused to allow federal actuaries to give Congress information that would reveal that the legislation under consideration would actually cost $100 billion more than claimed by officials from the Department of Health and Human Services. Likewise, information about the outsourcing of federal work, domestically and for defense purposes, has been routinely withheld from Congress, even when repeatedly requested.

Of great significance, and as described in chapter two, President Bush signed Executive Order 13233 (November 1, 2001), which curtailed access to presidential records by Congress or the citizenry. Under this order, such papers can be released only if the former president whose records are concerned and the current president agree, creating the possibility of a double veto. With this order the actions of the president, vice president, and dozens of senior officials can effectively be hidden forever. Moreover, the order provides that taxpayers will finance the legal defense of that censorship.

The issue is well stated in the 2006 Annual Report of the Information Security Oversight Office (ISOO), a twenty-five-person office in the National Archives and Records Administration: "We spend billions of dollars every year to classify information, much of which, as identified by the '9–11 Commission' and others, should never have been classified in the first place."

In that spirit, Congress and the next president should aggressively strip away the secrecy surrounding the operations of the government—past, existing, and future. Immediately upon assuming office, the next president should revoke President Bush's Executive Order 13233.

The Presidential Records Act of 1978 gives ownership of those records to the public. Congress should modify that act in a way that will allow the National Archives to access and release unclassified presidential papers immediately at the end of an administration and provide for a quick review of the papers that are classified. The 1978 act has multiple provisions to protect true national security documents.

The president and his advisers are doing the public's business; thus, the presumption about disclosure should be in favor of "sunshine." The principal excuse for such secrecy is that presidential aides will be reluctant to provide frank advice if it will become known. Ironically, many of those same advisers seem willing to rush their views into a book immediately upon leaving office. My view is that those who are too delicate to give frank advice to a president and have it known by the American people should remain in private life.

Our political system has also become sclerotic and undemocratic, principally because of the way we finance our elections and establish the boundaries of congressional districts. The result is undue influence on the electoral system by corporatism and elitism.

Though many solutions have been advanced to reduce the influence of special-interest money on our elections, public financing and short campaign cycles, such as six months, are the most direct solutions. Public financing would be far less expensive than the current system, which perverts national policy by putting most elected officials in a perpetual chase for campaign donations. As a consequence of Supreme Court decisions, the present system of private contributions seems incapable of being made honest without a constitutional amendment that would permit Congress to regulate political contributions. Worse, a majority in Congress oppose campaign finance reforms and have repeatedly sabotaged even the best-intentioned changes.

Members of the Federal Election Commission (FEC), whose commissioners are equally divided between the Republican and Democratic parties, are appointed with the explicit expectation that they will protect their parties' interests. Seemingly, the only offense perceived by that body is when third parties, independents, and good-government organizations become involved in national elections.

Fortunately, other steps can be taken to make our national government more responsive. Regardless of how the United States finances its presidential and congressional campaigns, an important technical question concerns the corrupt manner by which we delineate boundaries for the election of members to the House of Representatives. Admittedly, this may seem dull and perhaps irrelevant. It is not. How we draw congressional districts is a defining political matter that greatly determines whether we can have a competitive democracy and who will represent us in Congress.

Under existing law, each state can redraw its congressional district boundary lines whenever it wishes, though almost all states wait until after the Census every ten years. In practice, congressional boundary lines are most often drawn in a way that looks like the outline of a python digesting some large animal—a narrow line on a map will sometimes run down a highway or railroad for miles and then suddenly balloon to include a large area, then become a line again and move on to some other population area and balloon again. Districts are drawn to favor or disenfranchise ethnic groups, religious groups, political partisans, or other interests and to minimize the chance that incumbents will be defeated. This gerrymandering has produced a House of Representatives whose members are seldom challenged in political races. It is a major reason we have an unrepresentative democracy.

In 2004, a California-based political activist named Jim Mangia helped mount initiatives in California and Ohio to make the drawing of congressional and state legislative districts fair. He proposed that an independent commission be appointed in each state every ten years to draw boundaries that would then require approval by the governor and two thirds of the state legislature. The lines would be drawn in a way that would make the races more competitive, thereby encouraging elected representatives to pay more attention to their constituents.

Washington political interests, with close ties to the existing incumbents, made the defeat of the California and Ohio state initiatives a top priority, and they carried out massive negative campaigns that set back the measures in both states. Fair districting is a basic issue that, like suffrage and civil rights, may take decades to achieve. But also like suffrage and civil rights, the benefits are worth the time and effort.

Iowa is an example of what is possible. In 2001, the legislature adopted a new state legislative and congressional redistricting plan. The state assigned the nonpartisan Legislative Services Bureau the task of developing three redistricting plans for consideration by the legislature. Each plan was criteria-driven, with factors that were clear and measurable: (1) population equality, (2) contiguity, (3) unity of counties and cities (maintaining county and city boundaries), and (4) compactness. After due consideration, the legislature selected a plan, and, unlike the rest of America, Iowa now does not have irregularly shaped congressional districts that look like pythons in action.

· · ·

Voters cannot control their government if they do not vote and if their votes do not count when they do. The League of Women Voters, most major newspapers, and many civic groups have made recommendations for improvements in our voting processes. The 2004 *New York Times* forty-nine-part series "Making Votes Count" by Adam Cohen summarizes the best of these ideas.

A starting point would be for our national leaders to accept responsibility for devising and imposing uniform standards for presidential elections. The presidency and vice presidency are national offices, and the rules and practices for voting should be the same for every American regardless of where he or she lives. Such standards, set high, are likely to be adopted by the states and cities for most other elections as well. *The New York Times'* editorial recommendations are, in brief:

1. A holiday for voting. This would highlight the significance of voting and encourage a higher turnout.
2. Early voting. People should be allowed to go to a few places and cast their ballots in advance of election day.
3. Electronic voting machines with paper records and encouragement of shorter lines at polling places by allocating machines/polling places on a per capita basis.
4. Impartial election administrators.
5. Uniform and inclusive voter registration standards.
6. Accurate and transparent voting poll purges.
7. Uniform and voter-friendly standards for counting provisional ballots.
8. Upgraded voting machines, improved ballot designs, and paper records.
9. Fair and uniform voter ID rules.
10. Penalization of vote suppression.
11. Rescission of laws barring former felons from voting. They have paid their debt to society.
12. Streamlined absentee ballot procedures, including by Internet access, in a timely manner.

What is discouraging about these recommendations is that, though they are eminently practical, most are still not national law. Congress and the president seem to have forgotten the counting debacle associated with the 2000 election. The 2000 recount was a national humiliation; that U.S.

electoral mechanics have not been fixed in time for the 2008 elections is a political scandal of historic proportions. Americans cannot control their government if antivote schemes and incompetence are able to deny them a vote. Repairing the election mechanics of our democracy is a task that the next president and Congress should put at the top of their "100 days" agenda.

The low ethical standards our public officials impose on themselves have created a quagmire in which national interests are often bartered away for cash and other unprincipled considerations. The deepening involvement of the United States in the global economy creates numerous opportunities, large and small, for corruption, which is undermining our national sovereignty.

To that end, two basic actions seem timely. The first involves ethical standards for the president, vice president, and the officials appointed by them. Congress should put into law Executive Order 12834: "Ethics Commitments by Executive Branch Appointees," which President Clinton instituted when he entered office in 1993 and revoked when he left in 2001. This law requires all senior appointees in every executive agency of the U.S. government to sign a contract binding them for five years after the termination of their employment as a public official not to lobby any officer or employee of their agency or engage in any activity on behalf of any foreign government or foreign political party. This contract could also be strengthened to preclude providing postemployment lobbying advice to other clients and lobbying members of Congress on issues pertaining to their former employment.

In recent years, many former appointed or elected officials have become highly paid consultants to transnational corporations and foreign governments. As part of any ethics reform, senior officials such as former cabinet officers, national security advisors, and CIA and NSA directors should be required to file income and employment statements annually for five years after leaving office. Former presidents ought to make such disclosures for their lifetimes. The idea that ex-officials and ex-presidents are being paid millions of dollars by foreign governments and corporations is troubling in that it creates a possibility that the compensation could be viewed as delayed payment for some prior action or favor. Sunshine—open disclosure—remains the best "disinfectant" for such transactions.

Congress needs to impose upon itself the same open ethical standards it applies to the executive branch. Today, congressional self-regulation is a political joke.

An independent ethics body is also required to administer whatever standards Congress chooses to impose on its members. To be effective, such an authority must be able to receive complaints from the public as well as any other source it deems reliable, unlike the present situation, where only a member of Congress can bring a complaint against another member. Such a body requires the capacity to subpoena information and to take testimony under oath. The cat-and-mouse game that Congress plays on ethics is one of the main reasons its members are held in such low esteem by more than 80 percent of voters.

Global trade constitutes slightly more than one third of the U.S. GNP, and, though trade matters affect the daily lives of most Americans, most stakeholders are excluded when Washington sets its trade policies. The fact that the United States joined the WTO on terms that mock our most basic democratic principles reflects how far removed U.S. policy making on trade is from the citizenry.

In 2001, Bruce Stokes, a fellow at the Council on Foreign Relations, and I organized a study group of trade and congressional experts, drawn from all ideological spectrums, to identify how Congress could democratize U.S. trade policy making. We commissioned several papers from trade scholars, organized a series of conferences around the United States, and ultimately produced a report, *Democratizing U.S. Trade Policy.*

We concluded that the free-trade consensus that had undergirded U.S. trade policy making from the early 1930s onward was shattered and that the processes were gridlocked. We were correct about the consensus but premature in our conclusion about political obstruction.

President Bush used his Republican majority in Congress to get negotiating authority for a new round of trade talks at the WTO and several NAFTA-type regional trade pacts around the world. In November 2001, trade ministers from 142 WTO countries met in Doha, the capital of Qatar, and initiated a new round of negotiations on trade remedies, market access, and developing-country issues. As of mid-2008, the Doha Round negotiations were incomplete.

The last U.S. regional pact, the Central American Free Trade Agreement (CAFTA), passed by only one vote in 2006. In 2007, the Democrat-controlled House of Representatives refused to extend the president's authority to negotiate any more such deals. Thus, the nation is back to where it was in 2001 and the stalemate is even tighter.

Gridlock in global trade is a dangerous business. It polarizes positions at the extreme. Imagine a scenario in which global financial markets experience major setbacks, the value of the dollar slides, the United States is unable to finance its massive imports, and double-digit unemployment, similar to that of the early 1980s, puts seemingly irresistible political pressure on Congress to impose immediate protectionist measures such as currency exchange penalties and high tariffs on imports. The result would be the end of the second generation of globalization with unimaginable consequences, mostly undesired.

The principal impediment to breaking the current trade impasse is the way U.S. trade policy is made. The process is an artifact of an earlier time when trade consisted largely of the movement of goods and its regulation was exercised by Congress raising or lowering tariffs. Today's exclusionary policy-making procedures are not an accident of history; those in control are able to advance their interests, which they might not be able to do if open, democratic procedures were used.

As I described in *Agents of Influence* (1990), the old way often resulted in secret side deals never revealed to Congress. Of equal significance, the old way is unable to adequately consider the effects of trade on related matters such as environmental policy, the safety of imported medicines and foods, intellectual property rights, communications, immigration, water rights, technology standards, and foreign labor standards, among others.

The incompletion of the WTO Doha Round of trade negotiations and the elevenfold increase in the U.S. net trade deficit between 1993 and 2007 (from $70 million to $740 billion) strongly suggest that the policies, made in the old way, are creating undesirable outcomes and thus require change.

The institutional responsibility for any such structural and policy reform lies with Congress, which, under Article I, Section 8, of the Constitution, has the power "To regulate Commerce with foreign Nations, and among the several States, and with the Indian Tribes." For almost two hundred years, the work of Congress was divided among a few committees, in which the power of the chairmen was absolute. Robert Caro, in *The Path to Power*, the opening volume of his biography of Lyndon Johnson, recounts how Representative Carl Vinson, the longtime chairman of the powerful Naval Affairs Committee, restricted the right of committee members to ask questions: "In his first year on the committee, a member was allowed to ask one question, in his second year, two, and so on."

After the Watergate scandal in 1974, a coalition of newly elected members joined congressional reformers to make two landmark changes in the way that the House of Representatives is governed. First, seniority is no longer the sole means of determining leadership. Second, committee chairs must share their power with semi-independent subcommittees.

The 1974 reforms divided power in Congress among 8 select and special committees, 38 full committees, and 242 subcommittees. This division of authority makes trade decision-making correspondingly complicated and difficult, since most major congressional committees have authority over some issue involved with global trade.

Also absent in the closed and splintered structure and politics of trade decision-making is a way for all the various stakeholders in Congress to participate. Bruce Stokes and I recommended, and our study group endorsed the idea, that both the House and Senate form a Joint Trade Committee (JTC) to serve as "a neutral, advisory, oversight forum, involving the chair or sub-committee chairs of all Congressional committees with a trade interest."

This committee's role would be advisory, like that of the Joint Economic Committee and the Joint Committee on Taxation. We recommended that the JTC analyze whether trade pacts meet mandated objectives, assist in oversight, and analyze foreign compliance. The committee would provide Congress with additional expertise on matters now involved with trade such as environmental protection, intellectual property agreements, and safety of food imports and a place to reconcile differences in new negotiations. Hopefully, the JTC would help Congress avoid internecine disputes on trade matters, much as the Joint Committee on Taxation has done on tax issues.

We also recommended that Congress establish a Congressional Trade Office, much as it created a Congressional Budget Office (CBO) in the mid-1970s. As with the CBO, its purpose would be to provide Congress with independent data, plus expert, nonpartisan analysis of trade policy options. It could review the work of all trade advisory groups, calculate the effects of WTO decisions, and solicit and summarize public comments on proposed agreements. We also recommended that if Congress ever again gives the president fast-track authority to negotiate trade deals, it ought to require a 60 percent majority for approval. The presumption of a strong fight in Congress would give U.S. trade negotiators bargaining leverage they need.

Eight

SECURITY

The United States spends more on national security than all other nations combined. Its approach to globalization, however, massively undermines the very security that money supposedly buys.

The United States, for instance, allows other governments to buy key American defense suppliers. In 1995, Washington permitted the Chinese government to purchase a subsidiary of General Motors that produces special magnets used in precision-guided munitions. China's government-owned company now holds the Department of Defense contract to make the high-tech motors used in U.S. precision-guided smart bombs.

The GM subsidiary was the last U.S.-based producer of such technology. Once the Chinese completed the purchase, they closed the plant and moved its machines, technology, and production to Tianjin, China, where its magnets will also be used to improve China's smart bombs and long-range cruise missiles. Earlier, the Beijing government acquired the other two U.S. manufacturers of such magnets and also moved their technology to China. By these maneuvers, China obtained an exotic technology it lacked, and the United States now depends on China for a key component it needs for weapons systems.

Outsourcing the U.S. defense industrial base is so far along that the United States no longer has an assured capacity to manufacture enough ammunition for its forces. The Surge Roundtable, a group of ammunition producers, reported in December 2006 that of 302 items critical to ammunition production, the defense industrial base had deteriorated to the point that 71 had only one supplier. It also reported that 10 percent of U.S. ammunition components now come from thirteen different countries. No U.S. sources exist for those vital items.

Surprisingly, the Department of Defense does not know the extent of its supply vulnerability because it does not collect all the data. The Government Accountability Office (GAO) reported in January 2006 that, for data collection purposes, DOD defines a foreign contractor as a company that is not incorporated in the United States. DOD does not consider purchases from a company incorporated in the United States but owned by a foreign parent as "foreign."

DOD foreign subcontractor data also do not identify subcontracts beyond the second supplier tier, subcontracts worth less than $500,000, subcontracts in which less than $100,000 of work is done abroad, or subcontracts whose place of performance is abroad. The GAO also found that most of the top 100 defense contractors are not complying with requirements to report the details of their foreign subcontracts.

The Pentagon is not aware of the sources of thousands of components in the weapons it buys. Thus, it cannot guarantee the armed forces have an assured supply of parts or weapons needed for national defense. As President Dwight Eisenhower feared and warned against in his farewell address to the nation in 1961, the "military-industrial complex," what I term corporatism, has put their profits over the interests of national security. In other eras, this would have been viewed as criminal malfeasance.

Little discussed, but also eminently dangerous, America is increasingly vulnerable to "cyberwar," a tactic the United States used in the 1991 Iraqi conflict. In the 1980s, the United States supplied the Iraqi government with the computers, equipment, and software used in its military command and control systems. Unknown to the Iraqi leaders—and undetectable had they known—the United States had embedded "Trojan horse" viruses in that equipment. When the U.S. attack on Iraq began, American military hackers triggered the viruses and Iraqi military computers shut down permanently. Iraqi military chaos ensued.

China's People's Liberation Army has developed an extensive cyberwar capacity, which it constantly improves and tests. Chinese government hackers have repeatedly penetrated the computers of U.S. corporations, banks, regional power grids, telephone companies, federal agencies, and even the Pentagon. Yet the federal government, including the State and Defense Departments, buys computers from companies that rely heavily on Chinese and other foreign-made components susceptible to such rigging.

The U.S. government, moreover, does not routinely inspect such computers and software for "Trojan horse" viruses, which can be triggered by telephone, Internet, or remote control. In 2005, the State Department purchased from a Chinese-owned company 16,000 computers, all of which were potentially vulnerable to virus implants. The department eventually agreed not to use the computers in secure functions and to cut its order to 15,000, but only after a strong protest from Michael Wessel and other members of the United States–China Economic and Security Review Commission and Representative Frank Wolf (R-Va.), a powerful member of the House Appropriations Committee.

The unfettered, unexamined global integration of vital U.S. communication and computer networks, coupled with lax and ineffective security, gives a hostile foreign power or terrorist group the ability to shut down major parts of the U.S. economic and defense base almost at will, creating a fundamental threat to economic and military security.

As described in chapter one, another security threat stems from America's growing dependence on foreign-based producers for a large portion of the advanced technology products (ATPs) the nation requires—the newest, best, most sophisticated technologies and innovations essential to greater economic productivity and an assured national defense. For decades, domestic-based U.S. manufacturers dominated world production in opto-electronics, information and communications systems, advanced materials, life sciences, flexible manufacturing equipment, and other high-tech fields. By 2007, that dominance was lost. Instead, America imported more than $369 billion of such products, a serious dependency in this high-tech age. This shift is significant because the Defense Department encourages the development and use of dual technologies; that is, military technologies that can also be used in commercial products.

The primary source of these vital goods is China and the surrounding countries within the Chinese sphere of military and political influence. Of the $369 billion of ATP goods the United States imported in 2007, almost 52 percent came from that region. This production is now the only source of many vital advanced technology products. U.S. trade data provide a very detailed view of our growing industrial dependence in a widening field of economic sectors. The figures below are calculated from trade statistics compiled by the Department of Commerce. This vast body of data can be organized in ways that give a detailed, month-by-month, product-by-product, industry-by-industry view of the United States' position in global markets.

A deeper look into this trade data reveals that the United States is running trade deficits not only in high-tech industries, such as scientific instruments and airplanes, but in a majority of all industries. Of 1,344 separate major industries tracked by the Commerce Department at a four-digit code level, almost two thirds (851) had a trade deficit, for a total of $766 billion in 2005. This means that in these industries, producers were facing massive foreign competition within their own domestic market, a danger sign about their failing competitiveness globally.

U.S. industries with a positive trade balance are mainly commodities such as cotton, soybeans, corn, scrap paper, rice, coal, tobacco, hides, meat, and wheat.

The profile of the U.S. trade position today is that of a nation being economically colonized—one that is purchasing high-value-added commodities and manufactured goods from abroad and paying for them with the export of agricultural commodities, massive foreign borrowing, and the liquidation of its own national assets.

Although many advocates of unfettered globalization argue that trade in services—such as architecture, software, engineering, research and development, and finance—will provide a substitute for America's loss of its manufacturing industries, Commerce Department trade data refute that hope. Eighty percent of the U.S. workforce is employed in service work, but trade in services in 2007 produced a net surplus of only $104 billion, up from $40 billion in 2000, offsetting barely 12 percent of the overall $815 billion deficit in goods.

Alan Tonelson, at the U.S. Business & Industrial Council Educational Foundation, an association that represents small and medium-sized companies, reports that foreign import penetration is between 50 and 90 percent for 114 individual industries vital to the overall economy, including aircraft engines and parts, industrial valves, printed circuits, optical instruments, telephone switching equipment, broadcasting equipment, computers, tires, industrial controls, motor vehicle steering and suspension systems, X-ray equipment, semiconductor production equipment, and environmental controls.

Tonelson notes that such massive import penetration contradicts the argument that a strong dollar is the principal trade-related problem faced by U.S.-based manufacturers. The vast majority of U.S. industries lost market share both when the dollar was rising (1997–2002) and then when it was falling (2002–2004), indicating that other factors were in play. He also maintains that the issue of rising import penetration rates is not mainly cyclical in nature. U.S. industry lost position both when the economy was growing stronger and when it was becoming weaker. The changes under way, he concludes, are structural; that is, the very foundation of the economy is shifting, and in ways that are undesirable.

As Barry Lynn, a former executive editor of *Global Business* magazine, documented in *Harper's* (June 2006) and in his book *The End of the Line*, most of the corporations that supply U.S. manufacturing needs are increasingly shells whose headquarters staffs coordinate a flow of components from tens of thousands of independent suppliers located around the globe. The result of this business disintegration is an expanding vulnerability of supply equal to or greater than what Britain, Germany, and the United States faced in World War I, at the end of the first era of globalization.

As Lynn wrote, the hollowing U.S. industrial base undermines companies that retain their factories here, making them dependent on networks that stretch around the world and creating an unprecedented peacetime vulnerability to interrupted supplies. A Dell computer assembled in Texas, for instance, is composed of 4,500 parts produced by hundreds of suppliers, most of which are clustered in China and surrounding countries. Dell maintains a four-day parts supply. If that supply line is interrupted for five days, the company must close its assembly lines. The Dell example, moreover, is neither unique nor extreme.

As the United States loses its manufacturing base, it is also giving up related R&D activities and capacity to innovate. Case studies of innovation have repeatedly documented that the process is one of incremental losses. Japanese manufacturers, striving for constant improvement, have production workers directly involved in identifying innovations that can be implemented. Already, IBM, General Electric, Microsoft, Cisco Systems, and General Motors have shifted parts of their R&D activities to be close to the foreign locations where they do their manufacturing. The idea that the United States can remain a place where R&D and design are done, leaving to contractors in other countries the work of manufacturing, is simplistic and has limited application.

Equally disturbing, the outsourcing of jobs and work that has drawn so much attention for the past decade is probably only a foretaste of what lies ahead if present policies on globalization are continued. Alan S. Blinder, a Princeton University economist and former vice chairman of the Federal Reserve System, wrote in the March–April 2006 edition of *Foreign Affairs* that this offshoring of work will likely cost the remaining 14 million U.S. manufacturing jobs and up to three times that number in the service sectors.

As a result of this decline in manufacturing, the United States is increasingly unable to shift production from consumer goods to military goods in a time of emergency because neither the consumer nor the military goods are being made here. Year by year, there are fewer factories to convert and workers to staff them, as was possible in World War II, and what factories remain are capable of supplying only part of any potential military and civilian demand.

Current law requires the secretary of defense to submit an annual report to the defense committees in both the House and Senate. Section 2504 of Title 10, United States Code, provides all that the law needs to require the DOD to disseminate information about the state of the nation's defense industrial base. The George W. Bush administration has not been forthcoming with this information. In part, this lack of forthrightness can be traced to ideological opposition to "Buy America" laws by DOD and the Bush administration, and to politically active defense contractors who hold down costs by purchasing lower-cost components from overseas markets. Regardless of such ideological stances and corporate pricing strategies, a secure defense policy requires, at a minimum, reliable information on the sources of supply. To put this recommendation into some perspective again, Wal-Mart tracks every item of merchandise, on every shelf of every store everywhere in the world, on a real-time basis. Such basic information allows that corporation to control its inventory, manage its expenditures better, and save money. The technology and expertise exist to perform the same for the DOD.

Food-borne diseases cause 76 million illnesses, 325,000 hospitalizations, and 5,200 deaths in the United States each year, according to the Centers for Disease Control and Prevention. Despite this toll on the American people, food and medicine security in the United States is deteriorating rapidly, in large part because the federal government is underfunding the import inspection functions of the Food and Drug Administration (FDA) and the Department of Agriculture.

As earlier chapters document, the FDA also lacks the resources to inspect the thousands of foreign factories that supply the bulk ingredients for most of our medicines. The lack of U.S. food and medicine security reflects the ideological, Milton Friedman–like "let the buyer beware" attitude held by the Bush administration. What this ignores is that consumers do not possess the information they require to make safe, rational decisions about their purchases, largely because food producers have actively withheld such knowledge and their government refuses to collect and publish such information.

Congress should mandate the implementation of country-of-origin labeling (COOL) for all meats, fruits, vegetables, and related products, including all ingredients. Products for pets and other animals should also be covered. If countries such as China do not establish effective food and medicine safety regulations, many American consumers will not buy any product for personal or pet consumption that has any ingredient from that country. But before we can be aware, we need information.

Congress should also provide sufficient resources for the FDA and USDA to hire more talent and regularly inspect all foreign factories and processing plants that supply Americans with foods and should impose an inspection fee on imported foods and medicines sufficient to cover all such inspection costs fully.

Consumers Union (CU) has identified a number of other practical steps that Congress and the next administration can take. The first and most obvious is to hold accountable the importers, distributors, retailers, and manufacturers that by intention or lack of due diligence bring poisoned or dangerous goods into our market. Meaningful penalties would encourage preshipment testing and quality controls during production.

CU also calls for the creation of voluntary safety standards for imported products, such as those used by the Underwriters Laboratory for most electronics sold in the United States. Though voluntary standards may be sufficient for electronics, they should be mandatory for imported medicines and foods; that is, items that will be consumed by humans and animals.

Along with safety standards, the United States should require a certificate of authenticity and safety for all imports from importers, manufacturers, or foreign governments. A safety bond should accompany the certificate in case the product turns out to be dangerous. Bonding firms are skilled at inspection and are reluctant to stand behind companies that provide substandard products.

If a producer or country continues to send poisoned or defective goods into the U.S. market, its exports should be put on a list that mandates the inspection of all of its goods before they can enter the United States. If any of these producers or nations retaliates against such action, which is legitimate and congruent with WTO treaty obligations, the United States should immediately file a formal complaint at the WTO seeking full monetary damages. If this fails, the United States can reassess its WTO membership and once again rely on bilateral approaches.

Consumers Union recommends that the federal agencies responsible for the safety of imported goods should publicly disclose their findings and as quickly as possible. If my friend, mentioned in the introduction, had not immediately called me about the pet food recall, I might not have known for weeks, if at all. Ideally, Congress should require that this information be collected and posted on a federal Internet site in a timely manner.

The United States needs the capacity to trace unsafe products and components back to their sources with speed and accuracy. Then remedial actions can be taken. The Chinese reluctance to share information and identify the culprits in the pet food scandal resulted in needless deaths. We are truly lucky that it wasn't canned human food that was poisoned.

In sum, the next president and Congress must make abundantly clear to all U.S. trading partners that open trade is not an invitation to export unsafe foods, medicines, and other products into the United States.

U.S. immigration policies and practices now undermine security in two important ways. If denied a visa, a terrorist can simply go to Canada or Mexico and walk or ride across the border, which is only marginally defended. If for no reason other than keeping terrorists from entering the United States and attacking with relative ease, U.S. borders need to be secure, which they are not.

The other security threat comes from the illegal influx of millions of poor and unskilled foreign workers and their families. Even economists who are "intuitively, emotionally pro-immigration," such as Paul Krugman, conclude that the net benefits to the United States from the immigration of the poor and unskilled are tiny. These immigrants, Krugman writes, "have much less education than the average American worker and are driving down the wages of the worst-paid Americans."

The numbers of illegal immigrants attempting to enter the United States each year are staggering. Since the beginning of this decade, the Border Patrol has stopped more than 1 million people annually trying to cross without visas. An estimated 500,000 others managed to slip into the country. Altogether, an estimated 13 million people are in the United States illegally as of 2008.

These people are exploited by tens of thousands of U.S. employers.

Their pay is low. Their working conditions are substandard and often illegal. Their benefits are virtually nonexistent. Though such employment is unlawful and the Department of Labor has full authority to deal with exploitive, scofflaw employers, it has not. In 2004, the Department of Homeland Security cited only three employers for possible violations. The message is clear: exploiting illegal immigrants is acceptable to the government of the United States. The effect is also clear to people in other countries: if you can get into the United States, you can find a job if you are willing to work for less than American workers, and the government will look the other way.

Consequently, we are creating a massive new underclass, building new social tensions, and institutionalizing downward economic pressures that hold back poor Americans. But worst of all, our refusal to control our borders provides terrorists unlimited opportunities to enter our country and harm us.

Robert J. Samuelson, an op-ed columnist at *The Washington Post*, has argued that the United States should build a fence along the entire 1,989-mile border with Mexico because, he says, a genuine fence would probably work. He cites the 10 miles of up-to-fifteen-feet-high steel-and-concrete barriers in San Diego, which have reduced illegal crossings by a reported 95 percent. If we don't care that our immigration system is not working, he writes, "we should say so and open our borders to anyone but criminals and terrorists."

The failure of President Bush and the bipartisan group of Senate and House members to enact immigration legislation in 2007 means that an effective law may be years away. House Democratic Caucus Chairman Rahm Emanuel (D-Ill.) told Latino activists in July 2007 that a Democratic House, Democratic Senate, and Democratic president would not take up the immigration issue until the second term of a Democratic president, meaning 2013 at the earliest. Without any changes in U.S. policies and practices, the United States will have at least an additional 5 million illegal immigrants by then. Clearly, presidential leadership on this issue is required in 2009, as opposed to 2013.

A productive starting point for examining, and then changing, immigration policy is the work in the mid-1990s by the Commission on Immigration Reform, chaired by the late Barbara Jordan, a former congresswoman from Texas. The Jordan Commission, as it was known, gave special attention to the question of illegal immigration. The commission was composed of nine members: the chairperson, four Democrats, and four Republicans. Their recommendations were made unanimously and outlined a comprehensive approach divided into eight parts.

First, the commission set forth the principle that we are a nation of immigrants committed to the rule of law. It is necessary, therefore, to make distinctions between those who obey the law and those who violate it. The members concluded that attempts to control illegal immigration are not inherently anti-immigration, because unlawful entry is unacceptable.

Second, the commission acknowledged that half of all illegal immigrants in the United States come to get jobs. They believed that sanctions on employers for hiring illegal immigrants could be successful, but only with a reliable system of verifying the authorization to work.

Third, the commission urged Congress to make eligibility for public benefits consistent with immigration policy. It recommended against eligibility for illegal immigrants, except in extraordinary circumstances. Jordan also argued that it is in the national interest for immigrants to become citizens so they can be fully participating, voting members of our polity.

Fourth, the commission adopted as a principle that "those who should get in, get in; those who should be kept out, are kept out; and those who should not be here will be required to leave." Deportation is critical to a sound policy, Jordan testified.

Fifth, immigration emergencies happen, as with past events involving Haiti and Cuba and now with Iraqi immigrants, and the United States should have in place procedures on how to respond.

Sixth, policy makers require reliable data, including analysis of the economic and social consequences of illegal immigration.

Seventh, the United States should seek help from the other nations, particularly Mexico, whose people are illegally coming here in vast numbers.

Eighth and finally, the commission urged better border management that would stop illegal crossings and facilitate legal ones.

At the close of her February 1995 testimony before her former colleagues on the House Judiciary Committee, Jordan noted, "Immigration is far too important to who we are as a nation to become a wedge issue in presidential politics. I, for one, wish that we would do away with all the hyphenation and just be Americans, together."

One hopes that the collapse of immigration legislation in 2007 will become a political turning point on this issue and that the next president and Congress will dust off the Jordan report and reexamine its very wise recommendations to the nation.

Securing the U.S. border is essential whether such reforms come in 2009 or 2013. But, as Samuelson further wrote in *The Washington Post*, "I do not like advocating a fence. It looks and feels bad. It's easily stigmatized as racist. It would antagonize Mexico. The imagery is appalling, but it beats the alternative: a growing underclass and social tensions. Moreover, a genuine fence would probably work."

Perhaps a fence is necessary. But a fence and guards, in themselves, are insufficient in the short term and undesirable in the long term. More directly, employers who violate U.S. labor laws need to be identified and fined heavily for breaking statutes and exploiting workers.

The best antidote to massive illegal immigration, however, would be for the United States to help create millions of good-paying jobs in Mexico and the rest of Latin America, the primary sources of illegal immigration. Most people would prefer to remain at home if they could make a decent living. For that, a trade policy is required that would create the special relationship with Mexico that was promised by NAFTA but not instituted. As I will discuss in the next chapter, the time has come for the United States, Mexico, and Canada to renegotiate NAFTA.

Nine

PROSPERITY

The United States has a strong economy despite the many foolish mistakes our leaders have made over the past three decades. Equally important, the nation is fully able to correct those errors in a timely manner. The appropriate emotion is anger about such poor public stewardship, not despair.

The first step in restoring prudence and balance to America's economic affairs is to recognize that our present fiscal and trade policies are unsustainable and undesirable in the long run. At some point, other nations will stop selling the United States goods on credit. Even the most fanatic "no-new-taxes" advocates must surely be appalled that the value of the dollar against the euro declined by more than half between 2001 and 2008. An American who could buy $10,000 worth of European goods in 2001 can buy only $4,900 of foreign goods today. Without changes in U.S. fiscal and trade policies, the value of the dollar and its buying power will sink further.

Remember David Stockman? Remember the "supply-side" magic that as director of the Office of Management and Budget (OMB) he persuaded President Ronald Reagan to adopt? His actions are a useful lesson for those who would be president.

In a now-famous interview with the political writer William Grieder, "The Education of David Stockman," the little-known thirty-four-year-old former Republican congressman from Wisconsin acknowledged that when he ran the numbers of his "supply-side" plan through the computers at the OMB in 1981, they projected that the federal deficit would be $82 billion in 1982 and $116 billion in 1984, both unacceptable figures at the time.

Rather than adjust his ideology and plan, Stockman reprogrammed the OMB computer to get the results he needed to persuade Reagan and Congress to accept his proposed budget.

Stockman observed in the interview that had he been in the private sector and played so fast and loose with a corporate budget, he would have been indicted for fraud. It turned out that even the original OMB computer-generated numbers underestimated by 50 percent the fiscal consequences of Stockman's "supply-side" magic bullet: the federal budget deficit in 1982 was $128 billion, and in 1984 it soared to $185 billion—record amounts that continued to grow and grow, year after year.

The Stockman lesson is simple: No magic bullets, please. Hopefully, we will avoid such simple, single, or untested ideological solutions to our economic problems.

Ideally, the next president will have some of the political skills that Franklin D. Roosevelt exhibited throughout his administration. FDR realized that to overcome the Great Depression and later to defeat the Axis powers, the people of the United States needed to be as united as possible. Thus, he appointed to his cabinet talented and independently minded people from both major political parties. During World War II, FDR's secretary of war was Colonel Henry Stimson, who served every Republican president from Theodore Roosevelt to Herbert Hoover. His secretary of the Navy was Frank Knox, a "Rough Rider" in the Spanish-American War and the GOP vice presidential candidate in the 1936 election. After the 1940 election, Wendell Willkie, the Republican candidate for president, became FDR's personal representative to other nations.

Because of the cynicism that now pervades Washington and the wide acceptance of corrupt practices, a small, high-level corps of "untouchables" is needed to staff and administer the federal government's major programs. The one commitment each individual in this group should be asked for is that he or she not profit in any way from service to the nation—royalties from later books or fees from speeches would be donated to charity, no insider consultant deals or directorships would be accepted, no lobbying or advising of corporations or foreign governments would be undertaken. In sum, no cashing in, as General George C. Marshall refused to do after leaving government service.

Fortunately, the United States has a vast store of competent, talented, and honest citizens who would be honored to serve their nation for a period and seek nothing extra in return, except their government paycheck. And they must be paid well, so that all Americans with talent and integrity have the opportunity to serve our nation.

The larger point is that the United States badly needs the next president to bring us together as a people, explain the trap in which we find ourselves, call upon the best people we have to serve the nation, and then institute policies that can facilitate sustainable, noninflationary economic growth with benefits shared fairly among the American people.

For all political appointees, and for members of Congress, a uniform ethics code is required. The experience of recent years is that our national interests are ill served when they are crafted and administered by appointees who have personal or ideological agendas or who are using public service as a stepping-stone to private enrichment. Fortunately, this problem can be rather easily solved by real ethical standards and real enforcement.

President Bush and his former political adviser Karl Rove have used their appointee and contracting powers to bring about a de facto repeal of the Civil Service Act (Hatch Act) by replacing tens of thousands of federal employees with private contractors, many of whom are politically connected. These contractors and their employees are prime sources of campaign funds and, moreover, will just as willingly contribute to Democratic Party coffers as to those of the Republican Party. This problem is structural in nature and requires structural solutions.

The easiest way to stop the politicization of the federal workforce is to bring these contract workers under the provisions of the Hatch Act, which prohibits federal employees from becoming active campaign partisans. Then all the private contracts should be reviewed to determine what work civil servants should be doing.

Both Presidents Clinton and Bush relied on their vice presidents to supervise substantive work. In the next administration, the president will be fully engaged with the war in Iraq and related foreign policy issues. Ideally, that president will give the vice president a mandate to elevate the idea of public service, which has been so soiled over the past three decades, and begin recruiting a new generation of talented people into federal service.

We have seen the consequences of filling high public positions as a reward to campaign contributors and campaign staff members, such as the federal officials who dealt with the response to and aftermath of Hurricane Katrina, or with lobbyists from the industries an agency regulates. Placing people to lead programs they oppose ideologically does incalculable damage to the nation. If the next administration lifts the "iron curtain" of secrecy that has covered the Bush administration, Americans will surely see that government can be the solution to many problems—sometimes the only solution. A new spirit of public service and new people in the civil service would do much to restore competence in public programs and respect for the U.S. government.

Which brings us to questions of policy. Because unfettered globalization is unsustainable and the current results are unacceptable, new or at least different economic policies are required. The balance of this book describes ideas and policies that are basic to any long-term effort to rein in the excesses of globalization, while allowing the people of the United States to gain its benefits without risking economic ruin.

Foreign Taxes on U.S. Trade Ideally, the next president and Congress will agree to bring down the twin deficits—fiscal and trade—within a set time frame, such as five or seven years, with incremental annual goals. There are many ways to do this. Relying on a change in currency exchange rates with China, Japan, and Europe, which is the current policy, may be useful but is insufficient to solve the deficit problem and is not in the short-term interest of those nations.

As the Bush administration's tax breaks expire in the first years of the next administration, a spirited political fight on taxes is inevitable. Whether the cuts are extended or not, an unrelated tax issue merits immediate attention by the next president and Congress. It is the abusive use of the value-added tax (VAT) by foreign governments against U.S.-based producers.

Consider the European Union's case against the U.S. tax system at the WTO.

After World War II, the United States agreed, as part of a global trade agreement, to accept a provision that allowed other governments to rebate to their producers any indirect taxes paid on exported goods and impose an equal tax on imports from the United States into their countries. In that pact, the United States also agreed not to rebate any direct taxes on exports or to impose their equivalent on foreign imports.

This was a post–World War II U.S. tax loophole designed to speed Europe's recovery. Europe recuperated from that war decades ago, but the loophole has not only remained, it has been expanded and applied by 148 other nations.

In practical terms this means, for example, that the German manufacturer of a car, or any other product, exported into the United States gets a rebate from the German government equal to the indirect taxes paid on that product in Germany—the German value-added tax (VAT). The VAT rate in Germany is 19 percent, so German carmakers get a 19 percent tax rebate from their government on every vehicle exported to the United States. This is a big subsidy by any measure to German automakers.

Conversely, any U.S. carmaker exporting a vehicle to Germany must pay that government a VAT-equivalent tax of 19 percent of the price of the car, plus another 19 percent tax on the costs of all transport, insurance, docking, and duties involved in getting the car into Germany. Worse, the American company gets no credit in Germany for the corporate taxes it pays in the United States. This is a giant de facto tariff on imports.

The competitive impediments to American producers created by this tax discrimination and the use of the VAT as a trade barrier are enormous. In 2005, a foreign VAT was applied to 94 percent of all U.S. exports and imports. Foreign governments paid their domestic companies $239 billion of VAT rebates on goods and services exported to the United States. These governments also collected from U.S. producers $131 billion of VAT-equivalent taxes on goods and services imported from the United States, creating a $370 billion distortion in the international trade figures with the United States. By 2006, that distortion had grown to $428 billion per year.

Can anyone be surprised that U.S. exports are increasingly uncompetitive when they must overcome such enormous foreign subsidies and import taxes?

The WTO rules on the VAT, moreover, provide a powerful incentive for U.S.-headquartered companies to shift production and jobs from America to nations that use a VAT. Indeed, thousands of U.S.-headquartered companies have outsourced their production to foreign countries to get the VAT tax advantage in global trade.

Congress has repeatedly tried to eliminate the VAT disadvantage. In 1974, for instance, it directed the Nixon administration to negotiate America's VAT handicap away in the Tokyo Round of global trade talks. The other nations, however, ignored the United States' demand and refused to deal with the issue. The same thing happened in subsequent trade negotiations initiated in 1986 and again in 2002. Even today, foreign governments will not consider the issue.

In 1972 and again in 1984, Congress confronted this stonewalling by changing the tax system so U.S. exporters could exempt between 15 and 30 percent of their export income from U.S. taxes, thereby creating a VAT offset. In 1998, the European Union lodged a complaint with the newly created WTO, claiming that the tax benefit was an export subsidy that violated the WTO agreement.

The WTO formed a panel to hear the case. The panel met in closed session with the media excluded and the proceedings sealed, as is the practice in all WTO dispute cases. In October 1999, the WTO panel upheld the European position. With that, the United States had one year to change its contested tax law or pay WTO-sanctioned tariffs to Europe as compensation. U.S. post–World War II generosity was forgotten, it seems.

In November 2000, Congress enacted replacement legislation, which was again unsatisfactory to the Europeans, who filed another WTO case against the United States. In August 2001, a new panel upheld the European position, and in January 2002 the WTO's appellate body affirmed the panel's decision.

Congress ignored the WTO decision, which caused the organization to authorize the European Union to impose $4 billion of retaliatory tariffs per year on U.S. imports. This got the attention of the Bush administration, which responded by persuading Congress to enact, in October 2004, a substitute for its replacement bill of 2000. Meanwhile, the WTO sanctions were postponed.

Again the European Union filed a case at the WTO, arguing that the new legislation still provided export subsidies. A panel formed in Geneva, Switzerland, in September 2005 issued a thirty-four-page decision that concluded that the U.S. law enacted in 2004 still constituted an illegal subsidy that violated the United States' WTO obligations. The Europeans again threatened to impose sanctions. In 2006, President Bush and Congress gave up and stripped the offending tax provisions from U.S. law.

Throughout this almost-eight-year trade battle, the Europeans, like all other VAT-using countries, continued to provide full VAT rebates on their exports and impose a VAT-equivalent tax on all U.S. imports.

The simplest way to eliminate the VAT disadvantage, while not changing our complicated tax system, is for Congress to start the negotiations by imposing an equalizing fee on global imports of services equivalent to the individual exporting countries' VAT rebates on the same services, then provide an equalizing rebate on U.S. service exports equal to the importing nation's VAT charge on the U.S. producer for the same services.

If the United States were to adopt a consumption tax in lieu of the income tax, the problem would also be solved. Politically, this is unlikely to happen. To be very clear, that is not what I recommend. I propose creation of an offset fee—or tax if you prefer—on imported *services* for the sole pur-

pose of offsetting the foreign VAT advantage. When other nations eliminate their VAT on the import of U.S. services, the U.S. offset fee would automatically be dropped.

While doing something similar for the VAT on manufactured goods is
not permitted under the WTO agreement, such a U.S. action on trade in
services is. That step would force an opening of real negotiations with
other nations on what is now one of the principal trade disadvantages
imposed on U.S. producers and workers.

This proposed action is fully congruent with our obligations at the
WTO. Trade with nations that neither rebate a VAT on their exports to the
United States nor impose a VAT on their imports from the United States
will be exempt and totally unaffected. Legislation to allow this was introduced in the 109th and 110th Congresses but went nowhere, largely
because it was incorrectly seen as a tax on Americans, when it was really an
equalizing measure that would relieve U.S. producers and consumers of
foreign taxes.

Trade Today, U.S. trade policy is in a shambles. Not surprisingly, the trade
machinery of the U.S. government has proven unequal to the challenge.
The principal policy-making agency is the Office of the U.S. Trade Representative (USTR), which is located in the Executive Office of the President
and has a less-than-200-person staff, including clerks and drivers. This
office is responsible for negotiating, monitoring, and enforcing all U.S.
trade agreements. The mission has long been beyond the capacity of the
USTR to fulfill fully, and this has contributed greatly to the present U.S.
policies of unfettered globalization.

In 1974, Congress established an advisory system that would supposedly provide the thinly staffed USTR with expert advice. This system has
fallen into ruin as presidents have appointed their supporters to these
positions as political rewards. Worse, the system has been used not for the
collection of information but as a rubber stamp to lobby Congress on
behalf of the president.

The vacuum left by the collapse of the Doha Round of trade talks, coupled with the obvious weaknesses in the current global financial system,
will present the next president with an opportunity, much as FDR had in
1933, to make sweeping changes in how U.S. trade policies are made, their
substance, and their enforcement.

A visible signal that changes are meaningful would be to consolidate the
key institutions of the executive branch that set and administer trade pol-

icy. Specifically, the authority and staff of the USTR should be transferred to the Department of Commerce and the secretary made top trade negotiator and chairperson of an interagency policy committee that sets trade policy.

The Commerce Department is ideal for such a lead role since it is the agency that collects and analyzes trade data. Among the bureaus in Commerce are the Patent Office, National Institute of Standards and Technology, National Telecommunications and Information Administration, Minority Business Development Agency, Economic Development Administration, Census Bureau, Bureau of Economic Analysis, and National Oceanic and Atmospheric Administration. It also has the International Trade Administration, which operates offices in more than eighty nations, monitors foreign market access and compliance with existing trade agreements, and analyzes unfair foreign pricing and subsidies.

Enforcement of trade agreements needs to be separated from the negotiation of those agreements. In the present situation, in which U.S. trade policy making and trade pact enforcement reside in the same body, pulling and tugging between making new agreements and enforcing those made, a constant struggle ensues. It's elementary that a negotiator and a trade enforcer should not be the same person, as is now the case. Thus, a special trade enforcement unit should be established in the Justice Department and a sufficient number of lawyers and staff be employed to enforce trade policy actively and effectively.

When hundreds of corporations were reluctant to produce for the War and Navy Departments in the late 1930s, often out of their executives' loathing for FDR, the New Deal, and unions, Roosevelt recruited Thurman Arnold of Yale University to take charge of the Justice Department's Antitrust Division and provided enough money to hire three hundred lawyers. Arnold believed strongly in putting corporate executives into prison for violations of antitrust laws, which most corporations were then disobeying. After Arnold's appointment, corporations soon became willing to help the nation in its war effort.

An assured way to quickly eliminate many of the foreign trade barriers that companies, exporters, and workers now face would be to hire someone to head a trade policy enforcement unit who has the zeal for fair trade that Arnold had for competition, provide funding for that person to hire two or three hundred aggressive trade lawyers, and allow them to do what good lawyers do. After the initial political squealing from foreign governments, transnational corporations, and globalization ideologues, U.S. producers and workers would get more of the benefits from existing trade agreements than they realize now.

The present members of the Trade Advisory Committees, a system enacted by Congress that was originally intended to provide expert advice to the USTR, should be thanked for their service, given a certificate of appreciation, and then dismissed. Trade and trade deficit issues are too important to be left to individuals who fill positions given to them as political rewards, as they have often been. The next president and secretary of commerce will require the best advisers the nation has to offer, which may possibly include a few people now on those committees.

The World Trade Organization has proven unable to fulfill its intended function of facilitating international commercial negotiations and adjudicating trade disputes with objectivity and fairness. Moreover, it is unequipped to facilitate trade between differing economic systems.

In recognition of this institutional impotence, the Bush administration has negotiated a series of bilateral and plurilateral agreements outside the WTO. While the template for those negotiations was the failed NAFTA model, the idea of not waiting for the WTO to act and initiating negotiations with those who were willing to negotiate was appropriate.

While the WTO as we now know it is weak and too often used to advance the agendas of other governments and transnational corporations, it has a larger potential. In a world of unfettered corporate excesses, the WTO could be converted into an organization that member governments could use to restrain the abuses of globalization. Japan, China, and many European nations are accustomed to regulating the excesses of their corporations, as are most other industrial nations. Poor and developing countries have lacked the means to do this, but most seem willing to do so.

While the idea of regulating corporate behavior is not novel, the relevant question is, to what standard? Interestingly, Milton Friedman's answer is the most practical—the only responsibility of business, he wrote, is "to use its resources and engage in activities designed to increase its profits so long as it stays within the rules of the game, which is to say, engaged in open and free competition without deception and fraud."

Friedman's answer is that government's role is to set the "rules of the game," ensure that competition remains "open and free," and prevent "deception and fraud." Since the authority of a country's government ends at its borders, a multinational approach to setting such rules of the game is required. A revamped WTO could be that means.

The next U.S. president should work with his or her counterparts in Europe, Japan, and China to negotiate a global code of corporate "rules of the game." Among other activities, the WTO could develop a uniform tax regime that ensures corporations pay their fair share of taxes to the nations in which they do business. Corporate tax cheating is widespread and could be curtailed with uniform tax rules and multilateral monitoring.

Open competition is being quashed worldwide by unfettered globalization, which actually promotes monopolies in certain products. The principal monitor of antitrust issues today is the European Union. The WTO could usefully serve as the negotiating forum for creating a global competition policy, which its staff would monitor and then work with member governments to enforce.

"Sunshine" on international corporate activities would promote more competition and help governments avoid unwelcome economic surprises. The WTO should develop a worldwide disclosure system that applies to all stock corporations, hedge funds, investment banks, and other organizations engaged in multinational financial and corporate activities. The fact that thousands of hedge and investment funds are buying, selling, and revamping corporations on which the United States and other nations depend and subsidize, but doing so in secret without governments being aware of any contingent risks, is a formula for a global financial meltdown.

Deception and fraud in financial markets are now rampant. They are of a magnitude that threatens global economic stability. Controlling such undesirable activities is beyond the capacity of any single country, but working together, WTO members could bring offenders to the legal authorities of the member countries, where penalties can be imposed. Likewise, many transnational corporations are endangering the conditions that support life on this planet. A global regime of environmental monitoring and enforcement is essential. The WTO could provide that as well.

As to trade negotiations, the world may have reached the point when large multilateral agreements, such as the Doha Round, may be impossible. A new strategy is required. Step one in changing U.S. trade policy would be for the next administration to abandon the existing practice of seeking one solution or one policy that fits the Anglo-American model of trade and then trying to impose it on all other countries through the WTO.

As to why, the answer is reflected in the mathematics of our present trade deficit. Two thirds of the deficit in goods and services in 2006 was with only five countries: China, Japan, Canada, Mexico, and Germany. Therefore, it seems sensible to negotiate directly with those nations. With Germany, the bargaining could be expanded to include the European Union as a bloc.

While the economic models of Canada and Mexico are somewhat akin to that of the United States, those of China, Japan, and Germany are different, as previously discussed. Consequently, the approach to negotiating away the trade deficit for China should be different from the one for Japan or Germany. Future negotiations should be tailored to the circumstances. The only constant is that the deficits must be reduced on a set timetable by mutual action. Otherwise, the United States should reserve for itself the right to lower those deficits by unilateral actions, such as raising tariffs or setting import quotas.

Negotiations with NAFTA partners have been under way since 2005, when the leaders of Canada, Mexico, and the United States created the Security and Prosperity Partnership of North America (SPP), the pact that seeks to deeply integrate the economic and political systems of the three nations. The next president should aggressively continue to work with Mexico and Canada but change the SPP's structure, focus, and intended outcomes.

In an August 2007 conference in Washington, D.C., prior to the third annual meeting of the three heads of state to discuss the SPP, Dr. John Fonte of the Hudson Institute observed that the SPP as now operated is devoid of the "regular procedures of American constitutional democracy." Congress has neither authorized the SPP nor provided funding for any of its activities. There has been no congressional involvement, no public involvement, and no transparency. Yet the three heads of state are working together to create the trinational harmonization of regulations of all types, establish common tariffs, create a common border security effort, and redefine immigration procedures under the guise of labor mobility. From all of this, the many stakeholders in the three countries, except major business and foreign policy interests, are excluded.

Fonte described his vision of a future North America as "consisting of three independent democratic nation states, the United States, Canada, and Mexico. There would be reasonable cooperation, security, and trade, but as sovereign democratic states, they would rule themselves."

Today, the SPP does not have political legitimacy with the American people or the Congress; indeed, few voters are even aware of it. The obsessive secrecy surrounding this diplomacy and the dodgy excuses and explanations surrounding the SPP have cast a taint on whatever proposals might emerge from it. Yet the United States does have much to bargain with Canada and Mexico.

A starting point in bringing legitimacy to these negotiations, whether labeled as SPP, NAFTA, or simply "trilateral discussions," is to revert to what Dr. Fonte terms "the regular procedures of American constitutional democracy." This means making public all SPP documents; obtaining congressional authorization, funding, and oversight; conducting open meetings; and broadening the advisory panels to include the many stakeholders in the three nations, including unions, environmental groups, and consumer advocates. Before any recommendations are adopted by the United States, moreover, congressional ratification under normal legislative procedures should be mandated.

Among future agenda items that should be considered are uniform standards for the environment, workplace safety, employment benefits, taxes, competition, and labor law. These were major omissions in the original NAFTA pact. And unlike so many international negotiations over the past decade and a half that have served as political cover for ideologically driven deregulation, the United States should seek to harmonize those standards up to its own level, rather than down to some lower "international" level.

Since NAFTA was used as a trade model, a refocused NAFTA could also be the model for modifying the various other regional trade pacts in which the United States participates.

Private Capital—from Speculation to Investment The frenzied movement of capital in search of short-term returns is undermining our capacity to think and act for the long term. The fact that the entire value of the New York Stock Exchange is turning over every eleven-plus months is a clear signal that speculation has come to dominate long-term investment.

To make long-term investment more attractive to financial institutions, two changes are desirable. First, federal regulations should be instituted mandating that managers be compensated on the basis of some measure of long-term financial performance, rather than on a simple percentage of the funds managed and a major portion of any profits. A billion-dollar paycheck for a year's work by a fund manager, which often can involve little more than being in the right place when the economy is booming, is nothing more than looting other people's pensions and savings. The existing structure encourages speculation with other people's money.

A second viable means of creating an environment for long-term investment is to impose either a transaction tax on each corporate stock trade or a tax on short-term trades. Wall Street, of course, will oppose this as vigorously as it opposes paying the same taxes all other Americans pay. Alternately, a high downward sliding tax on short-term trades that would be reduced to zero over some period of time could encourage longer-term thinking and investing. The goal is to change the rules of the game in a way that would force fund managers to concentrate on a company's longer-term prospects—its capital management, research and development, worker training, management, and global competitiveness. This is a market solution to a market failure.

Public Capital—Twenty-first-Century Infrastructure The United States has invested trillions of dollars of public capital in roads, bridges, water and waste water systems, libraries, and schools, among dozens of other civil works. Collectively, these facilities are known as "public infrastructure" or simply "infrastructure." These works underpin the American economy and way of life.

Yet the United States is failing to invest adequately in the roads, bridges, airports, railways, and seaports we need to maintain a dynamic economy. The Federal Highway Administration estimates that there is almost a $460 billion backlog of investments on roads and bridges. The failure to make those expenditures in recent years has created a waste of fuel of more than $70 billion annually because of road congestion. Inefficiencies in freight movement cost another $200 billion each year. The point is that while good infrastructure may be expensive, poor infrastructure costs even more.

In 1981, Susan Walter and I wrote *America in Ruins,* which described the increasing lack of public investment in infrastructure and the consequences in that era. In part, our message was heard. A gas tax was enacted in 1982, and the public sector increased investments in highways; but that was not enough.

The no-new-taxes political policies of many contemporary office holders have prevented the generation of adequate investment for periodically updating infrastructure facilities and for new construction. As discussed, the governor of Texas is actually diverting highway funds to other purposes to create a road-financing crisis that he proposes to solve by leasing highways the state has already built and paid for to private toll companies.

In this infrastructure-financing vacuum, Wall Street is offering governors and mayors huge cash advances to lease publicly owned facilities to private companies that would be empowered to set whatever monopolistic fees they wish for as long as a century. As the story of the Texas Department of Transportation's Trans Texas Corridor illustrates, this could be the most expensive road tax any governor or mayor could impose on his or her citizens.

Though the pay-as-we-go policy long used by the United States to finance public capital projects, such as highways, remains attractive to voters, the nation lacks a long-term strategy for such public investment, especially as articulated in a national capital budget. The central recommendation of *America in Ruins* was that a systematic and orderly approach to public capital investment must replace the loose, give-and-take legislative procedures we have come to know. In 2007 alone, more than six thousand public infrastructure projects were set for funding not through some design but by congressional "earmarks."

Since Congress seems unable to control itself when allowing earmarks, the next president should collect the data required to make national infrastructure budgeting feasible. This would include an inventory of existing national public works and identification of short-term and long-term future needs. Then the executive branch should prepare a multiyear capital budget for the proposed phased capital investments that displays preconstruction, construction, maintenance, and operating costs, as well as the proposed financing.

Strikingly, every state government has such a capital budget, as does every corporation of any size. Only the federal government lacks this simple and basic tool of management. If such a budget existed, the question any earmarked project would face would be, is it in the plan or not? The answer to that question for most of the six thousand earmarked projects per year would be "no," which is why no such tool currently exists. At a time when America's public facilities are wearing out faster than they are being replaced, the moment has arrived for the next president to put into place a national capital budget and a process to update it continually.

Innovation The twenty-first century belongs to innovator nations. By innovation, I use the definition of James E. Malackowski, the founder of Ocean Tomo, a Chicago-based patent-consulting firm, who describes it as "the design, invention, development and/or implementation of new or altered products, services, processes, systems, organizational structures, or business models for the purpose of creating new value for customers and financial returns for the firm."

Ocean Tomo reports that as the U.S. economy has increasingly become driven by knowledge and innovation, rather than production and manufacturing, intellectual capital has "emerged as the leading asset class."

In support of this conclusion, the company notes that in 1975 the market value of the physical assets of the Standard & Poor's 500 corporations made up 80 percent of those corporations' value, and that the patents, copyrights, and trademarks—the intellectual capital—made up 20 percent.

Thirty years later, those ratios are reversed. In 2005, the buildings, machinery, and other physical facilities of the S&P 500 constituted 20 percent of the value of those corporations. Intellectual property (IP) made up 80 percent.

Robert J. Shapiro and Nam D. Pham confirm Ocean Tomo's work in their study *Economic Effects of Intellectual Property-Intensive Manufacturing in the United States.* Using a different set of companies, they calculate that "ideas," that is, the intellectual properties, of America's large businesses are now their principal assets. The share of corporate value represented by these intangible assets rose from 25 percent in 1984 to 64 percent in 2005.

Shapiro and Pham conclude that U.S. policy should encourage the creation of more intellectual properties and work harder to help the owners protect them. Alan S. Blinder, a former vice chairman of the Federal Reserve Bank, commented in the foreword to the study, "If America is to remain the leader of the economic pack, we must keep innovating in the future—just as we have done in the past. Shapiro and Pham are right that the incentive to create IP depends, in part, on our ability to protect it."

Former Federal Reserve Chairman Alan Greenspan has observed in several recent speeches and in his book *The Age of Turbulence* that "market economies require a rule of law . . . though laws can never be fixed in perpetuity." Though details of law need to change over time as societies and economies evolve, he writes, the United States has chosen "to lessen legal uncertainty by embedding our fundamental principles in a constitution, which we made difficult to amend."

No legal principle is more fundamentally embedded in U.S. law than that providing for the "right of exclusive use" by authors and inventors—copyrights and patents. It is explicitly provided for in the U.S. Constitution, which also authorizes Congress to set the terms of that "right."

Greenspan concluded that one of the basic challenges the United States faces over the coming quarter century is to sort out the laws governing and protecting intellectual property rights.

As to the goals of that "sorting out," maintaining a patent system that would encourage and defend U.S. innovation would be primary. Ideally, such a system should be able to process a patent in a short time after publication, such as three to six months. The cost of a patent should be low, so that small inventors (independent inventors, universities, small companies, and nonprofit research organizations) can fully participate. Today, such entities file 30 percent of patent applications. An ideal patent system would preserve for inventors as much of the twenty-year life of a patent for their exclusive use as possible. Such a system would not permit gaming through the use of litigation and would ensure that patent holders get quick resolution in the federal courts and are entitled to at least a fair royalty when infringers are found guilty of illegally using someone's patent.

So what is Congress doing about U.S. intellectual property policy? It is weakening U.S. patent and other IP protections in the guise of "harmonizing" them with those of other nations, all of which provide lesser protections. Legislation has been introduced in the last two Congresses that would double or triple the cost of a patent application, increase the time for processing applications, eliminate the assumption of validity when a patent is issued, make the collection of damages from guilty infringers difficult, reduce damage awards, and restrict where federal patent suits can be filed. In short, anti-innovation legislation is being pushed in Congress at just the moment we need more innovation, applied faster and more widely.

Not surprisingly, Japan, Europe, and many large U.S. corporations have long sought to water down U.S. patent protections. The reason is simple: large corporations (large entities) with intellectual property interests have many forms of power to promote and increase their business interests: market penetration, cash, many well-known products, political contacts, and legal representation, among others.

Yet the only real power most small-entity individuals and organizations have is the legal rights conferred by their ownership of a patent. Without a patent, most inventors cannot secure financing.

In 1999, Congress took a giant step backward in weakening U.S. patents by mandating that the Patent Office publish applications eighteen months from the filing date, even if a patent has not been awarded. The law allows inventors to opt out from such premature disclosure if they agree not to seek a patent outside the United States, which more than half of all small-entity inventors do. Otherwise, the most intimate secrets of U.S. inventors are now made available on the Internet before they have the protection of a patent. For many companies in China, India, and elsewhere, their entire R&D program consists of putting engineers into a room with high-speed Internet service where they troll U.S. patent applications.

In 2007, the House of Representatives voted for legislation that would allow third-party opposition while a patent was under review, reduce the damages a patent owner could collect from infringers, create a European-style postgrant judicial procedure that would allow a patent to be challenged repeatedly throughout its life at little cost to the challenger, and limit the federal courts in which patent lawsuits could be filed primarily to the hometowns of the infringers. This is judicial deck-stacking. The legislation would also eliminate the publication opt-out for those who agree not to patent their invention outside the United States, thereby forcing the Patent Office to make a premature publication of all patent applications. The same bill was reported out of the Senate Judiciary Committee.

In November 2007, Chen Yongshun, one of China's foremost patent experts and a former senior judge of Beijing High People's Court, did an analysis of the proposed patent law then being considered by Congress. He concluded that the proposed U.S. law would give China greater flexibility to challenge U.S. patents, weaken U.S. patent protections, and make it less costly to infringe. In sum, he concluded that the legislation was good for China and bad for America.

Why would the U.S. Congress systematically weaken U.S. patent protections for U.S. inventors at precisely the moment it should be strengthening them? The answer is globalization, elitism, and corporatism. The big technology companies and foreign governments behind this legislation want to make infringement easier and less expensive, and they simply do not care what other effects it might have on America's future. If the bill is not passed in 2008, advocates promise to bring it back in 2009.

If America is to remain an innovative nation, it requires a strong patent system, not some pale imitation of Japan's and Europe's. Some first steps are obvious. For example, the Patent Office should be directed to cease the publication of all unexamined patent applications. In a world of pirates and counterfeiters, often abetted by other governments, disclosure of the most valuable secrets of American inventors before they have the protection of a patent is beyond foolish.

During the Clinton and Bush administrations, part of the fees used to finance the work of the Patent Office was diverted to the general budget. Thus, the agency was unable to hire enough examiners to review all applications in a timely manner. The Patent Office now has a backlog of almost 800,000 applications, and the average time before a decision is made is thirty-one months from filing. Such delays are deadly in the global race to innovate. Congress should return to the Patent Office the diverted fees it took and then mandate that they be used to increase the number of examiners so the average processing time is cut to a year or less. The United States needs more and better innovations, and they are needed now.

Along with more money, the Patent Office requires improvements in management. For many years, too many high positions have been filled with unqualified political appointees who have no experience with patents. One result is a 30 percent turnover rate among employees and much discontent among those who remain.

Finally, the vast amount of intellectual property piracy and counterfeiting under way in the world requires an aggressive response by the United States. Under the WTO, the United States has the right to bring a case against nations that fail to meet their WTO obligations and seek damages. Since 2001, the United States has exerted that right only once. Protecting U.S. intellectual properties is central to the United States' future prosperity. The next president should proceed accordingly.

Human Capital Today's workers will still constitute almost 85 percent of the U.S. workforce a decade from now. Between now and well into the twenty-first century, therefore, the United States will succeed or fail with today's workforce. A bracing thought.

The educational profile of workers eighteen years of age and over is that 15 percent do not have a high school education and 75 percent have less than a bachelor's degree. Most will require booster shots of education and training throughout the remaining years of their working lives. Most will hold a number of jobs over their careers and have many employers. These workers require three things: health care financing; a universal, mandatory portable pension plan that is tied to the worker rather than the job; and access to education and training throughout their careers.

For almost two decades, our presidents and Congress have put globalist trade agreements into place while postponing the creation of the basic social programs that would help Americans make the hard transitions those policies created. The time has come to create and make work the social programs that a quickly changing economy requires. Put another way, there should be no more trade agreements until the social infrastructure is in place.

Unfettered globalization is shattering the health care and pension systems created in the United States after World War II. Though defining how a universal health care plan should work is not within the scope of this book, it is sufficient to say that such care for all Americans is needed and that many feasible cost-effective options exist. The provision of such should be a top priority for the next president.

Many proposals to provide universal portable pensions have been advanced, only parts of which have been enacted into law, such as 401(k) plans. By combining key elements from some of these plans and adding a few new elements, the United States can provide private pension coverage for all workers.

In outline form, a private pension system can be created that would supplement Social Security but not be integrated into it. A portable pension account would be established for every worker in America, and vesting would be immediate. Withdrawals before retirement would be restricted. Workers and employers could make matching tax-exempt contributions to the accounts, allowing workers to build up a private retirement fund throughout their lives, even as they shifted from job to job and employer to employer. The Thrift Savings Plan, a similar plan for U.S. government employees, already exists.

The U.S. Treasury or the Pension Benefit Guaranty Corporation could administer the funds, which would be invested by the administering agency in secure investments from a list of choices that workers would select from. Such a simple plan would give workers greater flexibility and allow them to build pension wealth for a dignified retirement. It would supplement their private savings and Social Security. It would increase national savings.

A national worker education and training strategy is also required for the vast number of people who are already working and need to improve their knowledge and skills. The challenge is to divide the responsibilities of such a program most efficiently between individuals and society.

The Labor Department and state employment offices are ideally suited to provide reliable, short-term information as to what jobs exist and what training is required. Their job is to answer the question: Train for what? The next president and Congress need to know how many workers with various higher skills are unable to find jobs for which they are already qualified. Such information will be invaluable for setting longer-term trade policy goals.

Employers, especially large companies, are generally in the position to provide much of the training that America needs. A traditional way to encourage such private investment in education is for governments to provide tax incentives to lower the costs to employers. Since many employers are reluctant to make such investments, fearing that the newly trained workers will go elsewhere, tax incentives can help.

State and local governments traditionally provide technical and vocational training that is often linked to the employers' needs. Job-training systems already put into place during the 1960s through the 1980s to help workers whose jobs have been outsourced can provide the structure for a massive training effort. After years of federal inattention, however, a quick analysis of the existing capacity and responsiveness of these systems, plus a strategy for refreshing those institutions and making them flexible and relevant to present and anticipated needs, is required.

Today, the United States provides only the most limited support for displaced workers, and that support is generally made available to those affected by specific trade. In fact, most American workers are going to be displaced at one point or another in this age of globalization. What they need is good information about jobs, relocation assistance, access to training and education, and counseling.

Many will require transitional financial assistance at low and affordable rates. It is in the national interest that these displaced workers become taxpayers again as quickly as possible. And all efforts should be made during their time of unemployment to help them stay out of the clutches of credit card and loan companies that charge interest of up to 30 percent or more.

All these actions require a federal government that is competently staffed by people who believe in the missions of the agencies that employ them. The incompetents and ideological saboteurs who have been placed in positions of power throughout the government during the past several years should be quickly returned to private life by the next administration, whether it be Republican or Democratic. Then the work of assuring American prosperity into the future can begin in earnest.

Epilogue

The Prologue ended with three questions. Here are my short answers.

1. Q: Why did the government of the United States, the world's trading and economic powerhouse, choose to integrate its economy with those of the rest of the world without providing the most basic safeguards for the nation and its people?
   A: Ideology. Corporatism. Elitism.
2. Q: Can the United States maintain its standard of living, pay its debts, retain its sovereignty, and ensure its national security under its present policies?
   A: No. As Herbert Stein, President Nixon's chairman of the Council of Economic Advisors, famously remarked, "Things that can't go on, don't."
3. Q: Can the United States gain the benefits of globalization without plunging into economic ruin?
   A: Of course it can. The recommendations in the last part of this book would make a good start to gain those benefits.

One of the principal reasons that globalization is in such disfavor in the United States is that the social, institutional, and regulatory decisions needed to lessen the force of that change were not considered when the U.S. policies on globalization were adopted. Those who benefited got theirs immediately. For the rest of America, it was jam yesterday, jam tomorrow, but never jam today.

The first lesson is that before the United States more deeply integrates its economy globally, the safety nets, social investments, and institutional changes that should have been put into place years ago must first be put into place now. Jam today for America's working people.

The second lesson is that the time has come for the United States to end its free-trade missionary work around the world. We should deal with the economies of other nations as they are, not as we would like them to be. And we should accept nothing less than full reciprocity in our global business dealings.

In conclusion, the challenges of unfettered globalization are minor compared to those faced by prior generations and previous presidents. Washington, Lincoln, Roosevelt, and the American people, moreover, all rose to the test at their moments of crisis. We are no less a generation. Indeed, ours is a far wealthier nation now than then and richer in so many ways. Mastering globalization is easily within our political and economic capacities.

The missing element is national leadership—public, political, corporate, financial, union, religious, educational, moral, and social. We need a Congress that will work together for the people of America and adopt political reforms that will bring voters back into our politics and governance. Equally important, we need a president who respects and appreciates what we, the American people, can do together through our government, who will thwart the corporatism and elitism that is undermining our national future, and who will in every decision put the interests of the United States above all others.

The reality of American politics is that none of us can know what any candidate for president will do once in office. Our hope must be that the person has the wisdom to understand the challenges and risks created by globalization, plus the character and political skills to overcome them. Mount Rushmore has enough space to honor one more great U.S. president.

Acknowledgments

These acknowledgments cannot convey the fullness of my appreciation to many people whose support, encouragement, and insights made possible my writing of this book. The first of these is Kay Casey, my wife, who patiently reordered her life and our leisure so that I had time to research and write this book.

George Becker, to whom this book is dedicated, urged me to write it, as did Michael Wessel, his fellow commissioner on the U.S.-China Economic and Security Review Commission. George was one of the great union leaders in U.S. history. Both he and Mike gave me wonderful insights that are incorporated into this book. I deeply regret that George did not live to see the publication of *Dangerous Business.*

Leo Gerard, international president of the United Steel Workers, and Jim English, international secretary-treasurer of the USW, arranged financial support for the research needed to do this book and have been very supportive of this project. Under Leo's leadership, the USW is building a network of thoughtful people, groups, and institutional arrangements that are coming forth with ideas and solutions that can help the United States put the well-being of workers and people into any future policies on globalization. Their work is heroic, and I hope other organizations and unions will emulate it.

Roger Milliken and Milliken & Co. again continued their support of my work, for which I am deeply grateful.

Sara Sherbill, Ashbel Green's editorial assistant, kept the mechanics of this process moving in a most diligent manner.

John Davis did his usual superb job of editing my work and helping me keep the words clear and to the point.

Andrew Miller provided valued editorial suggestions; Peter Mendel-sund designed a beautiful jacket; Anthea Lingeman designed an elegant layout; and Andrew Dorko, the production editor, pulled it all together in a timely manner. I thank them all for their superb work.

Many other people aided me in numerous ways but would prefer to remain anonymous. I thank them all.

Throughout the book and in the Notes, I highlight books, reports, and articles that I found interesting and informative. For those who wish to know more, those works are a good starting point.

Finally, I thank Ashbel Green for his support of this project and his many insights. Among those who write and publish books, he is considered "legendary," an apt description.

And as always, the views and positions advocated in this book are my own and not necessarily those of anyone else associated with this project. They can pick their own fights.

Washington, Virginia

Appendix

Special Interests and Washington's Revolving Door

"The real scandal in Washington is not what is done illegally, but what is done legally."

—The New Republic

The right to petition the government without fear of punishment or reprisal is one of an American's most basic freedoms. The First Amendment to the U.S. Constitution documents petition as one of five "freedoms"—the other four being religion, speech, a free press, and assembly. The petition clause permits lobbying, lawsuits, picketing, protests, ballot initiatives, letter or e-mail campaigns, ads, and testimony, among many other activities whose purpose is to shape or protest the actions of the legislative, executive, or judicial branches of the U.S. government.

The petitioning-for-pay done by the individuals and organizations identified in the following tables is entirely legal. Their work was done according to the rules and laws on lobbying established by the U.S. Congress, and this data exists because these lobbyists obeyed those laws and reported their activities.

Though legal, the breadth and magnitude of the lobbying activities documented in these tables reveal a policy-making and legislative process that is open to the highest bidders. No legislation and no policy are immune. "Structural corruption" is the way Japanese observers describe our situation.

The historian Arthur M. Schlesinger, Jr., captured the essence of the problem in his posthumously published *Journals, 1952–2000* with a quote from Senator Edward Kennedy, who in a 1978 discussion about the "collapse of Congress" observed that "the trouble with Congress is that it is owned, lock, stock and barrel by private interests." Schlesinger asked whether this was "more or less true than fifteen years ago (1963) when he had first come to the Senate." Kennedy said that it was more true because the private interests are better organized now.

Thirty years have passed since that interview. Not only are those private interests better organized and financed, they now dominate governance in the United States.

The corporatism and elitism described in this book, and the resulting unrepresentative democracy they engender, are obvious to both voters and public officials. In the 2008 presidential nominating process, each of the candidates from both parties asked voters to choose them to "fix" a broken Washington. While some of this was plainly political pandering, much was also an honest reaction by office seekers who knew very well how deeply our politics and governance are corrupted.

Intriguingly, these same candidates seemed loath to be more specific other than to flay at straw men—"big oil," "big banks," "special interests," "foreign interests," "Washington's revolving door," and "the massive amounts of money being spent on lobbying." Perhaps their reluctance is because those same lobbyists, representing those same interests, are guiding and financing those candidates' political careers and campaigns.

So who are these special interests? How much money are they spending? Which foreign interests are lobbying the U.S. government and how much are they spending? Who is going through Washington's revolving door? What public position did they hold, and where did they alight after leaving office? These are the questions that are never raised in political campaigns and thus are never answered.

These questions, however, are partially answered in this appendix. I note "partially" answered because much of the lobbying and political work done in Washington is never reported. The General Accountability Office in 1994 estimated that a fifth or more goes undocumented.

In the book, I write about "K Street" and "Wall Street." By K Street, I refer to the traditional lobbying of our government by people who register themselves with either the Congress or Justice Department as "lobbyists." K Street refers to a part of Washington, D.C., where dozens of lobbying and law firms have their offices—close to the White House and slightly more than one mile from the Capitol.

The Center for Responsive Politics did special data sorting for me and prepared Tables 1, 3, and 5 for this book. The Center for Public Integrity permitted me to draw on their data to make Table 2. For both centers, their data comes from registration forms filed by lobbyists and organizations. The information is as reliable as the reporting.

When I write about "Wall Street," it is about those whose revolving door spins between financial institutions and high public office, and often spins full circle—Wall Street to Washington and back to Wall Street. The Center for Responsive Politics provided the data for those who registered as lobbyists; the balance I collected from various public sources.

Table 1 identifies the 100 top lobbying expenditures by groups and corporations for the period 1998–2007. In that time, the "number one" special interest group was the U.S. Chamber of Commerce, which reported spending more than $338 million on lobbying. Though number 100 on the list, the National Federation of Independent Business spent $28.5 million for lobbying, which by any measure is an enormous amount of money.

Table 2 identifies, by nation, how much foreign governments and corporations spent for U.S. lobbying in the period 1998–2004. In that seven-year period, they spent almost $600 million. Of that, $60 million came from Switzerland, $166 million from the United Kingdom, and more than $59 million from Japan. Such large amounts can buy a great deal of influence, as this book describes.

Table 3 identifies the former government officials who move through Washington's revolving door. It identifies whether they worked in either the administrations of Bill Clinton or George W. Bush. It also identifies where they worked in government and where they subsequently worked as lobbyists. This data is mute testimony to a broken system of public service at the highest levels of our national government.

Table 4 identifies 121 former members of the U.S. House of Representatives and the U.S. Senate who have registered, and worked, as professional lobbyists some or most of the time in the period 1993–2007. As this data suggests, any special interest from anywhere in the world, for a high price, can pull together a skilled team of former Republican and Democratic legislators to lobby former colleagues on just about any issue that comes before Congress. Usually, this is an unbeatable combination.

Table 5 gives a hint of the personal connections between those who guide our national policies and those who profit from Wall Street deal making. It reflects the influence of financial interests in establishing our ad hoc, unfettered policies on globalization and the subsequent staffing of our government to implement those decisions. In light of the various financial debacles the U.S. government has tolerated, such as the S & L bailout and the subprime mortgage collapse, and often bailed out over the past three decades, this relationship is one that warrants far greater transparency than now exists.

The structural corruption documented in this appendix and described in this book can be fixed. *Dangerous Business* identifies specific actions that are politically feasible, practical, and will reverse our national slide into unrepresentative governance, economic decline, and national insecurity.

TABLE 1: WASHINGTON'S SPECIAL INTERESTS
(Top 100 Companies and Organizations Reported Lobbying)
(1998–July 2007)

Company or Organization	Amount
U.S. Chamber of Commerce	$338,324,680
General Electric	160,955,000
American Medical Assn.	157,247,500
American Hospital Assn.	138,084,144
AARP	116,452,064
Pharmaceutical Rsrch. & Mfrs. of America	115,008,600
Edison Electric Institute	107,132,628
National Assn. of Realtors	103,890,000
Northrop Grumman	102,969,474
Business Roundtable	101,660,000
Blue Cross/Blue Shield	90,163,317
Lockheed Martin	87,797,702
Freddie Mac	86,164,048
Verizon Communications	83,867,022
Boeing Co.	82,038,310
General Motors	77,620,483
Philip Morris	75,668,000
Roche Group	74,888,942
Fannie Mae	73,857,000
ExxonMobil	72,122,941
Ford Motor Co.	71,312,808
Southern Co.	69,850,694
Natl. Cmte. to Preserve Social Security	69,260,000
Microsoft Corporation	68,995,000
US Telecom Assn.	66,960,000
SBC Communications	64,713,327
National Assn. of Broadcasters	63,560,000
Citigroup, Inc.	62,555,000
American International Group	61,537,300

Company or Organization	Amount
Altria Group	$59,575,000
Securities Industry Assn.	59,364,293
American Council of Life Insurers	59,363,337
Alliance of Automobile Manufacturers	59,134,765
Assn. of American Railroads	58,742,869
American Farm Bureau Federation	57,670,217
IBM Corporation	56,581,643
General Dynamics	54,434,490
National Assn. of Manufacturers	53,420,585
Motorola, Inc.	53,340,369
Seniors Coalition	52,915,751
AT&T	52,723,499
AT&T, Inc.	51,907,376
National Cable & Telecommunications Assn.	50,530,000
BellSouth Corporation	50,399,824
Amgen, Inc.	49,920,000
AMR Corporation	49,741,456
DaimlerChrysler	49,633,295
United Services Automobile Assn. Group	48,825,015
Merck & Company	48,022,294
Pfizer, Inc.	48,010,000
Sprint Corporation	47,456,585
American Bankers Assn.	46,348,212
Bristol-Myers Squibb	45,760,579
Investment Co. Institute	45,535,574
Eli Lilly & Company	45,256,890
Textron, Inc.	44,376,000
Visa International	43,539,484
American Insurance Assn.	40,364,861
Mortgage Insurance Companies of America	39,880,000
Intel Corporation	39,209,000
Johnson & Johnson	38,730,000
Biotechnology Industry Organization	38,725,796
Asbestos Study Group	38,700,000
Abbott Laboratories	38,646,000
Aircraft Owners & Pilots Assn.	37,984,296
AFL-CIO	37,474,810
FedEx Corporation	37,352,500
Walt Disney Company	37,216,991
United Technologies	36,927,260
Raytheon	36,892,333
Metropolitan Life	36,493,750
Advanced Medical Technology Assn.	36,361,519
Shell Oil	35,669,007
Merrill Lynch	35,542,760
Honeywell International	34,840,000
JP Morgan Chase & Company	34,806,575

Company or Organization	Amount
EDS Corporation	$34,048,270
GlaxoSmithKline	33,841,000
Loews Corporation	33,550,000
PG&E Corporation	33,380,000
PriceWaterhouseCoopers	33,339,945
BP	33,053,294
Brown & Williamson Tobacco	32,202,000
Commonwealth of Puerto Rico	32,101,027
UAL Corporation	31,865,135
American Forest & Paper Assn.	31,673,940
Cellular Telecom & Internet Assn.	31,223,078
Novartis AG	31,222,729
News Corporation	31,184,000
Bond Market Assn.	30,775,850
Qwest Communications	30,611,480
America's Health Insurance Plans	30,530,000
FPL Group	30,416,967
Time Warner	30,162,954
American Chemistry Council	30,066,938
Union Pacific Corporation	30,044,821
Dow Chemical	29,397,270
Northwestern Mutual	28,464,976
Financial Services Roundtable	28,330,000
National Fedn. of Independent Business	28,250,773
Total	$6,600,017,491

Source: A special run prepared by the Center for Responsive Politics, Washington, D.C., January 2008.

TABLE 2: FOREIGN LOBBYING
IN THE UNITED STATES*
(1998–2004)

Country	Total Reported Expenditures
Antigua	$1,040,000
Argentina	700,000
Australia	1,695,000
Austria	120,000
Bahamas	230,000
Bahrain	20,000
Bangladesh	510,000
Belgium	896,447
Bermuda	32,098,000
Botswana	1,920,000
Brazil	860,000
Cambodia	100,000
Canada	47,268,411
Chile	240,000
China	4,225,282
Colombia	1,070,000
Costa Rica	74,000
Cyprus	240,000
Denmark	5,435,300
Dominica	10,000
Dominican Republic	930,000
Ecuador	270,000
Egypt	640,000
El Salvador	80,000
Ethiopia	700,000

Country	Total Reported Expenditures
Finland	1,342,000
France	48,729,562
Georgia	60,000
Germany	63,490,059
Gibraltar	1,500,000
Greece	520,000
Haiti	514,239
Honduras	30,000
Hong Kong	2,945,000
Hungary	40,000
Iceland	180,000
India	1,040,000
Ireland	360,000
Israel	3,640,000
Italy	3,407,000
Japan	59,620,223
Jordan	60,000
Kazakhstan	740,000
Kenya	280,000
Korea, North	160,000
Korea, South	5,080,000
Kuwait	884,500
Lebanon	20,000
Liberia	20,000
Luxemburg	620,000
Macedonia	260,000
Marshall Islands	500,000
Mexico	6,291,500
Netherlands	3,103,600
New Zealand	3,140,000
Nicaragua	180,000
Norway	4,768,000
Pakistan	540,000
Palau	180,000
Panama	60,000
Paraguay	100,000
Peru	710,000
Philippines	160,000

Country	Total Reported Expenditures
Poland	40,000
Portugal	365,000
Russian Federation	3,705,000
Saudi Arabia	245,000
Singapore	2,040,000
South Africa	280,000
Spain	268,000
Sri Lanka	300,000
Swaziland	180,000
Sweden	9,353,360
Switzerland	60,130,134
Taiwan	6,254,000
Thailand	970,000
Turkey	280,000
Ukraine	120,000
United Arab Emirates	20,000
United Kingdom	166,334,314
Venezuela	1,040,000
Yugoslavia	180,000
Zimbabwe	60,000
Foreign Lobbying Expenditures in U.S. (1998–2004)	$568,706,399
U.S. Organizations' Lobbying Expenditures (1998–2004)	11,361,273,880
Grand Total	$11,929,980,249

Source: "An Ongoing Investigation into the State of Federal Lobbying in the U.S., 1998–2004," LobbyWatch, Center for Public Integrity, Washington, D.C., January 2008. Reproduced with permission.

*The Center for Public Integrity downloaded every available lobbying disclosure record from the Senate Office of Public Records for the period 1998–2004. More than 2.2 million records were put into their database. It is a historic examination of lobbying at the federal level. Yet, as the Center notes, the data reported in these official records are a vast understatement of the real levels of lobbying expenditures; perhaps as much as one-fifth of all lobbying goes unreported. Nonetheless, the amount that is documented by the Center reveals the massive efforts that are made to influence the policies and decisions of the U.S. government. For more details, readers can go to the Center's Web site: http://www.publicintegrity.org.

TABLE 3: WASHINGTON'S REVOLVING DOOR

Between Public Position and Private Employment as a Lobbyist
(The administrations of Bill Clinton and George W. Bush)

Bill Clinton's Administration

Lobbyist	Employer—Private/Public	Title
Ackerman, Kenneth	Olsson, Frank & Weeda	Of Counsel
	Federal Crop Insurance Corporation	Manager
Akey, Steven	Bridgestone/Firestone Americas	Government Relations
	Dept. of Transportation	Asst. to Secretary
	Federal Highway Administration	Director of Public Affairs
	White House Office	Presidential Personnel
Alexander, Donald C.	Akin, Gump et al.	Partner
	Martin Luther King Jr. Federal Holiday Commission	Commissioner
Alford, Marty	Alford & Assoc.	Lobbyist
	Dept. of Navy	Director, Legislative Affairs
Amidzich, Gail	National Treasury Employees Union	Asst. Director, Legislation
	Office of National Drug Control Policy	Legislative/Congressional Affairs
Anderson, Michael	Monteau & Peebles	Partner
	Bureau of Indian Affairs	Deputy Asst. Secretary
Arthur, David	Dykema Gossett	Lobbyist
	Environmental Protection Agency	Employee/Staff
Ballantyne, Michelle	Recording Industry Assn. of America	Senior Vice President
	White House Office	Counsel to Chief of Staff
Ballentine, Roger S.	Green Strategies	Lobbyist
	White House Office	Legislative/Congressional Affairs
Berger, Samuel "Sandy"	Stonebridge International	Chairman, Cofounder
	National Security Council	National Security Advisor
	Presidential Transition Team	Asst. Transition Director, National Security

Lobbyist	Employer—Private/Public	Title
Biden, R. Hunter	Oldaker, Biden & Belair	Founding Partner
	AMTRAK	Board Member
	Dept. of Commerce	Executive Director, E-Commerce Policy
Blancato, Robert B.	Matz Blancato & Assoc.	President
	White House Office	Exec. Director, Conference on Aging
Blanchard, James J.	DLA Piper Rudnick et al.	Partner
	U.S. Diplomatic Missions	Ambassador to Canada
Bohannon, Mark	Software & Information Industry Assn.	General Counsel & VP
	Technology Administration	Counselor to Undersecretary
Boorstin, Robert	Center for American Progress	
	Dept. of State	Adviser
	Dept. of Treasury	Foreign Policy Adviser
	White House Office	Speechwriter
Bornstein, Theodore H.	Foley & Lardner	Partner
	Dept. of Defense	Director, Reinvestment Task Force
Brain, Charles M.	Capitol Hill Strategies	Principal
	White House Office	Legislative Affairs Director, House Liaison
Brinkman, Karen	Latham & Watkins	Partner
	Federal Communications Commission	Assoc. Chief, Wireless Telecom
Brophy, Susan	Glover Park Group	Partner, Legislative Affairs
	Presidential Transition Team	Clinton-Gore
	White House Office	Legislative/Congressional Affairs
Brown, Jesse	SPECTRUM Group	Lobbyist
	Veterans Affairs (executive offices)	Secretary of Veterans Affairs
Bueno, Irene	Nueva Vista Group	Cofounder & Partner
	Dept. of Health and Human Services	Deputy Asst. Secretary for Legislation
	White House Office	Special Asst. to President
Collier, Thomas C.	Steptoe & Johnson	Lobbyist
	Dept. of Interior	Chief of Staff/Chief Operating Officer
Connaughton, Jeffrey J.	Quinn, Gillespie & Assoc.	Lobbyist
	White House Office	Special Assistant
Corr, William V.	Campaign For Tobacco Free Kids	Exec. VP
	Daschle, Tom	Policy Director
	Dept. of Health & Human Services	Various Positions

Lobbyist	Employer—Private/Public	Title
Crater, Jeffrey C.	BWX Technologies	Mngr., Government Programs
	Dept. of Energy	Special Asst. to Secretary
Dalbello, Richard	Intelsat General Corp.	VP, Government Relations
	Dept. of Commerce	Director, Space Commercialization
	Office of Science & Technology Policy	Asst. Director, Aeronautics & Space
D'Amours, Norman E.	Norman E. D'Amours	Lobbyist
	National Credit Union Administration	Chairman
Daschle, Linda	Baker, Donelson et al.	Lobbyist
	Federal Aviation Administration	Deputy/Acting Administrator
DeGrazia, Bruce	Global Homeland Security Advisers	
	Dept. of Defense	Deputy Undersecretary, Defense
de Leon, Rudy F.	Boeing Co.	
	Dept. of Defense	Deputy Secretary
de Leon, Sylvia A.	Akin, Gump et al.	Lobbyist
	Presidential Transition Team	Coordinator
	White House Office	Member of a Task Force
Dhillon, Neil	Ruder Finn, Inc.	Managing Director, Washington Office
	Dept. of Transportation	Deputy Asst. Secretary, Governmental Affairs
Dover, Agnes P.	Hogan & Hartson	Lobbyist
	Dept. of Energy	Deputy General Counsel
Drazek, Paul	DTB Assoc.	President
	Dept. of Agriculture	Special Asst. to Secretary
Echaveste, Maria	Nueva Vista Group	Lobbyist
	White House Office	Deputy Chief of Staff
Eizenstat, Stuart	Covington & Burling	Lobbyist
	Bureau of Economic & Business Affairs	Undersecretary
	Dept. of State	Ambassador to European Union
	Dept. of Treasury	Deputy Secretary
	International Trade Administration	Undersecretary
Enright, Janice Ann	Ickes & Enright Group	Lobbyist
	White House Office	Asst. to Deputy Chief of Staff
Farquhar, Michele C.	Hogan & Hartson	Codirector, Communications
	Federal Communications Commission	Chief
	Natl. Telecom & Information Admin.	Deputy Secretary

Lobbyist	Employer—Private/Public	Title
Fitz-Pegado, Lauri	Livingston Group	Partner
	Dept. of Commerce	Asst. Secretary
Foley, Thomas S.	Akin, Gump et al.	Partner
	U.S. Diplomatic Missions	Ambassador to Japan/ House Majority Leader
Fontenot, Yvette	Jennings Policy Strategies	VP, Health Policy
	Office of Management & Budget	Medicare Specialist
Forbes, Jeff	Cauthen, Forbes & Williams	Lobbyist
	White House Office	Deputy Director of Scheduling
	White House Office	Legislative/Congressional Affairs
Fredrickson, Caroline	NARAL Pro-Choice America	
	White House Office	Legislative/Congressional Affairs
Frey, Scott	National Cmte. to Preserve Social Security	
	National Institutes of Health	Legislative/Congressional Affairs
Frost, Susan	Education Priorities	President
	Dept. of Education	Adviser to Secretary
Garvey, Jane	APCO Worldwide	Executive VP
	Federal Aviation Administration	Administrator
	Federal Highway Administration	Acting Administrator
Gebhard, Paul	Cohen Group	VP
	Dept. of Defense	Special Asst. to Secretary
Gilmartin, William	Jefferson Government Relations	VP
	Dept. of Housing & Urban Development	Asst. Secretary, Congressional/ Intergovernmental Rels.
Glickman, Daniel R.	Motion Picture Assn. of America	Chairman & CEO
	Dept. of Agriculture	Secretary of Agriculture/ Member of Congress
Godley, Patricia F.	Van Ness Feldman	Member
	Dept. of Energy	Asst. Secretary, Fossil Energy
Gold, Richard M.	Holland & Knight	Lobbyist
	Environmental Protection Agency	Special Asst. to Administrator
Gonzalez, Emilio	Verizon Communications	Director of Public Policy
	Technology Administration	Senior Policy Analyst
	Dept. of Education	Special Asst.
	Dept. of Commerce	Policy Adviser

Lobbyist	Employer—Private/Public	Title
Gorman, Matt	Fabiani & Co.	Lobbyist
	Presidential Transition Team	National Finance Director
	Dept. of Treasury	Director, Office of Business Liaison
Gould, J. Eric	Tew Cardenas LLP	Lobbyist
	White House Office	Associate Director, Domestic Policy
Gray, William H., III	Buchanan, Ingersoll & Rooney	Lobbyist
	Dept. of State	Special Adviser, Haitian Affairs
	White House Office	Special Adviser, Haitian Affairs
Griffin, Patrick J.	Johnson, Madigan et al.	Lobbyist
	White House Office	Asst. to the President, Legislative Affairs
Guidos, Robert J.	Infectious Diseases Society of America	
	Food & Drug Administration	Legislative/Congressional Affairs
Hale, Marcia	McKenna, Long & Aldridge	Lobbyist
	White House Office	Legislative/Congressional Affairs
Halpin, Peter G.	Dutko Worldwide	Senior VP
	Dept. of Transportation	Legislative/Congressional Affairs
	Overseas Private Investment Corporation	Legislative/Congressional Affairs
Hardock, Randolf H.	Davis & Harman	Lobbyist
	Dept. of Treasury	Benefits Tax Counsel
Harris, Scott Blake	Harris, Wiltshire & Grannis	Lobbyist
	Bureau of Export Administration	Chief Counsel
	Federal Communications Commission	Bureau Chief
Hayes, David	Latham & Watkins	Partner
	Dept. of Interior	Deputy Secretary
Haynes, Audrey	YMCA of the U.S.A.	Chief of Government Affairs
	Office of Women's Initiatives & Outreach	Director
	White House Office	Chief of Staff, Tipper Gore
Henneberry, Brian	Calpine Corp.	
	Bureau of Alcohol, Tobacco & Firearms	Inspector
Hicks, Vicki J.	Van Scoyoc Assoc.	Lobbyist
	Farm Service Agency	Deputy Administrator
	International Trade Administration	Policy Analyst

Lobbyist	Employer—Private/Public	Title
Hilton, Steven M.	Buchanan Ingersoll	Lobbyist
	White House Office	Deputy Assistant to President
Hoffman, Gail H.	Hoffman Group	Lobbyist
	Office of the Attorney General	Legislative/Congressional Affairs
	White House Office	Employee/Staff
Holder, Eric H., Jr.	Covington & Burling	Partner
	U.S. Attorney's Office	U.S. Attorney
	Office of the Attorney General	Deputy Attorney General
	Criminal Division	Clerk
Ibarra, Mickey	Mickey Ibarra & Assoc.	President
	White House Office	Asst. to President
Jacoby, Peter	AT&T, Inc.	VP, Federal Relations
	White House Office	Congressional Affairs/ Asst. to President
Jaskot, John J.	Jones, Walker et al.	Partner
	U.S. Coast Guard	Legislative/Congressional Affairs
Jennings, Christopher C.	Jennings Policy Strategies	Lobbyist
	White House Office	Adviser
Johnson, Joel P.	Glover Park Group	Partner
	White House Office	Senior Adviser to President
Jones, James R.	Manatt, Phelps & Phillips	Partner
	U.S. Diplomatic Missions	Ambassador to Mexico/ Member of Congress
Jones, Leroy, Jr.	Andrews & Bowe	Lobbyist
	Office of National Drug Control Policy	Legislative/Congressional Affairs
Kant, Peter	OSI Systems	VP, Government Affairs
	Dept. of Agriculture	Confidential Assistant
Kantor, Michael	Mayer, Brown et al.	Partner
	Dept. of Commerce	Secretary of Commerce
	Office of U.S. Trade Representative	U.S. Trade Representative
Kassir, Allison	King & Spalding	Government Relations Adviser
	Dept. of Defense	Staff Assistant
Keating, Timothy	Honeywell International	Senior VP, Governmental Affairs
	White House Office	Legislative/Congressional Affairs
Klepner, Jerry	BKSH & Assoc.	Managing Director
	Dept. of Health & Human Services	Asst. Secretary, Legislation
	Presidential Transition Team	Transition Director

Lobbyist	Employer—Private/Public	Title
Kohlmoos, James W.	National Educ. Knowledge Industry Assn.	
	Dept. of Education	Asst. Secretary, Elementary/Secondary Education
Kountoupes, Lisa	Clark & Weinstock	Lobbyist
	Office of Management & Budget	Asst. Director
Kristoff, Sandra J.	C&M International	Senior Adviser
	Dept. of State	Ambassador to APEC
	National Economic Council	Director, Asian Affairs
	National Security Council	Director, Asian Affairs
Kuwana, Eric A.	Katten, Muchin & Rosenman	Partner
	Dept. of Transportation	Employee/Staff
Lance, Linda	Wilderness Society	
	Council on Environmental Quality	Associate Director
	Vice President's Office	Senior Policy Analyst
LaRocco, Matthew L.	Arnold & Porter	Lobbyist
	Dept. of Interior	Special Assistant
LaRussa, Robert	Shearman & Sterling	Lobbyist
	International Trade Administration	Undersecretary
Laughlin, Keith	Rails to Trails Conservancy	
	White House Office	Employee/Staff
	Council on Environmental Quality	Associate Director
Lawler, Gregory E.	Lawler, Metzger et al.	Lobbyist
	White House Office	Senior Policy Adviser
Lawrence, Jeffrey	National Group	Partner
	National Aeronautics & Space Admin.	Assoc. Administrator, Legislative Affairs
Leach, Barbara M.	Leach, Barbara M.	Lobbyist
	Dept. of Transportation	Director, Intergovernmental Affairs
	Risk Management Agency	Chief of Staff
Levy, Michael B.	Brownstein, Hyatt et al.	Policy Director
	Dept. of Treasury	Senior Adviser to Secretary
Lynn, William J.	Raytheon Co.	Sr. VP, Government Operations & Strategy
	Dept. of Defense	Dir., Program Analysis & Evaluation
	Dept. of Defense	Undersecretary (Comptroller)
Magana, Mark	Raben Group	Lobbyist
	Dept. of Health & Human Services	Legislative/Congressional Affairs
	White House Office	Legislative/Congressional Affairs

Lobbyist	Employer—Private/Public	Title
Manning, Meredith	Hogan & Hartson	Partner
	Civil Division	Asst. U.S. Attorney
	U.S. Attorney's Office	Special Asst. U.S. Attorney
	Food & Drug Administration	Associate Chief Counsel
Marshall, Thurgood, Jr.	Bingham McCutchen LLP	Partner
	Vice President's Office	Director, Legislative Affairs
	Vice President's Office	Cabinet Secretary
Mason, Keith W.	McKenna, Long & Aldridge	Lobbyist
	White House Office	Legislative/Congressional Affairs
McCurry, Mike	Public Strategies	
	White House Office	Press Secretary
Medish, Mark C.	Akin, Gump et al.	Lobbyist
	White House Office	Special Asst. to President
	National Security Council	Senior Director, Eurasian Affairs
Michel, Kyle G.	Kyle Michel Law Firm	Lobbyist
	White House Office	Special Asst. to Vice President
Mikrut, Joseph	Capitol Tax Partners	Lobbyist
	Dept. of Treasury	Legislative/Congressional Affairs
Miller, Marcia	Kelley, Drye et al.	Senior Adviser
	U.S. International Trade Commission	Chair/Commissioner
Montgomery, John B.	Tighe, Patton et al.	Lobbyist
	Dept. of Defense	Special Asst. to Secretary
	Dept. of Navy	Director of Legislation
	Dept. of Navy	Special Counsel to the General Counsel
Morris, Evan	Hoffmann-La Roche	
	White House Office	Employee/Staff, Presidential Advance
Munoz, Kathy Juardo	Alcalde & Fay	Lobbyist
	Dept. of Veterans Affairs	Asst. Secretary, Public/ Intergovernmental Affairs
Murguia, Janet	National Council of La Raza	President & CEO
	White House Office	Deputy Dir., Legislative Affairs
Nichols, Johnnie	Potomac Advocates	Lobbyist
	Dept. of Air Force	Special Asst. to Secretary
	Dept. of Defense	Special Asst. to Secretary
Nordhaus, Robert	Van Ness Feldman	Member
	Federal Energy Regulatory Commission	General Counsel

Lobbyist	Employer—Private/Public	Title
Norton, Karin	Covington & Burling	Special Counsel
	U.S. International Trade Commission	Senior Investigative Attorney
Onek, Joseph	Constitution Project	
	Dept. of Justice	Employee/Staff
	Dept. of State	Employee/Staff
Pai, Jackson	Aegis Group	Lobbyist
	Dept. of State	Employee/Staff
Painter, Sally	Dutko Worldwide	Principal & Managing Director
	Dept. of Commerce	Deputy Director, Business Liaison
	White House Office	Senior Adviser
Palmer, Steven O.	Van Scoyoc Assoc.	VP
	Dept. of Transportation	Asst. Secretary, Govenmental Affairs
Palmieri, Jennifer	Center for American Progress	Sr. VP, Communications
	White House Office	Asst. to Chief of Staff
	White House Office	Deputy Press Secretary
Paster, Howard	Hill & Knowlton	Lobbyist
	White House Office	Legislative/Congressional Affairs
Permuy, Pedro Pablo	Greenberg Traurig LLP	Director, Government Affairs
	Dept. of Defense	Deputy Asst. Secretary, Inter-American Affairs
Perry, Mark	Gibson, Dunn & Crutcher	Partner
	Office of the Solicitor General	Attorney
Plebani, Jon	Buchanan Ingersoll	Lobbyist
	White House Office	Deputy Special Adviser on Haiti
Podesta, John	Center for American Progress	President & CEO
	White House Office	Assistant to President
	White House Office	Chief of Staff
Portman, Robert M.	Jenner & Block	Partner
	Dept. of Labor	Deputy Asst. Secretary, American Workplace
Powell, Paul	National Assn. of Chain Drug Stores	
	Dept. of Health & Human Services	Deputy Asst. Secretary, Congressional Liaison
Quinn, John M. "Jack"	Quinn, Gillespie & Assoc.	Founder & Cochairman
	Vice President's Office	Chief of Staff
	White House Office	Counsel to the President
Rasco, Carol	Reading Is Fundamental	
	Dept. of Education	Senior Adviser
	White House Office	Employee/Staff

Lobbyist	Employer—Private/Public	Title
Ratchford, William	Jefferson Government Relations	VP
	General Services Administration	Assoc. Administrator, Congressional Affairs
Reeder, Joseph R.	Greenberg Traurig LLP	Lobbyist
	Dept. of Army	Judge Advocate Undersecretary
Reid, Scott	Boston Scientific Corp.	
	Federal Judicial Center	Employee/Staff
Reinsch, William A.	National Foreign Trade Council	
	Bureau of Export Administration	Undersecretary
Ricchetti, Steve	Ricchetti, Inc.	President
	White House Office	Deputy Chief of Staff
	White House Office	Senate Lobbyist
Richard, Anne	International Rescue Committee	VP, Government Relations
	Dept. of State	Adviser for Budget and Planning
	Peace Corps	Deputy Chief Financial Officer
Robertson, Peter D.	Pillsbury, Winthrop et al.	Partner
	Environmental Protection Agency	Chief of Staff/Acting Deputy Administrator
Robinson, Jeffrey	Baach, Robinson & Lewis	Lobbyist
	Office of the Attorney General	Legislative/Congressional Affairs
Rohde, Gregory L.	e-Copernicus	President
	Natl. Telecom & Information Admin.	Administrator
Rotunno, Cynthia	Dewey Square Group	Principal
	White House Office	Political Affairs Office, Chief of Staff
	White House Office	Special Asst.
Rudman, Mara	Cohen Group	Lobbyist
	National Security Council	Legislative/Congressional Affairs
Santa, Donald	Interstate Natural Gas Assn.	President
	Federal Energy Regulatory Commission	Commissioner
Scher, Peter	Mayer, Brown et al.	Managing Partner
	Office of U.S. Trade Representative	Chief of Staff
	Office of U.S. Trade Representative	Special Trade Negotiator
	Dept. of Commerce	Chief of Staff
Scheunemann, Randy	Orion Strategies	President
	Dept. of Defense	Consultant, Iraq Policy
Schloss, Howard M.	National Assn. of Securities Dealers	Senior VP, Government Relations
	Dept. of Treasury	Asst. Secretary, Public Affairs

Lobbyist	Employer—Private/Public	Title
Seltman, Paul	Drinker, Biddle & Reath	Counsel
	Dept. of Health & Human Services	Special Asst.
Shearer, P. Scott	Bockorny Petrizzo, Inc.	Lobbyist
	Dept. of Agriculture	Counsel
Sheketoff, Emily	American Library Assn.	
	Occupational Safety & Health Admin.	Deputy Asst. Secretary
	Office of Personnel Management	Director, Interagency Affairs
Sibbison, V. Heather	Patton Boggs LLP	Lobbyist
	Dept. of Interior	Special Asst.
	Dept. of Justice	Counsel
Skol, Michael	Skol & Assoc.	President
	Dept. of State	Deputy Asst. Secretary, Inter-American Affairs
	U.S. Diplomatic Missions	Ambassador to Venezuela
Slater, Rodney E.	Patton Boggs LLP	Partner
	Dept. of Transportation	Secretary of Transportation
	Federal Highway Administration	Administrator
Smith, Brian D.	Covington & Burling	Lobbyist
	White House Office	Asst. to the Special Counsel
	Dept. of Labor	Special Asst. to Secretary
Smith, Jeffrey H.	Arnold & Porter	Partner
	Joint Security Commission	Chairman
	Central Intelligence Agency	General Counsel
	Dept. of Defense	Commission Member
	Presidential Transition Team	Chief, Defense Dept. Team
Stuart, Sandra	Clark & Weinstock	Lobbyist
	Dept. of Defense	Asst. Secretary, Legislative Affairs
Sussman, Robert M.	Latham & Watkins	Lobbyist
	Environmental Protection Agency	Deputy Administrator
Talisman, Jonathan	Capitol Tax Partners	Lobbyist
	Dept. of Treasury	Asst. Secretary, Tax Policy
Tate, Dan C., Jr.	Capitol Solutions	Lobbyist
	White House Office	Special Asst. to President, Legislative Affairs
	Dept. of Energy	Deputy Asst. Secretary, Congressional Relations
Terrell, Michael	Van Ness Feldman	Associate
	Council on Environmental Quality	Special Asst. for Outreach
Todd, Sean	Fox Potomac Resources	Lobbyist
	Dept. of Energy	Employee/Staff

Lobbyist	Employer—Private/Public	Title
Trapasso, Joseph S.	Pillsbury, Winthrop et al.	Senior Counsel
	Dept. of State	Legislative/Congressional Affairs
	Office of Personnel Management	Special Counsel to President
Turner, Leslie M.	Akin, Gump et al.	Lobbyist
	Dept. of Interior	Counselor to Secretary
Varney, Christine A.	Hogan & Hartson	Partner
	Federal Trade Commission	Commissioner
	White House Office	Secretary to the Cabinet
Velasquez, Joe	Velasquez & Lausell	Lobbyist
	White House Office	Deputy Political Director
Venable, Nicole	U.S. Chamber of Commerce	Director, International Trade
	Office of U.S. Trade Representative	Congressional Affairs Specialist
Vickery, Raymond E., Jr.	Vickery Intl.	Principal
	Dept. of Commerce	Asst. Secretary, Trade Development
Walke, John	Natural Resources Defense Council	Clean Air Director
	Environmental Protection Agency	Attorney, Office of General Counsel
Wexler, Daniel	Capitol Assoc.	VP
	White House Office	Special Asst. to the President
Wiginton, Joel	Sony Electronics	
	White House Office	Legislative/Congressional Affairs
Williams, Andrea	Cellular Telecom Industry Assn.	Asst. General Counsel
	Federal Communications Commission	Attorney/Adviser
Williamson, Thomas, Jr.	Covington & Burling	Lobbyist
	Mine Safety & Health Administration	Solicitor
Witt, James Lee	James Lee Witt Assoc.	CEO
	Federal Emergency Management Agency	Director

George W. Bush's Administration

Lobbyist	Employer—Private/Public	Title
Abernathy, Wayne	American Bankers Assn.	Exec. Director, Financial Institutions
	Dept. of Treasury	Asst. Secretary, Financial Institutions
	Senate Banking Committee	Staff Director

Lobbyist	Employer—Private/Public	Title
Ashcroft, John	Ashcroft Group	Principal
	Office of the Attorney General	Attorney General of the U.S.
	U.S. Senate	Senator
Atwood, Deborah M.	C&M Capitolink	Partner
	Dept. of Agriculture	Special Asst., Deputy Secretary
	National Oceanic & Atmospheric Administration	Staff
Becker, Brenda L.	Boston Scientific Corp.	Sr. VP, Global Government Affairs
	Dept. of Commerce	Asst. Secretary, Legislative/ Intergovernmental Affairs
	Vice President's Office	Asst., Legislative Affairs
Becker, Glynda	McBee Strategic Consulting	Exec. VP
	Dept. of Commerce	Adviser, Legislative/Inter- governmental Affairs
	White House Office	Associate Political Director
Benitez, Juan Carlos	Cassidy & Assoc.	Senior VP
	Office of the Attorney General	Special Counsel, Immigration Policy
Blackwill, Robert	Barbour, Griffith & Rogers	Lobbyist
	U.S. Diplomatic Missions	Ambassador to India
	National Security Council	Iraq Policy Deputy
Blalock, Kirk	Fierce, Isakowitz & Blalock	Partner
	White House Office	Special Asst. to President
Blank, Tom	Wexler & Walker Public Policy Assoc.	Principal
	Transportation Security Administration	Deputy Administrator
Bond, Phillip	Information Technology Industry Council	
	Dept. of Commerce	Undersecretary, Technology
Bonilla, Carlos	Washington Group	Lobbyist
	White House Office	Economic Adviser to President
Boyd, Thomas M.	DLA Piper	Partner & Cochair, Governmental Affairs
	Homeland Security Advisory Council	Member
Brenner, Scott	O'Neill & Assoc.	VP, Federal Relations
	National Highway Traffic Safety Admin.	Assoc. Administrator, External Affairs
	Federal Aviation Administration	Asst. Administrator, Public Affairs

Lobbyist	Employer—Private/Public	Title
Brouillette, Dan	Ford Motor Co.	VP, Washington Affairs
	Dept. of Energy	Asst. Secretary, Congressional/ Intergovernmental Affairs
Brown, Reginald	WilmerHale	Partner
	White House Office	Assoc. Counsel to the President
Bryant, Daniel	PepsiCo, Inc.	VP, Government Affairs
	Office of the Attorney General	Assistant Attorney General, Legislative Affairs
Bryson, Nancy S.	Venable LLP	Partner
	Dept. of Agriculture	Counsel
	Occupational Safety & Health Admin.	Staff Attorney & Assistant Counsel
Buchholz, Carl	Blank Rome Government Relations	Managing Partner, CEO
	Dept. of Homeland Security	Exec. Secretary
	White House Office	Special Asst. to President
Burgeson, Eric	Barbour, Griffith & Rogers	VP
	Dept. of Energy	Chief of Staff
	White House Office	Various Positions
Campoverde, Rebecca	Kaplan, Inc.	VP, Government Relations
	Dept. of Education	Asst. Secretary, Legislative/ Congressional Affairs
Card, Andrew H., Jr.	Fleishman-Hillard, Inc.	Member, International Advisory Board
	White House Office	Chief of Staff
	Dept. of Transportation	Secretary of Transportation
Carter, Thomas L.	Commonwealth Consulting	President
	Columbia Accident Investigation Board	Asst. to the Chairman
	Office of Foreign Missions	Counsel for Ambassador Bremer
Chadwick, Kirsten	Fierce, Isakowitz & Blalock	Partner
	White House Office	Special Asst., Legislative Affairs
Christie, Ronald I.	DC Navigators	Lobbyist
	White House Office	Special Asst. to President
Cole, Ray	Van Scoyoc Assoc.	VP
	Presidential Transition Team	Adviser, Dept. of Commerce

Lobbyist	Employer—Private/Public	Title
Colucci, Marlene M.	American Hotel & Lodging Assn.	Executive Vice President
	Domestic Policy Council	Special Asst.
	Dept. of Labor	Employee/Staff
Comstock, Barbara	Comstock Corallo	Partner
	Office of the Attorney General	Director, Public Affairs
Conklin, Brian	Urban Superintendents Assn. of America	VP, Federal Affairs
	White House Office	Special Asst., Legislative Affairs
Cooney, Philip	ExxonMobil	Lobbyist
	Council on Environmental Quality	Chief of Staff
Cox, Chris	DC Navigators	Principal
	Saxby Chambliss	Legislative Director
	White House Office	Special Asst., Legislative Affairs
Cragin, Maureen	Boeing Co.	VP, Communications
	Dept. of Veterans Affairs	Asst. Secretary, Public/ Intergovernmental Affairs
Craig, Daniel	Akerman Senterfitt	Lobbyist
	Federal Emergency Management Agency	Director, Recovery Division
Criss, Eric	Intermedia Communications	
	Consumer Product Safety Commission	Employee/Staff
Cunniffe, Amy Jensen	Advanced Medical Technology Assn.	Director, Government Affairs
	White House Office	Special Asst., Legislative Affairs
Cunningham, Bryan	Morgan & Cunningham	
	Central Intelligence Agency	Intelligence Officer
	National Security Council	Deputy Legal Adviser
Dahlberg, Gregory	Lockheed Martin	VP, Legislative Affairs
	Dept. of Army	Under Secretary of the Army
	Transportation & Related Agencies	Appropriations Subcommittee
Daniels, Deborah J.	Krieg Devault	Lobbyist
	Executive Office for Weed & Seed	Director
Davidson, Peter	Verizon Communications	Senior VP, Federal Government Relations
	Office of the Attorney General	Employee/Staff, Office of Legal Counsel
	Office of U.S. Trade Representative	General Counsel

Lobbyist	Employer—Private/Public	Title
Davis, Ashley	Blank Rome Government Relations	Principal
	Dept. of Homeland Security	Special Asst. to Director
Day, Lori Sharpe	Ashcroft Group	Lobbyist
	Office of the Attorney General	Associate Adviser
	White House Office	Director, Intergovern-mental/Public Liaison
Deere, Bill	U.S. Telecom Assn.	VP, Governmental Affairs
	Dept. of State	Deputy Asst. Secretary, Legislative Affairs
Delrahim, Makan	Brownstein, Hyatt et al.	Partner
	National Institutes of Health	Tech Licensing Analyst
	U.S. Antitrust Modernization Cmsn.	Commissioner
	Office of U.S. Trade Representative	Deputy Director, Intellectual Prop. Rights
	Office of the Attorney General	Deputy Asst. Attorney General
Duncan, John	Wexler & Walker Public Policy Assoc.	Lobbyist
	Dept. of Treasury	Asst. Secretary, Legislative Affairs
Fahmy Hudome, Randa	Fahmy Hudome International	Lobbyist
	Dept. of Energy	Foreign Policy Counselor
Faughnan, Brian	Electronic Industries Alliance	Sr. Manager, Government Relations
	U.S. Diplomatic Missions	Speechwriter to Ambassador to Mexico
Ferree, Kenneth	Sheppard, Mullin et al.	Partner
	Federal Communications Commission	Chief, Media Bureau
Frahler, Jori	Medical Device Manufacturers Assn.	Director, Federal Affairs
	Centers for Medicare & Medicaid Services	Employee/Staff
Fuller, James	Public Strategies	
	Transportation Security Administration	Chief of Staff
	Consumer Product Safety Commission	Chief of Staff
Furey, Jessica	Whitman Strategy Group	Partner
	Environmental Protection Agency	Associate Administrator
Gilbert, Alan	Pharmaceutical Rsrch. & Mfrs. of America	
	White House Office	Special Assistant to President
Glassco, Timothy	Patton Boggs LLP	Associate
	Federal Trade Commission	Law Clerk

Lobbyist	Employer—Private/Public	Title
Grubb, Darren	Bryan Cave LLP	Lobbyist
	Dept. of Commerce	Deputy Chief of Staff
	White House Office	Assoc. Director, Office of Global Communications
Hartley, Gregg L.	Cassidy & Assoc.	Vice Chairman & COO
	House Majority Whip	Chief of Staff (Roy Blunt)
Hauer, Jerome	Hauer Group	CEO
	Dept. of Health & Human Services	Sr. Health & Emergency Preparedness Adviser
Hay, John	P3 Consulting	Lobbyist
	Army Science Board	Member
	Dept. of Defense	Adviser to the Secretary
	Presidential Transition Team	Adviser
Heikkila, Heath	Ball Janik LLP	Lobbyist
	National Oceanic & Atmospheric Administration	Policy Adviser
Hobbs, David	Hobbs Group	Lobbyist
	White House Office	Chief Liaison to Congress
	White House Office	Legislative/Congressional Affairs
Hoffman, Bruce	Hunton & Williams	Lobbyist
	Federal Trade Commission	Deputy Director, Bureau of Competition
Holder, Eric H., Jr.	Covington & Burling	Partner
	Criminal Division	Clerk
	Office of the Attorney General	Deputy Attorney General
Hollis, Andre	Van Scoyoc Assoc.	VP
	Dept. of Defense	Deputy Asst. Secretary for Counternarcotics
Holman, Mark	Blank Rome Government Relations	Lobbyist
	Office of Homeland Security	Deputy Asst. to the President
Hotmire, Erik	Clark & Weinstock	Lobbyist
	White House Office	Communications Director, USA Freedom Corps
Howard, Jack	Wexler & Walker Public Policy Assoc.	President
	White House Office	Legislative/Congressional Affairs
Hughes, R. Douglas	Raytheon Co.	
	Navy (executive offices)	Director, Congressional Appropriations Liaison
Jackson, Paul	News Corporation	Lobbyist
	Federal Communications Commission	Legislative/Congressional Affairs

Lobbyist	Employer—Private/Public	Title
Jaeger, Lisa M.	Bracewell & Giuliani	Partner
	Environmental Protection Agency	Deputy General Counsel
	White House Office	Assoc. Director, Cabinet Affairs
	Environmental Protection Agency	Acting General Counsel
Jochum, James J.	Mayer, Brown et al.	Partner
	Dept. of Commerce	Asst. Secretary, Import Administration
Johnston, Ann Thomas	Capitol Hill Consulting	Lobbyist
	Dept. of Energy	Deputy Asst. Secretary, Congressional/ Intergovernmental Affairs
Jones, Alison	Ford Motor Co.	Legislative Manager
	White House Office	Legislative/Congressional Affairs
Jones, Elizabeth C.	APCO Worldwide	Executive VP
	Dept. of State	Asst. Secretary, Europe & Eurasia
Kelly, James A.	Phoenix Strategies	Lobbyist
	Dept. of Veterans Affairs	Deputy Asst. Secretary, Legislative Affairs
	White House Office	Special Asst. to President
Khatchadurian, Michael	American Defense International	Director, Government Affairs
	Joint Chiefs of Staff	Public Affairs Specialist
Kimbell, Jeffrey J.	Jeffrey J. Kimbell & Assoc.	President
	Dept. of Health & Human Services	Member, Transition Team
Kirk, Matthew	Hartford Financial Services Group	VP, Federal Government Affairs
	White House Office	Legislative/Congressional Affairs
Klitenic, Jason	McKenna, Long & Aldridge	Partner
	Dept. of Homeland Security	Deputy General Counsel
	Office of the Attorney General	Deputy Assoc. Attorney General
Krenik, Edward	Bracewell & Giuliani	Senior Principal
	Environmental Protection Agency	Legislative/Congressional Affairs
Lehman, Dirksen J.	Clark & Weinstock	Lobbyist
	White House Office	Special Asst. for Legislative Affairs
Lenti, Sarah	Bryan Cave Strategies	Sr. Adviser
	National Security Council	Director, Iraq Reconstruction

Lobbyist	Employer—Private/Public	Title
Lichtenbaum, Peter	Steptoe & Johnson	
	Bureau of Export Administration	Asst. Secretary
Litterst, Nelson	C2 Group	Lobbyist
	Presidential Transition Team	House Legislative Liaison
	White House Office	Legislative/Congressional Affairs
Loper, Ginger	Timmons & Co.	Lobbyist
	White House Office	Legislative/Congressional Affairs
	Lott, Trent	Legislative Asst.
Loy, James	Cohen Group	Senior Counselor
	Dept. of Homeland Security	Deputy Secretary
	Transportation Security Administration	Asst. Secretary of Homeland Security for TSA
	U.S. Coast Guard	Commandant
Lugar, Kelly	KSL Consulting	Principal
	Dept. of Energy	Deputy Asst. Secretary, Budget/Appropriations
Mackenzie, Cameron	Cohen Group	Sr. Assoc.
	U.S. Diplomatic Missions	Counselor, Togo Embassy
Maddox, Mark	Livingston Group	Lobbyist
	Dept. of Energy	Asst. Secretary, Fossil Energy
Martin, Aurene	Holland & Knight	Lobbyist
	Bureau of Indian Affairs	Deputy Asst. Secretary, Inter-American Affairs
Martinez, Jorge	Interamerica, Inc.	VP, Government & Public Affairs
	Office of the Attorney General	Spokesperson
McConnell, Mark S.	Hogan & Hartson	Partner
	Office of U.S. Trade Representative	Transition Advisory Cmte.
McHale, Stephen	Patton Boggs LLP	Lobbyist
	Dept. of Treasury	Acting General Counsel
	Transportation Security Administration	Deputy Administrator
McLean, Donna	Donna McLean Assoc.	President
	AMTRAK Reform Board	Member
	Dept. of Transportation	Asst. Secretary, Budget/ Programs
	Federal Aviation Administration	Chief Financial Officer
McSlarrow, Kyle	National Cable & Telecommunications Assn.	President & CEO
	Dept. of Energy	Deputy Secretary
Meece, Michael E.	Meece Enterprises LLC	Lobbyist
	Dept. of Commerce	Employee/Staff
	White House Office	Employee/Staff

Lobbyist	Employer—Private/Public	Title
Melley, Brendan	Cohen Group	Associate VP
	National Security Council	Director for Counterproliferation
Mencer, C. Suzanne	Brownstein, Hyatt et al.	Policy Director
	Dept. of Homeland Security	Director, Domestic Preparedness
Mendenhall, James	Sidley, Austin et al.	Partner
	Office of U.S. Trade Representative	General Counsel
Merola, Barbara	Loeffler Group	Legislative Asst.
	Office of Management & Budget	Procurement Policy Staff
Miller, Lisa	Tomb & Assoc.	
	Dept. of Housing & Urban Development	Director, Scheduling and Advance
Moffitt, Stephen	Whyte, Hirschboeck & Dudek	Principal
	Dept. of Defense	Deputy Asst. Secretary, Senate Affairs
Moore, Powell	McKenna, Long & Aldridge	Lobbyist
	Dept. of Defense	Asst. Secretary, Legislative Affairs
	White House Office	Legislative/Congressional Affairs
Moran, Robert L.	Perennial Strategy Group	Lobbyist
	Dept. of Education	Policy Adviser to Undersecretary
Morello, Steven J.	Native Law Group	Principal
	Dept. of Army	General Counsel
Morrell, Jim	HDMK	Partner
	White House Office	Spokesperson
Mulvaney, Susan	Whitman Strategy Group	Principal
	Environmental Protection Agency	Deputy Chief of Staff
Murphy, Dan	Barbour, Griffith & Rogers	Principal
	Dept. of Housing & Urban Development	Chief of Staff
Neely, Susan	American Beverage Assn.	President and CEO
	Dept. of Homeland Security	Asst. Secretary, Public Affairs
	White House Office	Special Asst. for Homeland Security
Nesmith, Steven	Blank Rome Government Relations	
	Dept. of Housing & Urban Development	Asst. Secretary, Congressional/Inter-governmental Affairs
	Economic Development Administration	Deputy Asst. Secretary, Legislative/Congressional Affairs

Lobbyist	Employer—Private/Public	Title
Newman, Constance	Carmen Group	Lobbyist
	Dept. of State	Asst. Secretary, African Affairs
	U.S. Agency for International Development	Assistant Administrator
Niemeyer, Matt	ACE INA	
	Office of U.S. Trade Representative	Legislative/Congressional Affairs
Norton, Karin	Covington & Burling	Special Counsel
	U.S. International Trade Commission	Senior Investigative Attorney
Olson, Pamela	Skadden, Arps et al.	Partner
	Dept. of Treasury	Asst. Secretary, Tax Policy
Pelletier, Eric	General Electric	
	Office of Management & Budget	Legislative/Congressional Affairs
	Solomon, Gerald B.H.	Legislative Asst.
	White House Office	Legislative/Congressional Affairs
Peltier, Benjamin	Arent, Fox et al.	Associate
	Dept. of Justice	Clerk
Pemberton, John L.	Southern Co.	VP, Governmental Affairs
	Environmental Protection Agency	Chief of Staff to Asst. Administrator
Phelps, Anne	Washington Council Ernst & Young	Lobbyist
	White House Office	Special Asst. to President
Pisano, Paul	National Beer Wholesalers Assn.	VP, Industry Affairs
	Bureau of the Census	Director, Congressional Affairs
	Economic Development Administration	Director, Intergovern-mental Affairs
Primrose, Steve	TriAdvocates	Principal
	Resolution Trust Corporation	Congressional Affairs
Principi, Anthony J.	Pfizer, Inc.	VP, Government Affairs
	Dept. of Veterans Affairs	Staff Director (Republican)
Radus, Seth	Advanced Medical Technology Assn.	VP, Government Affairs
	Dept. of Health & Human Services	Office Asst. Secretary Management & Budget
Reardon, Brian	Venn Strategies	Principal
	National Economic Council	Special Asst. to the President

Lobbyist	Employer—Private/Public	Title
Reinhart, Anthony	Ford Motor Co.	South Central Regional Government Affairs Mngr.
	Office of the Attorney General	Employee/Staff
Riley, Dawn R.	Triangle Associates	Associate
	Dept. of Agriculture	Special Asst., Deputy Secretary
Rogan, James	K&L Gates	Partner
	Patent & Trademark Office	Director
	Dept. of Commerce	Undersecretary
Rossetti, Michael G.	Akin, Gump et al.	Partner
	Dept. of Interior	Counsel
Rudolf, Paul	Avalere Health	
	Food & Drug Administration	Senior Adviser, Medical & Health Policy
Sailor, Angela	JC Watts Cos.	Partner, HR Empowerment
	Dept. of Education	Deputy Chief of Staff
	Office of Public Liaison	Assoc. Director
Schlapp, Matthew	Koch Industries	Executive Director of Federal Affairs
	White House Office	Deputy Director of Political Affairs
Schuchart, Cathy	School Nutrition Assn.	VP, Government Affairs
	Food Safety & Inspection Service	Legislative Division Chief
Schwerin, Eric	Oldaker, Biden & Belair	Partner
	Dept. of Commerce	Senior Policy Adviser
Sell, Tom	Combest Sell & Assoc.	Lobbyist
	Dept. of Agriculture	Director, Intergovern- mental Affairs
	Presidential Transition Team	Member, Bush II
Siff, Andrew	Siff & Cerda	Lobbyist
	Dept. of Labor	Chief of Staff
Sigal, Jill	EnergySolutions	Senior VP, Government Relations
	Dept. of Energy	Special Assistant
Sims, James	Policy Communications Colorado	President
	White House Office	National Energy Policy Task Force
Spellacy, Daniel	Dts Solutions	President
	Dept. of Agriculture	Sr. Adviser to Undersecretary, Food
Stroud, D. Michael, Jr.	American Cancer Society	Counsel for Federal and Regulatory Affairs
	Dept. of Commerce	Attorney

Lobbyist	Employer—Private/Public	Title
Styles, Angela B.	Crowell & Moring	Partner
	Office of Management & Budget	Administrator, Federal Procurement Policy
Thurmond, J. Strom, Jr.	J. Strom Thurmond, Jr.	Lobbyist
	U.S. Attorney's Office	U.S. Attorney, Dist. of South Carolina
Toner, Michael	Bryan Cave LLP	Partner
	Federal Election Commission	Commissioner
	Presidential Transition Team	General Counsel
Torrey, Michael	Michael Torrey Assoc.	Principal
	Dept. of Agriculture	Deputy Chief of Staff
Van Tine, Kirk	Baker Botts LLP	Lobbyist
	Dept. of Transportation	Deputy Secretary & General Counsel
Vennett, David	Toyota Motor Manufacturing North America	Lobbyist
	U.S. Diplomatic Missions	Special Adviser, Ambassador to Netherlands
	White House Office	Staff, White House Liaison
Verdery, C. Stewart, Jr.	Monument Policy Group	Lobbyist
	Dept. of Homeland Security	Asst. Secretary, Border/ Transportation Policy
Verveer, Alexandra	Discovery Communications	Professional/Lobbyist
	Federal Communications Commission	National Coordination Committee
Victory, Nancy	Wiley, Rein & Fielding	Lobbyist
	White House Office	Telecommunications Policy Adviser
	Dept. of Commerce	Asst. Secretary, Communications/ Information
Wallace, Mark	Akerman Senterfitt	Lobbyist
	Federal Emergency Management Agency	General Counsel
	U.S. Citizenship & Immigration Services	Principal Legal Adviser
	U.S. Immigration & Customs Enforcement	Principal Legal Adviser
Whitley, Joe D.	Alston & Bird	Partner
	Dept. of Homeland Security	General Counsel
Wilcox, Gary	Morgan, Lewis & Bockius	Partner
	Internal Revenue Service	Deputy Chief Counsel
Wild, Brian	Nickles Group	Lobbyist
	Vice President's Office	Asst.
Wolf, Chad	Wexler & Walker Public Policy Assoc.	Principal
	Transportation Security Administration	Asst. Administrator for Policy

Lobbyist	Employer—Private/Public	Title
Wood, Robert	Barbour, Griffith & Rogers	President
	Dept. of Health & Human Services	Chief of Staff
Yates, Steve	Barbour, Griffith & Rogers	Lobbyist
	Vice President's Office	Deputy Asst.
Yeager, Karen	Dutko Worldwide	VP
	Dept. of Homeland Security	Adviser to the Undersecretary
	White House Office	Deputy Assoc. Director, Presidential Personnel
Yu, Shannon	Metropolitan Life Insurance	Head, International Affairs
	International Trade Administration	Director, Office of Financial Services

Source: A special run by the Center for Responsive Politics, Washington, D.C., January 2008.

TABLE 4: THE CONGRESSIONAL REVOLVING DOOR

(Former Members of Congress, Their Committee Assignments, Their Lobbying Firms, and the Firm's Client Count)*

Firm's Client Count	Former Members of U.S. Congress	Employer	Committee 1	Committee 2	Committee 3	Committee 4	Committee 5
24	Alexander, William	Advantage Assoc	Appropriations				
12	Andrews, Michael	Michael A. Andrews					
14	Anthony, Beryl Franklin, Jr.	Sundquist Anthony	Ways & Means	Select Children, Youth & Families			
185	Archer, Bill	PriceWaterhouse Coopers	Ways & Means	Joint Taxation			
154	Armey, Dick	DLA Piper	Government Reform	Education & the Workforce	Budget	Banking, Finance & Urban Affairs	Joint Economic
20	Ashcroft, John	Ashcroft Group	Commerce, Science, & Transportation	Labor & Public Welfare	Judiciary	Foreign Relations	
346	Bacchus, James	Greenberg Taurig LLP	Select Children, Youth & Families	Banking, Finance & Urban Affairs	Science		
3	Barr, Bob	Liberty Strategies	Veterans' Affairs	Government Reform	Judiciary	Banking, Finance & Urban Affairs	Financial Services
931	Bell, Chris	Patton Boggs LLP	Financial Services				

Firm's Client Count	Former Members of U.S. Congress	Employer	Committee 1	Committee 2	Committee 3	Committee 4	Committee 5
19	Bentley, Helen Delich	Helen Bentley & Assoc.	Public Works & Transportation	Merchant Marine & Fisheries	Select Aging	Appropriations	Budget
1	Bentsen, Kenneth E.	Equipment Leasing Assn. of America	Small Business	Banking, Finance & Urban Affairs	Appropriations	Budget	Financial Services
83	Bliley, Thomas J., Jr.	Steptoe & Johnson	District of Columbia	Energy & Commerce	Select Children, Youth & Families		
16	Borski, Bob	Borski Assoc.	Standards of Official Conduct	Public Works & Transportation	Foreign Affairs	Transportation & Infrastructure	Select Aging
0	Breaux, John	Breaux-Lott Leadership Group	Special Aging	Commerce, Science, & Transportation	Rules & Administration	Finance	
78	Brewster, Bill K.	Capitol Hill Consulting	Transportation & Infrastructure	Public Works & Transportation	Ways & Means	Veterans' Affairs	
20	Bryan, Richard H.	Lionel, Sawyer & Collins	Commerce, Science, & Transportation	Armed Services	Joint Economic	Select Intelligence	Finance
2	Bryant, Edward G.	Bryant, Edward G.	Energy & Commerce	Judiciary	Agriculture		
264	Bumpers, Dale	Arent, Fox et al.	Small Business	Energy & Natural Resources	Appropriations		
136	Burns, Max	Thelen, Reid & Priest	Agriculture	Transportation & Infrastructure	Education & the Workforce		
33	Callahan, Sonny	Sonny Callahan & Assoc.	Merchant Marine & Fisheries	Energy & Commerce	Appropriations		

Firm's Client Count	Former Members of U.S. Congress	Employer	Committee 1	Committee 2	Committee 3	Committee 4	Committee 5
366	Campbell, Ben Nighthorse	Holland & Knight	Environment & Public Works	Indian Affairs	Banking, Housing & Urban Affairs	Veterans' Affairs	Energy & Natural Resources
52	Carr, Bob	Dow, Lohnes & Albertson	Appropriations	Armed Services			
135	Chapman, James L.	Bracewell & Guiliani	Appropriations				
117	Christensen, Jon L.	Buchanan, Ingersoll & Rooney	Ways & Means				
133	Coats, Daniel R.	King & Spalding	Armed Services	Select Intelligence	Labor & Public Welfare		
212	Coleman, E. Thomas	Livingston Group	Education & the Workforce	Agriculture			
10	Coleman, Ronald D.	Shawn Coulson Law Firm	Appropriations	Permanent Select on Intelligence			
9	Combest, Larry	Combest, Sell & Assoc.	District of Columbia	Permanent Select on Intelligence	Small Business	Agriculture	
40	D'Amato, Alfonse	Park Strategies	Banking, Housing & Urban Affairs	Appropriations	Select Intelligence	Finance	
81	Darden, George W.	McKenna, Long & Aldridge	Standards of Official Conduct	Armed Services	Appropriations	Interior & Insular Affairs	
145	DeConcini, Dennis	Parry, Romani et al.	Joint Library of Congress	Joint Printing	Veterans' Affairs	Appropriations	Select Intelligence
19	Derrick, Butler	Nelson, Mullins et al.	Administration	Rules	Select Aging	Natural Resources	
13	Dickey, Jay	JD Consulting	Appropriations	Small Business	Agriculture		
160	Dole, Bob	Alston & Bird	Joint Taxation	Agriculture, Nutrition & Forestry	Select Intelligence	Rules & Administration	Finance

Firm's Client Count	Former Members of U.S. Congress	Employer	Committee 1	Committee 2	Committee 3	Committee 4	Committee 5
1	English, Glenn Lee, Jr.	National Rural Electric Cooperative Assn.	Ways & Means		Joint Economic	Small Business	
87	Ewing, Thomas W.	Davis & Harman	Science	Administration	Transportation & Infrastructure	Agriculture	Joint Economic
426	Faircloth, Lauch	Akin, Gump et al.	Small Business	Banking, Housing & Urban Affairs	Appropriations	Armed Services	Environment & Public Works
1	Fawell, Harris W.	Harris W. Fawell	Science	Select Aging	Select Children, Youth & Families	Education & the Workforce	Economic & Educational Opportunities
426	Fazio, Victor H.	Akin, Gump et al.	Standards of Official Conduct	Appropriations	Select Hunger	Oversight	
25	Fields, Jack	Twenty-First Century Group	Merchant Marine & Fisheries	Energy & Commerce			
25	Flanagan, Michael P.	Flanagan Consulting	Government Reform	Veterans' Affairs	Judiciary		
426	Foley, Thomas S.	Akin, Gump et al.	Interior & Insular Affairs				
5	Forbes, Michael P.	PR/Strategies International	Banking, Finance & Urban Affairs	Appropriations			
13	Ford, Harold Sr.	Harold Ford Group	Select Aging	Ways & Means			
115	Ford, Wendell H.	Dickstein, Shapiro et al.	Energy & Natural Resources	Joint Printing	Commerce, Science, & Transportation	Rules & Administration	
1	Franks, Robert D.	Healthcare Institute of New Jersey	Budget	Transportation & Infrastructure	Public Works & Transportation		

Firm's Client Count	Former Members of U.S. Congress	Employer	Committee 1	Committee 2	Committee 3	Committee 4	Committee 5
21	Funderburk, David	Perennial Strategy Group	Economic & Educational Opportunities	Interior & Insular Affairs	Small Business		
3	Gephardt, Richard	Gephardt Group	Permanent Select on Intelligence	Budget			
16	Gibbons, Sam M.	Gibbons & Co.	Joint Taxation	Ways & Means			
1	Glickman, Daniel R.	Motion Picture Assn. of America	Permanent Select on Intelligence	Judiciary	Agriculture	Science	
0	Goodling, William	Goodling Institute	Education & the Workforce	Foreign Affairs	Interior & Insular Affairs	Budget	Economic & Educational Opportunities
1	Gorton, Slade	K&L Gates	Select Intelligence	Armed Services	Agriculture, Nutrition & Forestry	Labor & Public Welfare	Budget
28	Grams, Rodney R.	Hecht, Spencer & Assoc.	Energy & Natural Resources	Joint Economic	Banking, Housing & Urban Affairs	Budget	Foreign Relations
1	Greenwood, James C.	Biotechnology Industry Organization	Energy & Commerce	Economic & Educational Opportunities	Education & the Workforce		
110	Hayes, James A.	Adams & Reese	Transportation & Infrastructure	Science	Government Reform	Public Works & Transportation	
172	Hilleary, Van	Sonnenschein, Nath & Rosenthal	Education & the Workforce	Science	Small Business	Natural Resources	Budget
0	Hoagland, Peter	Advocacy, Inc.	Ways & Means	Judiciary	Interior & Insular Affairs	Small Business	Banking, Finance & Urban Affairs

Firm's Client Count	Former Members of U.S. Congress	Employer	Committee 1	Committee 2	Committee 3	Committee 4	Committee 5
213	Hochbrueckner, George J.	O'Connor & Hannan	Armed Services	Merchant Marine & Fisheries	Veterans' Affairs	Select Narcotics Abuse & Control	Permanent Select on Intelligence
0	Hutchinson, Asa	Hutchinson Group	Judiciary	Veterans' Affairs	Transportation & Infrastructure	Government Reform	
115	Hutchinson, Tim	Dickstein, Shapiro et al.	Public Works & Transportation	Veterans' Affairs	Agriculture, Nutrition & Forestry	Special Aging	Labor & Public Welfare
173	Johnson, Nancy	Baker, Donelson et al.	Standards of Official Conduct	Ways & Means		Special Aging	
105	Johnston, J. Bennett	Johnston & Assoc.	Select Intelligence	Energy & Natural Resources	Appropriations		Budget
1	Kennelly, Barbara	Natl. Cmte. to Preserve Social Security	Administration	Budget	Permanent Select on Intelligence	Ways & Means	
3	Klein, Herbert C.	Nowell, Amoroso et al.	Banking, Finance & Urban Affairs	Science			
212	Klink, Ron	Livingston Group	Education & the Workforce	Banking, Finance & Urban Affairs	Energy & Commerce	Small Business	
134	Klug, Scott	Foley & Lardner	Education & the Workforce	Energy & Commerce	Select Children, Youth & Families	Government Reform	
7	Kopetski, Michael J.	Kopetski, Michael J. Strategic Marketing Innovation	Science	Judiciary	Ways & Means	Agriculture	
185	Kuykendall, Steven T.		Transportation & Infrastructure	Armed Services	Science		
0	LaFalce, John J.	HoganWillig	Small Business	Banking, Finance & Urban Affairs	Financial Services		

Appendix

Firm's Client Count	Former Members of U.S. Congress	Employer	Committee 1	Committee 2	Committee 3	Committee 4	Committee 5
1	Largent, Steve	Cellular Telecom & Internet Assn.	Science	Energy & Commerce	Budget		
267	LaRocco, Lawrence P.	Fleishman-Hillard Inc.	Banking, Finance & Urban Affairs	Interior & Insular Affairs	Natural Resources		Merchant Marine & Fisheries
77	Laughlin, Gregory H.	Pillsbury, Winthrop et al.	Transportation & Infrastructure	Public Works & Transportation	Permanent Select on Intelligence	Post Office & Civil Service	Aviation
117	Lightfoot, James	Buchanan, Ingersoll & Rooney	Select Aging	Interior & Insular Affairs	Public Works & Transportation	Appropriations	
212	Livingston, Robert L.	Livingston Group	Permanent Select on Intelligence	Appropriations	Administration	Appropriations	
1	Luther, Bill	Fleishman-Hillard Govt Relations	Energy & Commerce	Science	International Relations		
133	Mack, Connie	King & Spalding	Armed Services	Joint Economic	Select Intelligence	Finance	Appropriations
1	McCurdy, Dave	Alliance of Automobile Manufacturers	Permanent Select on Intelligence	Science	Armed Services		
61	McDade, Joseph M.	Ervin Technical Assoc.	Appropriations	Small Business			
112	McGrath, Raymond J.	Downey McGrath Group	Government Operations	Science & Technology	Ways & Means		
171	McIntosh, David M.	Mayer, Brown et al.	Government Reform	Economic & Educational Opportunities	Small Business	Education & the Workforce	
471	Michel, Robert H.	Hogan & Hartson	Minority Leader				
154	Mitchell, George J.	DLA Piper	Veterans' Affairs	Environment & Public Works	Finance	Select Intelligence	

Firm's Client Count	Former Members of U.S. Congress	Employer	Committee 1	Committee 2	Committee 3	Committee 4	Committee 5
81	Miller, Zell	McKenna, Long & Aldridge	Banking, Housing & Urban Affairs	Veterans' Affairs	Agriculture, Nutrition & Forestry		
152	Molinari, Susan	Washington Group	Budget				
513	Myers, John	Cassidy & Assoc.	Post Office & Civil Service	Standards of Official Conduct	Appropriations		
19	Nethercutt, George	BlueWater Strategies	Appropriations	Science			
35	Nickles, Don	Nickles Group	Budget	Joint Taxation	Rules & Administration	Appropriations	Indian Affairs
24	Orton, Bill	Advantage Assoc.	Budget	Banking, Finance & Urban Affairs	Foreign Affairs	Small Business	
18	Packard, Ron	Packard Government Affairs	Science	Public Works & Transportation	Select Children, Youth & Families	Appropriations	
24	Packwood, Bob	Sunrise Research Corp.	Finance	Commerce, Science, & Transportation	Joint Taxation		
27	Parker, Mike	Welch Resources	Transportation & Infrastructure	Veterans' Affairs	Budget	Public Works & Transportation	Education & the Workforce
471	Porter, John Edward	Hogan & Hartson	Select Aging	Labor, Health & Human Services, Education & Related Agencies	Appropriations		
0	Pressler, Larry	Pressler International	Small Business	Foreign Relations	Commerce, Science, & Transportation	Finance	Special Aging
77	Riegle, Don	APCO Worldwide	Special Aging	Banking, Housing & Urban Affairs	Finance	Budget	

Firm's Client Count	Former Members of U.S. Congress	Employer	Committee 1	Committee 2	Committee 3	Committee 4	Committee 5
1	Rogan, James	K&L Gates	Judiciary	Energy & Commerce		Administration	
22	Rose, Charlie	Rose & Hefner Consulting	Agriculture	Joint Printing	Joint Library of Congress		
25	Roth, Toby	Roth Group	Banking, Finance & Urban Affairs	Foreign Affairs	Interior & Insular Affairs		
2	Salmon, Matthew J.	CompTel	Science	Small Business	Interior & Insular Affairs	Education & the Workforce	
267	Sandlin, Max	Fleishman-Hillard, Inc.	Ways & Means	Transportation & Infrastructure	Banking, Finance & Urban Affairs	Financial Services	
24	Sarpalius, Bill	Advantage Assoc.	General Farm Commodities	Select Children, Youth & Families	Small Business	Rural Enterprises, Exports & the Environment	
1	Schroeder, Patricia	Assn. of American Publishers	Armed Services	Select Children, Youth & Families			
142	Sharp, Philip R.	Van Ness Feldman	Interior & Insular Affairs	Natural Resources			
13	Shuster, Bud	Strategic Advisory Group	Transportation & Infrastructure	Public Works & Transportation	Permanent Select on Intelligence		
52	Simpson, Alan K.	Tongour Simpson Group	Veterans' Affairs	Finance	Judiciary	Environment & Public Works	Special Aging
120	Slattery, James	Wiley, Rein & Fielding	Energy & Commerce	Banking, Finance & Urban Affairs	Budget	Veterans' Affairs	
117	Stenholm, Charles W.	Olsson, Frank & Weeda	Agriculture	Armed Services	Budget	Veterans' Affairs	

Firm's Client Count	Former Members of U.S. Congress	Employer	Committee 1	Committee 2	Committee 3	Committee 4	Committee 5
14	Stokes, Louis B.	Squire, Sanders & Dempsey	Standards of Official Conduct	Appropriations			
14	Sundquist, Don	Sundquist Anthony	Ways & Means				
6	Swift, Al	Colling, Swift et al.	Administration	Transportation & Hazardous Materials			
7	Tate, Randy	Tate Strategies	Government Reform	Transportation & Infrastructure			
1	Tauzin, Billy	Pharmaceutical Rsrch. & Mfrs. of America	Resources	Energy & Commerce	Merchant Marine & Fisheries		
1	Thompson, Fred	Offices of Fred D. Thompson	Governmental Affairs	Finance	Select Intelligence	Judiciary	Select Presidential Campaign Activities
3	Thurman, Karen	Thurman, Karen	Agriculture	Government Reform	Ways & Means		
141	Turner, Jim	Arnold & Porter	Government Reform	Armed Services			
195	Walker, Robert S.	Wexler & Walker Public Policy Assoc.	Science	Budget			
0	Wallop, Malcolm	Frontiers of Freedom Institute	Small Business	Energy & Natural Resources	Finance	Select Intelligence	Armed Services
41	Watts, J. C.	J. C. Watts Cos.	Transportation & Infrastructure	Natural Resources	Banking, Finance & Urban Affairs	Armed Services	
182	Weber, Vin	Clark & Weinstock	Appropriations				

Firm's Client Count	Former Members of U.S. Congress	Employer	Committee 1	Committee 2	Committee 3	Committee 4	Committee 5
58	Wheat, Alan	Wheat Government Relations	District of Columbia	Select Children, Youth & Families	Rules	Select Hunger	
212	Zeliff, William H.	Livingston Group	Small Business	Government Reform	Public Works & Transportation	Transportation & Infrastructure	
65	Zimmer, Dick	Gibson, Dunn & Crutcher	Ways & Means	Select Aging	Science	Government Reform	

Source: A special run by the Center for Responsive Politics, Washington, D.C., January 2008.

*This table lists all former members of Congress turned lobbyists in the era of the administrations of Bill Clinton and George W. Bush. It identifies up to five of their most recent committee assignments. Those former members who served in the Executive Branch are identified in Table 3. For cases where the firm's client is listed as 1, the former MC works in-house at a trade association or company, most often. For cases where the firm's client is 0, it is usually the case that the firm was recently formed.

TABLE 5: THE WALL STREET–WASHINGTON CONNECTION

(Former Public Officials and Post-Governmental Employment in Financial Institutions)

Bill Clinton's Administration

Name	Employer	Title	Registered Lobbyist
Anderson, Karen	Citigroup, Inc.	VP	y
	Environmental Protection Agency	Legislative/Congressional Affairs	
	White House Office	Employee/Staff	
Blocker, Anaias III	New York Stock Exchange	Vice President, Government Relations	y
	White House Office	Legislative/Congressional Affairs	
Clinton, Bill	Yucaipa Companies	Investor/Adviser	n
	President of the United States		
Dalton, John	Financial Services Roundtable	President, Housing Policy Council	y
	Dept. of Navy	Secretary of the Navy	
Gore, Albert	Generation Investment Management LLC	Chairman	n
	Vice President of the United States		
Healy, Monica M.	Community Associations Institute	VP, Government & Public Affairs	y
	Dept. of Labor	Adviser to the Secretary	
Levitt, Arthur	The Carlyle Group	Senior Adviser	n
	SEC (1993–2001)	Chairman	

Name	Employer	Title	Registered Lobbyist
Lowrey, Carmen Guzman	Fannie Mae		y
	Office of U.S. Trade Representative	Deputy Asst. Trade Representative	
	Dept. of Commerce	Acting. Asst. Secretary, Legislative Affairs	
	Patent & Trademark Office	Associate Commissioner	
Marchick, David	The Carlyle Group Senior Presidential Adviser	Head, Regulatory Affairs	n
McLarty, Thomas F.	The Carlyle Group Senior Presidential Adviser	Adviser on Mexico Investments	n
Rubin, Robert E.	Citigroup	Director/Chairman	n
	U.S. Treasury	Secretary	
Stein, Larry	Capital One Financial	Senior VP	y
	White House Office	Legislative/Congressional Affairs	

George W. Bush's Administration

Name	Employer	Title	Registered Lobbyist
Abernathy, Wayne	American Bankers Assn.	Exec. Director, Financial Institutions	y
	Dept. of Treasury	Asst. Secretary, Financial Institutions	
Bolten, Joshua	White House 2006– OMB (2003–2006)	Chief of Staff Director	n
	White House (2001–2003)	Deputy Chief of Staff	
	Goldman Sachs (1994–1999)	Legal/Government Affairs	
	White House (1989–1993)	USTR Counsel/Deputy Asst., Legislative Affairs	
Burgeson, Christine	Citigroup, Inc.	VP, Federal Affairs	y
	Office of Management & Budget	Legislative Affairs	
	White House Office	Legislative/Congressional Affairs	
Duvall, Doug	Freddie Mac		
	Dept. of Housing & Urban Development	Deputy Asst. Secretary, Public Affairs	
Grubbs, Wendy	Citigroup, Inc.	VP, Federal Government Affairs	y
	White House Office	Liaison to Senate	

Name	Employer	Title	Registered Lobbyist
Keniry, Daniel J.	Teachers Insurance & Annuity Assn.	VP, Federal Relations	y
	White House Office	House Liaison & Deputy Asst., Legislative Affairs	
O'Neill, Paul H.	Blackstone Group	Special Adviser	n
	U.S. Treasury	Secretary	
Ruhlen, Stephen S.	JPMorgan Chase & Co.	Head of Federal Government Relations	y
	Vice President's Office	Deputy Asst.	
Sampson, David A.	Property Casualty Insurers Assn./America	President & CEO	
	Economic Development Administration	Asst. Secretary, Economic Development	
	Dept. of Commerce	Deputy Secretary	
Snow, John	Cerebus Capital Mgt.	Chairman	n
	U.S. Treasury	Secretary	
Whitfield, Sam	National Assn. of Realtors	Legislative Representative	y
	Dept. of Defense	Press Officer, Coalition Provisional Authority Iraq	
Zoellick, Robert	World Bank 2007–Present	President	n
	Goldman Sachs (2006–07)	Senior Intl. Adviser	
	Dept. of State	Undersecretary State	
	White House	Deputy Chief of Staff/Adviser	
	Dept. of State (2005–06)	Deputy Secretary	
	USTR (2001–05)	U.S. Trade Representative	
	Federal National Mortgage Association (1993–1997)	Executive VP	

Ex-Members of Congress

Name	Employer	Title	Registered Lobbyist
Bradley, Bill	J.P. Morgan & Co. (1997–1999)	Senior Adviser	n
	Allen & Company, LLC	Managing Director	n
	U.S. Senator (D-N.J.)		
Gramm, Phil	UBS Investment Bank	Vice Chairman	n
	U.S. Senator (R-Tx.)		

Source: A special run by the Center for Responsive Politics and public source materials. Several people who shifted from public position to private employment became lobbyists. Others took major positions in Wall Street and other financial institutions. This is a partial count since U.S. officials have no post-employment reporting requirements.

Notes

Prologue

3 "The extraordinary enigma": Sir James Goldsmith, *The Trap* (New York: Carroll & Graf, 1994), cover.

4 Surely, he said: Ibid., p. 28.

4 The domestic social compact: Calculated from "Mass Layoff Statistics," Bureau of Labor Statistics, U.S. Department of Labor, October 24, 2007.

4 Lifetime jobs: Tom Mullikin, *Truck Stop Politics* (Charlotte, N.C.: Vox Populi), pp. 7–37.

4 The U.S. trade deficit: "U.S. Trade in Goods and Services, 1960 through 2006," U.S. Census Bureau, Foreign Trade Statistics, June 8, 2007.

Introduction: AND HOLD THE MELAMINE, PLEASE

6 Relieved that: "Recall-Firm Press Release, 'Menu Foods Issues Recall of Specific Can and Small Foil Pouch Wet Pet Foods,' " U.S. Food and Drug Administration (FDA), March 16, 2007.

7 "Yesterday, I did": Paul Krugman, "Fear of Eating," *The New York Times*, May 21, 2007.

7 The Bush administration's: Anna Edney, "FDA Staffers Allege Agency Intimidation," *Congress Daily*, July 25, 2007.

8 Altogether, Menu Foods: Charlie Gillis and Anne Kingston, "The Great Pet Food Scandal: How One Supplier Caused a Huge Crisis, and Why It's Just the Tip of the Iceberg," available at Macleans.ca., April 30, 2007.

8 The scientists isolated: David Barboza and Alexei Barrionuevo, "Filler in Animal Feed Is Open Secret in China," *The New York Times*, April 30, 2007.

8 The American Veterinary: "Melamine and Cyanuric Acid Interaction May Play Part in Illness and Death from Recalled Pet Food," American Veterinary Medical Association, May 1, 2007.

9 ChemNutra had won: Gillis and Kingston, "The Great Pet Food Scandal."

9 By mid-April: Ibid.

9 FDA officials announced: "FDA and USDA Determine Swine Fed Adulterated Product" (April 26, 2007); "FDA/USDA Update on Tainted Animal Feed" (April 28, 2007); "FDA

and USDA Trace Adulterated Animal Feed to Poultry" (April 30, 2007); "Scientists Conclude Very Low Risk to Humans from Food Containing Melamine" (May 7, 2007), FDA.

9 But agency officials: Rick Weiss, "20 Million Chickens Given Tainted Feed," *The Washington Post*, May 5, 2007.

9 Simultaneously, that government: "China Bans Melamine in Food, but Denies It Caused Pet Deaths," Associated Press, April 26, 2007.

10 By late April: "Search for Pet Food Recalls," FDA, May 4, 2007.

10 On May 7, 2007: Walt Bogdanich and Jake Hooker, "From China to Panama, a Trail of Poisoned Medicine," *The New York Times*, May 7, 2007.

10 in May 2004: Simon Pitman and Danny Vincent, "China Faces Fake Baby Milk Scandal," *Food Products Daily*, May 22, 2004.

11 In 2005, the government: Joyce Primo-Carpenter and Milissa McGinnis, "Matrix of Drug Quality Reports in USAID-Assisted Countries," United States Pharmacopeia, Rockville, Md., July 1, 2007, p. 16.

11 The same year: Ibid., p. 17.

11 Of the 530 destroyed: Jonathan Watts, "Drug Pirates Leave Death in Their Wake," *The Guardian*, December 4, 2006.

11 As for the scandal: Bogdanich and Hooker, "From China to Panama."

11 Among the seized goods: Rick Weiss, "Tainted Chinese Imports Common," *The Washington Post*, May 20, 2007.

12 In the twelve months: Andrew Martin and Griff Palmer, "Times Report: Miscounted Refusals of Foreign Shipments," *The New York Times*, July 28, 2007.

12 Most worrisome: Andrew Martin and Griff Palmer, "China Not Sole Source of Dubious Food," *The New York Times*, July 12, 2007.

12 The agency's 2,000: "Government Fails Seafood Inspections," *Food & Water Watch*, Washington, D.C., July 2007, p. 3.

12 In 2006: Ibid.

12 Of the 190,000: "Federal Oversight of Food Safety," Report, GAO-08-435T, U.S. Government Accountability Office, Washington, D.C., January 29, 2008, p. 6.

12 As one FDA: Alexei Barrionuevo, "Food Imports Often Escape Scrutiny," *The New York Times*, May 1, 2007.

13 The two U.S.-based companies: "U.S. Group Says China's Meat Import Ban Groundless," Reuters, July 16, 2005.

13 Thus, most U.S. shoppers: Weiss, "Tainted Chinese Imports Common."

13 Now the Chinese: Ibid.

13 To evaluate: "Food from China: Can We Import Safely," Staff Trip Report, House Commerce and Energy Committee, October 4, 2007.

14 Significantly, the FDA: "Performance Plan: 2002," FDA, December 2002, p.7.

14 Yet agency officials: Committee on Commerce and Energy, "Statement of John Dingell (D-MI)," Hearing on Counterfeit Bulk Drugs, U.S. House of Representatives, June 8, 2000.

14 The FDA also: Ibid.

14 Over the next four months: David Barboza, "China Arrest 774 in Crackdown on Food and Drugs," *The New York Times*, October 29, 2007.

15 President Bush announced: David Stout, "Bush Forms Cabinet Committee to Study Safety of U.S. Imports," *The New York Times*, July 19, 2007.

15 A White House: Marilyn Geewax, "Bush Creates Panel to Ensure Safety of Imported Food and Products," Cox Newspapers, Washington Bureau, July 19, 2007.

15 In November 2007: "FDA Science and Mission at Risk," Confidential Report, FDA Science Board, FDA, November 2007, pp. 1–6.

16 For most of the twentieth: Thomas W. Gilligan, "Industrial Concentration," *The Concise Encyclopedia of Economics,* available at www.econlib.org/library/CEE.html, 2007.

17 Between 1994 and 2005: Eric Nelson, Testimony Before U.S. Senate Committee on Agriculture, Nutrition & Forestry, Regional Farm Hearing, Ankeny, Iowa, July 24, 2006.

18 By 1990: Bruce A. Babcock and Roxanne Clemens, "Beef Packing Concentration: Limiting Branded Product Opportunities?," *Iowa Agricultural Review,* Fall 2005, p. 1.

18 The number was 84: "Economic Concentration and Structural Change in the Food and Agricultural Sector: Trends, Consequences and Policy Options," prepared by the Democratic Staff, Committee on Agriculture, Nutrition and Forestry, United States Senate, October 29, 2004, p. 5.

18 A 1999 Senate hearing: Statement of Senator Tom Harkin, Hearing on Economic Concentration in Agriculture, Committee on Agriculture, Nutrition and Forestry, U.S. Senate, January 26, 1999.

18 Nestlé: "Industrial Concentration in the Agri-food Sector," International Federation of Agricultural Producers, United Nations, May 2003, pp. 1–3.

18 Cargill supplies: Ibid., pp. 1–5.

18 Four corporations: Ibid.

18 Four companies control: Ibid., p. 5.

19 Royal Ahold: Ibid.

20 In August 2007: Chris Waldrop, Director, Food Policy Institute, Consumer Federation of America, "Country of Origin Labeling Program," letter of comment to the U.S. Department of Agriculture, August 20, 2007.

21 "We don't plan": "What Is the Real Health of the Defense Industrial Base?," *Manufacturing and Technology News,* February 22, 2005, p. 1.

22 By May 2004: Renae Merle, "Running Low on Ammo," *The Washington Post,* July 22, 2004.

22 "Reliable foreign suppliers": "Assessing Defense Industrial Capabilities: A DOD Handbook," Office of the Under Secretary of Defense for Acquisition and Technology, Department of Defense, Washington, D.C., April 1996, p. 34.

One: MODERN MERCANTILISM

27 In 1989: Confirmed in telephone conversation with Allan M. Webber, February 2008.

28 China is actively: "Nation to Improve Market System," *China Daily,* October 21, 2003.

29 The Chinese government: "China Tightens Control over Key State-owned Industries," *China Times,* December 22, 2006.

29 In a nation of 1.3: "China," *The World Fact Book,* Central Intelligence Agency, United States, and "Politics of the People's Republic of China," Wikipedia.

29 One of these nine: "The State Council," Gov.cn, Chinese Government's official web portal, June 5, 2007.

29 All have: "China Factfile," Gov.cn, July 5, 2007.

29 For instance, Minister Wu Yi: "Paulson: Wu Yi Is 'Force of Nature,' " *China Daily,* May 5, 2007.

30 In 2002: "SASAC's Responsibilities & Targets," *People's Daily,* May 22, 2003.

30 The chairman is: Li Rongrong, curriculum vitae: www.chinavitae.com, accessed June 4, 2007.

30 At the first: "SASAC's Responsibilities & Targets," May 22, 2003.

31 In mid-December 2006: "Press Conference on State-Owned Assets Management System," Gov.cn, December 20, 2006.

31 Currently, foreign-invested: John Whalley and Xian Xin, "China's FDI and Non-FDI Economies and the Sustainability of Future High Chinese Growth," Working Paper 12249, National Bureau of Economic Research, Cambridge, Mass., May 2006, p. 1.

32 In 2006: Peter Navarro, *Report of "The China Price Project,"* Merage School of Business, University of California–Irvine, Irvine, California, 2006.

32 In all: Ibid., p. 1.

32 Navarro calculates: Ibid.

33 Their most recent: "Joint Press Release: ILO/WHO Number of Work Related Accidents and Illnesses Continues to Increase; ILO and WHO Join in Call for Prevention Strategies," International Labor Organization, April 28, 2005.

33 This contributes: Navarro, *Report of "The China Price Project,"* p. 1.

33 At the same time: "China Confronts Growing Environmental, Health Concerns," Woodrow Wilson International Center for Scholars, Washington, D.C., April 2007.

33 Navarro calculates the absence: Navarro, *Report of "The China Price Project,"* p. 1.

34 In a 2006 report: Terence P. Stewart, Esq., "China's Industrial Subsidies Study: High Technology," Trade Lawyers Advisory Group, April 2007, p. 33.

34 Foreign companies: Ibid., pp. 34–41.

34 Overall, Professor Navarro: Navarro, *Report of "The China Price Project,"* p. 1.

34 Navarro estimates: Ibid.

34 Navarro concludes: Ibid.

35 Then, in 1992: Goldsmith, *The Trap,* p. 32.

35 Walton died: I have had several conversations with Roger Milliken, a cofounder of the "Made in the USA" program and the long-term CEO of Milliken & Company, about Sam Walton, whom he knew well. He strongly believes that Sam Walton would not have made the dramatic shift to low-cost imports that his successors did.

35 In 2007: "Trade in Goods (Imports, Exports and Trade Balance) with China: 1985–2007," Foreign Trade Statistics, U.S. Census Bureau, 2007.

36 Paul Otellini: "Intel Announces a $2.5 Billion Chip Project in China," Xinhua, March 23, 2007.

36 Specifically, foreign: Stewart, "China's Industrial Subsidies Study," pp. 34–41.

37 Overall, the United States: "ATP by Country and Country by ATP," Country and Product Trade Data, Federal Trade Statistics, U.S. Commerce Department, 2007.

37 In 2007: Pat Choate and Edward A. Miller, "U.S.-China Advanced Technology Trade: An Analysis for U.S.-China Security Review Commission (USCC)," 2005, updated in 2007.

38 by the end of 2010: Brad Setser, "The Extent of the Government's Control of China's Economy and Its Impact on the United States," testimony before the U.S.-China Economic and Security Review Commission, May 24, 2007.

38 The total value: "Market Capitalization of NYSE Companies," New York Stock Exchange, www.nyse.com, November 4, 2007.

39 With the purchase: "Frequently Asked Questions About Lenovo," Lenovo Group, available at www.pc.ibm.com/ww/lenovo/faq.html.

39 Now China's largest: "Lenovo Reports Fourth Quarter and Full-year 2006/07 Results," Lenovo Group, available at www.lenovo.com.

39 After the completion: Lenovo Group Fact Sheet, Lenovo Group, available at www.lenovo.com.

39 Also, Bank of America: Cathy Chan and Adrian Cox, "China Gambit Paying Off for Goldman Sachs," *International Herald Tribune,* October 24, 2006.

40 In late 2006: Cathy Chan and Zhao Yidi, "China to Bar Foreign Brokerages from Setting Up," *International Herald Tribune,* October 3, 2007.

40 In 2006, and again: Steve Gelsi, "U.S. Calls for 'Market Discipline' in Hedge Funds," *MarketWatch,* February 10, 2007.

41 According to Fingleton: Eamonn Fingleton, *In the Jaws of the Dragon* (New York: Thomas Dunne Books–St. Martin's Press, 2008), pp. 233–243.

43 Murdoch and: "Media Magnate Murdoch 'Building China Home,' " *China Daily,* December 22, 2004.

43 Eamonn Fingleton: Fingleton, *In the Jaws of the Dragon,* p. 243.

43 When a majority: Richard McCormack, "Domestic Manufacturers Force the National Association of Manufacturers' Big Members to Take a Stand on China; Multinationals Lose Vote and Are Accused of Defending Chinese 'Protectionism,' " *Manufacturing News,* June 7, 2006.

Two: CORPORATISM

45 The consumer advocate: Patrick J. Buchanan, "Patriotism in the Boardroom," Internet Brigade, March 2000.

46 David M. Rubenstein: "Perception and Irony at Davos," Andrew Ross Sorkin, *The New York Times,* January 29, 2008.

47 As R. J. Hillhouse: R. J. Hillhouse, "Who Runs the CIA?," *The Washington Post,* July 8, 2007.

47 Among the private contractors: Ibid.

47 A campaign for: "Stats at a Glance: 2006 Election Overview," Center for Responsive Politics, www.opensecrets.org, accessed July 3, 2007.

48 Warren Buffett: Simon Bowers, "Buffett Attacks American Spending Junkies," *The Guardian,* March 7, 2005.

48 Walter Reed includes: "Military Medical Care: Questions and Answers," CRS Report for Congress, Congressional Research Service, March 7, 2007, pp. 2–3.

48 After the United States: Kelly Kennedy, "Wounded and Waiting," *The Washington Post,* February 20, 2007.

49 That story: Philip Mattera, "Outsourcing Walter Reed," March 6, 2007, available at www.tompaine.com/articles/2007/03/06/outsourcing_walter_reed.php.

49 The new president: "The President's Management Agenda: Fiscal Year 2002," Executive Office of the President, p. 17.

50 The GAO dismissed: B-295529.6, Alan D. King, February 21, 2006: Decision, U.S. Government Accountability Office, February 21, 2006.

50 At this point: Ibid.

51 Meanwhile, the number: Letter to Major General George W. Weightman, Commander (former) Walter Reed Army Medical Center, from Henry A. Waxman, Chairman of the House Committee on Oversight and Government Reform, and John Tierney, Chairman, House Subcommittee on National Security and Foreign Affairs, March 2, 2007.

51 She also told: Jeanne Cummings, "Walter Reed Inquiry Targets GOP," *The Politico,* March 21, 2007.

51 The board also: "Who We Are: Leadership," IAP Worldwide Services, www.iapws.com/who/about.aspx, accessed July 2, 2007.

52 It also owns: "About: Company Profile," Cerberus Capital Management, L.P., www.cerberuscapital.com/about_comp_prof.html, accessed July 2, 2007.

52 In January 2006: Matt Kelley, "The Congressman & the Hedge Fund," *USA Today*, January 19, 2006.

52 *The New York Times:* Editorial: "Politics and the Corruption Fighter," *The New York Times*, January 18, 2007.

52 In 2001: Cummings, "Walter Reed Inquiry Targets GOP."

53 Based on State: Jeremy Scahill, *Blackwater: The Rise of the World's Most Powerful Mercenary Army* (New York: Nation Books, 2007), pp. 370–382.

53 Scahill testified: Jeremy Scahill, "Outsourcing the War," *The Nation*, www.thenation.com, May 11, 2007.

53 The United States now: Ibid.

53 Scahill reports: Scahill, *Blackwater*, p. 372.

54 Thus, military contracts: Ibid.

54 We know only: "Report on Competitive Sourcing Results," White House Office of Management & Budget, May 2, 2007.

55 In the first: "Secrecy in the Bush Administration," United States House of Representatives, Committee on Government Reform, Minority Staff, Special Investigations Division, September 14, 2004, p. vi.

55 The administration: Ibid.

58 A public toll: "The Indiana Toll Road," www.wikipedia.org/wiki/Indiana-Toll-Road, accessed November 26, 2007.

58 Daniels resigned: Mitch Daniels, "Major Moves Statement," Office of the Governor, State House, Indianapolis, Indiana, January 23, 2006.

58 The state then: Daniels, "Major Moves Statement."

58 To make the arrangement: "Indiana Toll Road," Wikipedia, accessed July 6, 2007.

59 After 2010: Ryan Dvorak, "Contract to Lease the Indiana Toll Road Is Full of Holes," SouthBendTribune.com, February 15, 2006.

59 Using information: Ibid.

60 In 1989: "Rick Perry," Wikipedia, accessed November 11, 2007.

61 The Trans Texas Corridor: "Crossroads of the Americas: Trans Texas Corridor Plan," Texas Department of Transportation, Austin, Texas, June 20, 2002, pp. 1–6.

61 The Texas corridors: Ibid.

62 The official name: www.fhwa.dot.gov/hep10/nhs/hipricorridors/hipri-big.pdf.

62 In his 2002 plan: "Crossroads of the Americas: Trans Texas Corridor Plan."

63 The act was: "Driver Responsibility Program," Texas Department of Public Safety, Austin, Texas, August 19, 2003.

63 Krusee tricked: Peggy Fikac, "Higher Fines Eyed for Rowdy Motorists," *San Antonio Express-News*, May 8, 2003.

63 At its core: H.B. No. 3588, An Act Relating to the Construction, Acquisition, Financing, Maintenance, Management, Operation, Ownership, and Control of Transportation Facilities, and the Progress, Improvement, Policing, and Safety of Transportation in the State; Imposing Criminal Penalties, Texas Legislature, June 2003.

63 Under the quick-take: Ibid.

63 The legislation: Ibid.

64 The Nossaman firm: *Super Lawyers*, www.superlawyers.com.

64 TxDOT refuses: Eilen Welsome, "Aching Assets," *The Texas Observer,* March 1, 2007.

64 On August 20, 2003: Pre-Proposal Workshop Transcript, Texas Department of Transportation I-35 High Priority Trans-Texas Workshop, Commission Room, C. Greer Building, Austin, Texas, August 20, 2003.

64 The legislation: Ibid.

65 He told the group: Ibid.

65 "It would require": Ibid.

65 The state now: Nancy Smith, "2003 Transportation Short Course: Comprehensive Development Agreements," Nossaman Guthner Knox Elliott LLP, Work product for TxDOT, Austin, Texas.

66 Prior to that job: "Mary Peters, Secretary of Transportation," the White House, Washington, D.C., accessed November 5, 2007.

66 Prior to joining: "Who's Who in Transportation: David James Gribbin, IV," Corridor Watch.org, accessed November 5, 2007.

67 He shared it: Telephone interview with David and Linda Stall, July 4, 2007.

67 TxDOT sent: Ibid.

68 The auditors concluded: John Keel, "An Audit Report on the Department of Transportation's Reported Funding Gap and Tax Gap Information," State Auditor's Office, Austin, Texas, p. 1.

68 She found: Telephone interview with David and Linda Stall, July 4, 2007.

69 With that: Ibid.

71 Giuliani Capital Advisors: Mark Coultan, "Macquarie Takes the Bank as Giuliani Runs for President," *The Sydney Morning Herald,* March 7, 2007.

71 Peters went to: "Mary E. Peters, Secretary of Transportation," official biography, U.S. Department of Transportation, www.dot.gov/bios/peters.htm, accessed April 29, 2008.

71 Gribbin became: "Who's Who in Transportation: David James Gribbin, IV."

72 When Perry finally: Telephone interview with David and Linda Stall, July 4, 2007.

72 One "good government": "Big Money Paves the Way for the Trans Texas Corridor," Campaigns for People, Austin, Texas, May 12, 2005, p. 1.

72 Before the legislature: Macquarie Media Group, "Acquisition and Ownership," Macquarie.com, accessed November 5, 2007.

73 So many: Telephone interview with David and Linda Stall, July 4, 2007.

73 He sent a: Jere Thompson, Jr., "We Would Forfeit Billions with Private Partnership on 121," *The Dallas Morning News,* March 23, 2007.

73 In a further twist: Letter from James D. Ray, Chief Counsel, FHWA, to Michael Behrens, Executive Director, Texas Department of Transportation, undated, and Letter from Janice Weingart Brown, Executive Director, Texas Division, FHWA, April 26, 2007.

73 U.S. Senator Kay: Letter from Senator Kay Bailey Hutchison to FHWA Administrator J. Richard Capka, May 1, 2007.

73 Although the NTTA: Letter from J. Richard Capka, Administrator, Federal Highway Administration, to Michael W. Behrens, Executive Director, Texas Department of Transportation, August 16, 2007.

75 David Stall: "TxDOT Hits the Toll Road Running," testimony of David Stall, Texas Senate Transportation and Homeland Security Committee, Austin, Texas, August 7, 2007.

76 Foremost of these: "Forward Momentum, Texas Department of Transportation," Austin, Texas, February 28, 2007, pp. 10–11.

76 Additionally: Ibid., p. 9.

Three: ELITISM

78 In a provocative: Samuel Huntington, "Dead Souls: The Denationalization of the American Elite," *The National Interest,* www.freerepublic.com, accessed spring 2004.

79 In 2007: Ibid.

79 The U.S. government: Ibid.

79 As Barry C. Lynn: Barry C. Lynn, "War, Trade, and Utopia," *The National Interest,* December 2005, available at www.nationalinterest.org.

83 It is a $10-billion: Jeffrey H. Birnbaum, "Lobbyists Foresee Business as Usual," *The Washington Post,* June 22, 2005.

83 GOP control: Ibid.

83 Data produced: Calculated from data provided on the Web site of the Center for Public Integrity, Washington, D.C., www.publicintegrity.org, accessed January 7, 2008.

84 More than 250: "Congressional Revolving Doors: The Journey from Congress to K Street," Congress Watch, Public Citizen July 2005.

84 One particularly: Congressman Frank Wolf (R-Va.), "5 Year Wait Before Ambassadors Can Lobby," Congressional Statement, May 23, 2007.

85 In 2004: "U.S. Senators Join the U.S. Senate India Caucus," news release, U.S. India Political Action Committee, September 23, 2004.

85 In June 2007: Jill Gardiner, "Indian Americans Raise $2 Million at Clinton Event," *The New York Sun,* June 25, 2007.

88 The ethics truce: "Memorandum to the Members of the Committee: Recommendation for disposition of the complaint filed against Representative DeLay," Joel Hefley, Chairman, and Alan B. Mollohan, Ranking Minority Member, House Ethics Committee, October 6, 2004.

89 In 2006, James: "Hedge Fund," Wikipedia, accessed November 7, 2007.

89 When the Blackstone Group: David Cay Johnston, "Tax Loopholes Sweeten a Deal for Blackstone," *The New York Times,* July 13, 2007.

89 As these funds: "Common Approach to Private Pools of Capital Guidance on Hedge Fund Issues Focuses on Systemic Risk, Investor Protection," news release, President's Working Group, U.S. Treasury, February 22, 2007.

90 The Conference Board reports: "U.S. Institutional Investors Continue to Boost Ownership of U.S. Corporations," Conference Board, www.conference-board.com, accessed January 22, 2007.

90 Today: "Facts and Figures," New York Stock Exchange, www.nyse.com, accessed November 5, 2007.

90 At the 1970s pace: Ibid.

93 The U.S. cochairman: "Building a North American Community, Report of an Independent Task Force on the Future of North America," Council on Foreign Relations, May 2005.

96 On March 23, 2005: www.spp.gov.

97 "as well as": www.spp.gov.

97 Campbell Soup: www.spp.gov.

98 "The ability to": Enhancing Competitiveness in Canada, Mexico, and the United States," North American Competitiveness Council, U.S. Department of Commerce, February 2007, p. 32.

Four: PARADISE: CREATED AND LOST

103 Indeed, the entwining: Erik Rauch, "Is 'Globalization' Exaggerated?,"
      www.swiss.ai.mit.edu, accessed June 6, 2006.

104 Great Britain sold: John Maynard Keynes, *The Economic Consequences of the Peace* (New
      York: Harcourt, Brace and Howe, 1920), p. 17.

104 "What an extraordinary": Ibid., pp. 11–12.

105 When the war began: Pat Choate, *Hot Property* (New York: Alfred A. Knopf, 2005),
      pp. 103–104.

106 Even by the end: Ibid., pp. 104–109.

107 Keynes, who was: Keynes, *The Economic Consequences of the Peace*, p. 8.

109 The problem with: Alfred E. Eckes, Jr., *Opening America's Markets* (Chapel Hill:
      University of North Carolina Press, 1995), pp. 86–97.

109 Neither did the law: Ibid., pp. 100–139.

110 The coalition that: Ibid., pp. 141–157.

111 He made unilateral: Ibid., pp. 144–148.

112 The U.S. Senate: Pat Choate and Juyne Linger, "Tailored Trade: Dealing with the World
      as It Is," *Harvard Business Review,* January–February 1988, p. 2.

113 Britain got: Ibid.

113 In 1958: Eckes, *Opening America's Markets*, p. 165.

114 During that same period: Ibid., pp. 172–173.

Five: FRIEDMAN I (MILTON)

117 What eventually: Lynn Downey, Company Historian, "Levi Strauss: A Short Biography,"
      Levi Strauss & Co., 2005.

118 By 1996: Judy Mares-Dixon, Julie A. McKay, and Scott R. Peppet, "Building Consensus
      Within a Major Corporation: The Case of Levi Strauss & Co.," *The Consensus Building
      Handbook* (SAGE Publications, 1999), p. 1.

118 The Levi Strauss factories: "Values and Visions," Levi Strauss & Co.,
      www.levistrauss.com, accessed November 27, 2007.

118 In 1992: Ibid.

118 The company was also: Milton Friedman, "A Friedman Doctrine: The Social
      Responsibility of Business Is to Increase Its Profits," *The New York Times*, September 13,
      1970.

119 "There is one": Ibid.

119 "The core ethical": Karl Schoenberg, *Levi's Children: Coming to Terms with Human Rights
      in the Global Marketplace* (New York: Grove/Atlantic Press, 2000).

120 By 1982, "Civilian Unemployment Rate," Bureau of Labor Statistics, U.S. Department of
      Labor, November 2007.

122 Forgetting how: Ann Crittenden, "In for a Dime, In for a Dollar," *The New York Times*,
      July 8, 1984.

122 Henry Kaufman: Darrell Delamaide, *Debt Shock* (New York: Anchor Books, 1985), p. 8.

122 A Washington Post Book: Roger J. Vaughan and Edward Hill, *Banking on the Brink*
      (Washington, D.C.: Washington Post Book Company, 1992).

122 "the views of": Moisés Naim, "Washington Consensus or Washington Confusion?,"
      Foreign Policy, Spring 2000, p. 91.

125 The control of: Andrew Wheat, "Mexico's Privatization Piñata," *Corrupting Democracy* 17, no. 10 (October 1996), at www.multinationalmonitor.org/hyper/mm1096.00.html.

126 The bulleted information comes from: Ross Perot and Pat Choate, *Save Your Job, Save Your Country: Why NAFTA Must Be Stopped* (New York: Hyperion, 1993), pp. 1–12.

127 Before NAFTA: I was closely involved in the battle to defeat NAFTA. In the summer of 1993, I also coauthored the book cited above with Ross Perot that argued against congressional ratification. Subsequently, John R. MacArthur wrote *The Selling of "Free Trade": NAFTA, Washington, and the Subversion of American Democracy* (New York: Hill and Wang, 2000). I have drawn from his book to refresh my memories of those events.

129 Two days after Christmas: MacArthur, *The Selling of "Free Trade,"* p. 306.

129 The Department of Agriculture: Skip Jonas, Florida Tomato Committee, "WTO Listening Session," United States Department of Agriculture, June 4, 1999.

129 The CTC can: Peter Cooper and Lori Wallach, *NAFTA's Broken Promises* (Washington, D.C.: Public Citizen, 1995), pp. 1–58.

130 In 1995, the Mexican: MacArthur, *The Selling of "Free Trade,"* pp. 276–307.

131 In the thirty-two: Juan Forero, "As China Gallops, Mexico Sees Factory Jobs Slip Away," *The New York Times*, September 3, 2003.

132 Since 1974: "Facts from EBRI," Employee Benefit Research Institute, Washington, D.C., www.ebri.org, accessed November 12, 2007.

132 The threat held: David Lazarus, "Bank of America: Train Your Replacement or No Severance Pay for You," *San Francisco Chronicle*, June 9, 2006.

133 Do not work: "Levi Strauss & Co. Global Sourcing and Operating Guidelines," Levi Strauss and Co., www.levistrauss.com, accessed November 8, 2007, p. 2.

134 Robert E. Scott: Robert E. Scott, "The High Price of Free Trade," Economic Policy Institute, Washington, D.C., November 17, 2003.

Six: FRIEDMAN II (THOMAS)

136 He identifies: Thomas L. Friedman, *The World Is Flat: A Brief History of the Twenty-First Century* (New York: Farrar, Straus and Giroux, 2006), pp. 51–200.

137 "There it produces": Ibid.

137 Ultimately, Friedman's: Ibid., p. 263.

137 The solution: Ibid.

138 President Theodore Roosevelt: Patrick Buchanan, "Free Trade and Funny Math," *Human Events*, February 27, 2007.

139 Advantage today: Paul Craig Roberts, Statement Before the U.S.-China Economic and Security Review Commission, Washington, D.C., September 25, 2006.

140 In a 2006 CNBC: "Caught on Tape," www.davidsirota.com/index.php/2006/07/24/, July 24, 2007.

140 Only one of nine: Pat Choate, review of *Opening America's Market: Foreign Trade Policy Since 1776, Chronicle Magazine*, Winter 1995, p. 1.

142 By 2003: Auggie Tantillo, Testimony of AMTAC Executive Director Auggie Tantillo, U.S.-China Economic and Security Review Commission Public Hearing, Washington, D.C., February 3, 2005.

142 Equally significant: Ibid.

144 In 2005: Ibid.

144 Several recent studies: Ibid.

145 "It is easier": James Mann, *The China Fantasy* (New York: Viking Penguin, 2007), pp. 80–84.

146 more trade: Ibid.

146 "detained, sequestered": Congressional-Executive Commission on China, Section V, "Monitoring Compliance with Human Rights, Freedom Religion," 2006 Annual Report, pp. 2–3.

148 "The history of": Clarence E. Ayres, *Toward a Reasonable Society: The Values of Industrial Civilization* (Austin: University of Texas Press, 1963).

151 The practice is: Akio Morita, Edwin M. Reingold, and Mitsuko Shimomura, *Made in Japan* (Fontana Press, 1988).

155 "What is good": Ralph E. Gomory, Testimony before the Committee on Science and Technology, U.S. House of Representatives, Washington, D.C., July 12, 2007.

Seven: SOVEREIGNTY

159 "to focus on": "10 Benefits of the WTO Trading System," www.wto.org, accessed November 2007.

159 By joining: Final Act of the 1986–1994 Uruguay Round of Trade Negotiations, World Trade Organization, Geneva, Switzerland, November 11, 2007.

162 "Clearly, one": Robert E. Lighthizer, Testimony, Subcommittee on Trade of the House Committee on Ways and Means, Washington, D.C., August 2, 2007.

162 Repeatedly, according: Ibid.

167 Iowa is an: "Iowa's Redistricting Information," www.fairvote.org.

172 Bruce Stokes and I: Bruce Stokes and Pat Choate, "Democratizing U.S. Trade Policy" (New York: Council on Foreign Relations, 2001), pp. 1–3.

Eight: SECURITY

173 By these maneuvers: Choate, *Hot Property* (New York: Alfred A. Knopf, 2005), pp. 176–177.

173 It also reported: "Surge," Conference Report of the Surge Roundtable, IAM, December 2007.

174 The Government Accountability: Defense Trade Data, GAO report number GAO-906-319R, January 27, 2006.

174 In the 1980s: Off-the-record interview, July 2007.

175 Of the $369 billion: Calculated from "Advanced Technology Products, Data, Monthly December 2003–present," Foreign Trade Statistics, U.S. Census Bureau, November 2007.

175 The figures below: Calculated from Foreign Trade Statistics, U.S. Census Bureau, Washington, D.C.

176 Alan Tonelson: Alan Tonelson and Peter Kim, "U.S. Domestic Producers Lose Increasing Share of Home Market to Foreign Competition," AmericanEconomic Alter.org, accessed December 26, 2006.

180 "have much less": Paul Krugman, "North of the Border," *The New York Times*, March 27, 2007.

180 Since the beginning: "Border Patrol Operations," Federation for American Immigration Reform, Washington, D.C., 2007.

180 Altogether, an estimated: "How Many Illegal Aliens?," American Federation for Immigration Reform, Washington, D.C., 2007.

181 "We should say so": Robert J. Samuelson, "Build a Fence—and Amnesty," *The Washington Post*, March 8, 2006.

181 House Democratic Caucus: Stephan Dinan, "Border Reform Not a Priority for Democrats," *The Washington Times*, July 25, 2007.

182 Their recommendations: Barbara Jordan, Testimony before the U.S. House of Representatives, Committee on the Judiciary, Subcommittee on Immigration and Claims, Washington, D.C., February 24, 1995.

182 "Immigration is far too important": Ibid.

183 "I do not like advocating": Samuelson, "Build a Fence—and Amnesty."

Nine: PROSPERITY

184 In a now-famous: William Grieder, "The Education of David Stockman," *Atlantic Monthly*, December 1981.

186 Ideally, that President: This practical idea comes from Bruce Stokes.

187 In that pact: Terence P. Stewart, "The Costs of Differential Tax Treatment," Law Offices of Stewart and Stewart, Washington, D.C., January 2007. This study was done on behalf of Milliken & Company and the U.S. Business and Industrial Council. I am grateful to them for allowing me to draw materials from their study.

188 This is a giant: Ibid.

189 A panel formed: Ibid.

192 "to use its resources": Friedman, "A Friedman Doctrine."

194 In an August 2007: John Fonte, "After Montebello: The View from the Summit—and Where We Go from Here," Newswithviews.com, accessed August 26, 2007.

196 The failure: Samuel Sherraden, "Sustaining an Infrastructure for Success," *The Washington Post*, October 17, 2007.

197 By innovation: "Innovation Measurement," James E. Malackowski, Ocean Tomo, LLC, Chicago, Ill., 2007.

198 Robert J. Shapiro: Robert J. Shapiro and Nam D. Pham, *Economic Effects of Intellectual Property-Intensive Manufacturing in the United States* (Washington, D.C.: Sonecon, LLC, 2007).

198 "market economies require": Alan Greenspan, "Intellectual Property Rights" (speech, Stanford Institute for Economic Policy Research Summit, Stanford, Calif., February 27, 2004).

200 In November 2007: Chen Yongshun, "The Greatest Changes of the U.S. Patent System in the Last 50 Years," *China Intellectual Property News*, November 7, 2007.

EPILOGUE

204 "Things that can't": Clyde Prestowitz, "Things That Can't Go On, Don't," www.yaleglobal.yale.edu, accessed February 3, 2008.

APPENDIX

209 The petition clause: Elisa Hahnenburg, "The Right to Petition Government," www.learningtogive.org, accessed March 8, 2008.

Index

A NOTE ABOUT THE AUTHOR

Pat Choate is the author of *Hot Property* and *Agents of Influence* and the coauthor of *The High-Flex Society; America in Ruins; Being Number One;* and *Save Your Job, Save Our Country* with Ross Perot. In 1996, he was Ross Perot's vice presidential running mate. He lives with his wife outside Washington, D.C.

A NOTE ON THE TYPE

This book was set in Tyfa, originally the winning design for a Czech typeface for book composition, made into fonts for Linotype and released in 1959. Designed by Josef Tyfa, it was popular in Czechoslovakia but little used elsewhere owing to communication difficulties during the "Cold War," until another Czech designer started digitizing it under Tyfa's direction in 1995 for the International Typeface Corporation. Tyfa is based on classical form but is quirky and modern in nature.

Composed by North Market Street Graphics, Lancaster, Pennsylvania
Printed and bound by Berryville Graphics, Berryville, Virginia
Designed by Anthea Lingeman